Copyright © 2003 by Peter Hiett.

Published by Integrity Publishers, a division of Integrity Media, Inc.,
5250 Virginia Way, Suite 110, Brentwood, TN 37027.

HELPING PEOPLE WORLDWIDE EXPERIENCE *the* MANIFEST PRESENCE *of* GOD.

Unless otherwise indicated, Scripture quotations used in this book are from The Revised
Standard Version of the Bible (RSV). Copyright © 1946, 1963, 1972 by the Division of
Christian Education of the National Council of the Churches of Christ in the USA. Used by
permission.

Other Scripture references are from the following sources:

The Holy Bible, New International Version (NIV), copyright © 1973, 1978, 1984,
International Bible Society. Used by permission of Zondervan Bible Publishers. The King
James Version of the Bible (KJV). The New King James Version (NKJV), copyright © 1979,
1980, 1982, Thomas Nelson, Inc., Publishers. New American Standard Bible (NASB),
© 1960, 1977 by the Lockman Foundation.

Published in association with the literary agency of Alive Communications, Inc.,
7680 Goddard Street, Suite 200, Colorado Springs, Colorado 80920.

Cover Design: UDG | Designworks
            www.udgdesignworks.com

Interior: Inside Out Design & Typesetting

Library of Congress Cataloging-in-Publication Data

Hiett, Peter.
Eternity now! : encountering the Jesus of Revelation / by Peter Hiett.

p. cm.
Includes bibliographical references.
ISBN 1-59145-085-3 (hardcover)

1. Bible. N.T. Revelation—Criticism, interpretation, etc. I. Title.
BS2825.52H54 2003
228'.06–dc21   2003012869

Printed in the United States of America
03 04 05 06 07 LBM 9 8 7 6 5 4 3 2 1

ETERNITY NOW!

PETER HIETT

INTEGRITY®

PUBLISHERS

Nashville

To Dan Hiett: my father, friend, and pastor—who is a revelation of Jesus.

Contents

CONTENTS

Contents

PREFACE

IF SOMEONE HAD TOLD ME several years ago that I'd write a book on the Revelation, I would have laughed in his face or been filled with fear that in the future I was destined to freak out totally. Had you looked at my Bible sideways at that time, you would have seen that the first two-thirds of the pages (the Old Testament) were somewhat smudge free. Then you would see a section of very, very smudged pages (the New Testament, minus the last book). This would be followed by a short section of a few very white pages—the Revelation.

Do you have a Bible? What does it look like when you turn it sideways?

I saw the movie *The Omen* in high school, in which Damien shaves his head, finds the number 666 tattooed on his scalp, and realizes he's the antichrist. It filled me with fear and I wanted to shave my head just to make sure I was okay (eventually I did shave my head, in case you're wondering. Praise God, I had no weird tattoos. But my wife did make me grow my hair back.) In my church youth group, we saw the movie *A Thief in the Night,* and about all that I remembered of it was that a bunch of bad stuff happened, and some people got raptured but others didn't.

I knew that Jesus could say some really tough stuff, as He did in the Gospels, but He was always willing to die for you. This Jesus in the Revelation, however, didn't seem like the Jesus I had come to know and love. The end-times Jesus seemed capricious and freaky mean. I figured that the Revelation was for scaring bad youth group kids into repenting.

As I got older, went through seminary, and studied Scripture in more depth, the Revelation seemed even stranger. Well, actually it wasn't the Revelation, but all the strange things people were saying about it. G. K. Chesterton wrote, "And though St. John the Evangelist saw many strange monsters in his vision, he saw no creature so wild as one of his own commentators."[1] Unfortunately, I reacted by avoiding the Revelation or reading it out of guilt—but with great speed, so that it wouldn't damage my faith in the Jesus revealed in the rest of Scripture.

A few years ago I found myself reading the Revelation in a time of stress—not because I understood it but because I began more and more to believe it—not the commentators, not the movies, not the fiction series, but the book itself. I began to believe more and more that Jesus is trustworthy, and the Revelation reveals that He is in charge and He has won.

At the time I was also gaining faith in a great truth: If we're willing to go to weird and frightening places with faith in Jesus, He is waiting for us there with the most glorious revelations of Himself. The light shines in the darkness. If you're willing to go to the cross, you get to see Easter. That's true in theology, true in our personal lives, and also true in Scripture.

So a few years ago I confessed to my church, "I really don't know what I'm doing"—nobody was surprised at that—and then we took a plunge into the Revelation. To my absolute delight, I found that the Revelation really is *the revelation* of Jesus, just like the first line of the book says. Since then, I've read tons of stuff about it, gobs of commentaries, both critical and popular, and heard a million different arguments. I still don't have all the answers. And yet I do: *The answer is Jesus.*

Now the last few pages of my Bible are really smudgy, and even the Old Testament is much more smudgified. You see, the Revelation reveals that Jesus is everywhere and every*when,* and that He always wins. The Gospels and the Epistles reveal that as well—we just haven't taken them seriously enough for it to hit home.

If you are a believer in Jesus, I bet you'll find that the Revelation reveals that all the stuff you've believed is true, is far truer than you ever knew. Jesus is so much larger and better and kinder, and more gracious, glorious, and true, than we ever imagined.

I'm beginning to see it because of the Revelation. I hope you do too. I hope the last few pages of your Bible get really smudgy.

—Peter Hiett
Golden, Colorado
April 2003

ONE

THE TIME IS AT HAND

(Revelation 1:1–8)

REVELATION 1:1: *The revelation of Jesus Christ, which God gave him to show to his servants what must soon take place.*

WHERE IS GOD? DOES HE KNOW MY NAME? *Does He even care? How can He be good when life is painful and the journey is confusing? Is this whole Jesus thing a cruel joke? Is the presence of His Spirit just wishful thinking or religious hype?*

That's what seven little churches in Asia Minor must have been asking nearly two thousand years ago. Each one stood seemingly alone against the mightiest empire the world had ever known, against a culture that labeled them as insane or seduced them into impotence, and against the hierarchy of the ancient religion that branded them heretics and crucified their founder. Their questions are our questions.

DO YOU EVER FEEL as if your life is like a lost page from a book with no plot—you have no idea where you fit and why? Story—plot—gives meaning to each page. If you could number all the pages so that you knew their exact sequence and which page was yours, life would still be meaningless if you didn't know what the book was about.

The apostle Paul prayed for the little bands of believers in Asia that they would have a spirit of revelation, and the eyes of their hearts would be enlight-

1

ened (Ephesians 1:17–18). Then the apostle John sent them "The revelation of Jesus Christ" (Revelation 1:1). In Greek, it is the "apocalypse" of Jesus, which means the "unveiling" of Jesus. I believe this is the same John who wrote the Gospel according to John. He begins his Gospel with "In the beginning was the Word" (1:1)—that is, the *Logos,* the Logic, the Meaning, the Plot.

The Revelation of Jesus is the revelation of the Story. Jesus is the Plot. This was God's plan for the fullness of time, writes Paul: "to unite all things in him, things in heaven and things on earth" (Ephesians 1:10).

Perhaps the Revelation reveals far more than the order of page numbers. Maybe page numbers aren't the point anyway; perhaps the *plot* is the point. Maybe it's not for us to know the order of all the pages. Perhaps the order of the pages is even something of an illusion for creatures stuck in time. The point is, we know the Plot. They wrapped Him in swaddling clothes and laid Him in a manger. He's risen from the dead and lives in the manger of our hearts . . . *now.* Eternity touches time now.

Einstein argued that at the speed of light there is an eternal *now.* He postulated that time and space are relative to the speed of light; light is the constant. We modern people think he thought that up. Yet two thousand years earlier, John wrote, "God is light" (1 John 1:5), and he recorded Jesus saying, "I am the light of the world" (John 8:12). John taught that Jesus is the Word, and the Word is the Light. All things are made through Him and are relative to Him.

It's been said that time is simply God's way of keeping everything from happening all at once. Of course, for Him it *does* happen all at once; it's always here and now. But for us, God stretches out time so long and space so deep that we can learn of His wonder and sing His song of grace . . . we can read not history as much as His Story.

Yet we ignore the Story and argue about the order of pages in the book. We quarrel over which pages belong to the future or to the past, missing the Story and therefore living without the Plot—and therefore without its meaning for our lives now. If we don't know the Plot now, how can we know Him in the future? He is a person and He is Spirit.

We obsess over dates and times as if *they* are the solid things and everything spiritual is metaphor—as if the Word of the Lord will pass away and *this* world will abide forever. We take space and time far too seriously. Scripture says more than once that a day is like a thousand years and a thousand years like a day. In the middle of the Revelation, an angel flies through midheaven with an "eternal gospel" to proclaim. Eternal! How sad that we take our calendars more seriously than the gospel.

In the Bible we've been given the Gospel according to Matthew, to Mark, to Luke, and to John. But there is *also* a Gospel according to Jesus: the Revelation. In the other Gospels, Jesus was incarnated (in-fleshed) in our space and time, speaking *our* language. In the Revelation, John is *out*-carnated (out-fleshed) from our space and time so that Jesus can reveal the eternal gospel in the language of heaven.

In the Revelation, the stars fall from the sky more than once. Christmas seems to happen in chapter 12 *after* all creatures worship Jesus in chapter 5. In chapter 6, the sky rolls up like a scroll before most of the action even starts. The Revelation is obviously so much more than a time line. What if we believed it as an unveiling of the realities that surround us *right now?* What if we took it more seriously than our antiquated, supposedly scientific view of reality?

What if . . .

the New Jerusalem really *is* coming down (Revelation 3:12; 21:2, 10);

Jesus really *is* coming on the clouds of heaven (1:7);

the time really *is* at hand (1:3 KJV)?

What if God is answering Paul's prayer for the church by giving *you* a spirit of revelation (apocalypse) in the knowledge of Him? What if He is unveiling the Plot in a way you have never seen it before, such that the eyes of your heart are enlightened and you know the hope to which He has called you, the riches of His glorious inheritance in the saints, and the immeasurable greatness of His power in those who believe?

What if the apocalypse is now? What if eternity is now?

TEN YEARS AGO WITH A HIGH SCHOOL YOUTH GROUP, I introduced a study on the letters to the seven churches in the Book of Revelation. I began by talking about how confusing these times are in which we live, and wouldn't it be great to have a chronology with all the details of the future?

Then I introduced the Revelation. I told them I had been doing some amazing research, illuminating harmonic convergence in the seven bowls of wrath. I showed them two graphs which systematically plotted these convergences in the systems of the apocalyptic vision as it related to the sociopolitical issues of our day, which all pointed clearly to the year of the antichrist's appearance: *that* year.

Then I revealed to them the remarkable numeric acuity so prevalent in the last eleven chapters. On the overhead we began to fill in the blanks of the name of the antichrist, all according to numeric, acuitive construction.

Before our very eyes the name took shape: Saksuork Mij. I said, "I just don't know what this name means. What if we turned the overhead over, reversing polarity?"

We did, and all at once it became clear. The staff screamed as they read the name Jim Krouskas—our new high school intern, sitting in the back row! The kids started looking at me as if I had made up all that harmonic numeric acuity stuff.

We ran to the back of the room, grabbed Jim, and dragged him up front. We ripped off his shirt, and sure enough—he was wearing some satanic, heavy-metal T-shirt underneath. When we ripped that off, Jim's chest was covered with thick, black, curly, Greek hair. Fortunately, we just happened to have an electric razor handy. I yelled to another leader, "Let's look for the mark!"

We began shaving off chest hair, and there on the right side of his chest was a huge, black, numeral six. We gasped and shaved more, revealing another numeral six. "Oh, Jim, we're really disappointed," we said. Then we shaved the other side of Jim's chest, revealing . . . a numeral five.

"Oh man, Jim," I exclaimed, "I'm *so* sorry. I miscalculated. I was off by one."

Was I off by only one? Did I miscalculate, or misunderstand? Whatever the case, I wasn't the first to get it wrong. . . .

- Remember all the books a few years ago about Saddam Hussein and the end times? You could get them really cheap right after the Persian Gulf War. Maybe we'll see some sequels soon.
- Before that it was Gorbachev.
- Somehow Ronald Wilson Reagan added up to 666, according to some.
- Before that folks were convinced it was Hitler.
- During the Revolutionary War, many Americans were convinced that the antichrist was King George the Third.
- For most of Protestant history, the pope was considered the antichrist.
- The church father Hippolytus taught the world would end in A.D. 500
- People were going nuts around 1000 A.D., even more than in A.D. 2000
- Jehovah's Witnesses have projected end-times events in 874, 1878, 1881, 1910, 1914, 1918, 1925, 1975, and 1984.

When I was in high school, Hal Lindsey's *The Late Great Planet Earth*[1] was the rage, along with his *The 1980s: Countdown to Armageddon*.[2] Both were full of frightening statistics on how the USSR and China fulfill Bible prophecy.

In 1988 Edgar Whisenant sold over three million copies of *88 Reasons Why the Rapture Could Be in 1988*[3] (one forty-year generation after Israel became a nation in 1948.) In late December 1988, bookstores were offering substantial discounts.

In 1989 Whisenant came out with *89 Reasons Christ Could Return in 1989.*[4] People didn't buy as many that time around. He obviously did some miscalculating. Or did he misunderstand?

The cumulative batting average of all these chronologists throughout history is .000. In Matthew 24 Jesus says, "Of that day and hour no one knows, not even the angels of heaven, nor the Son, but the Father only" (v. 36). Jesus does say we can know seasons, but then He seems to say *now* is the season, so *always* be ready. Keep your lamps burning, foolish virgins, or you will not be ready when the bridegroom arrives in the middle of the night (see Matthew 25:1–13).

Why are we so concerned to get the day and hour?

A friend sent me one of her prophecy newsletters. On the first page it quoted Revelation about famines and earthquakes. The rest of the newsletter addressed canning fruit, food storage, and nutritional concerns during the tribulation.

Is this what Revelation is about—why we'll be "blessed" if we read it? We'll get the chronology so we can prepare for the last days with canned goods, secret hideouts, and shotguns? I'll tell you this: The last place I want to be when Jesus comes back is sitting on a pile of food in a secret hideout holding a shotgun while people starve to death in the streets.

In the best-selling *Left Behind* fiction series,[5] the great Bible scholar Tsion Ben Judah sits in a safe house, unlocking the chronology of Revelation, then posting it on the Internet, so that the one billion tribulation saints can be prepared for the coming woes . . .

> And count down to the day of the glorious appearing
> When Jesus will come on the white horse.

In Revelation 16:15 Jesus says very clearly, "Behold, I come like a thief! Blessed is he who stays awake" (NIV). In Matthew 24:36 Jesus says, "Of that day and hour no one knows."

I don't think I ever held the attention of the youth group like I did when I told those teenagers I knew who the antichrist was and when the world would end. I remember being fascinated with the subject as a teenager, because I had two important things to accomplish before Jesus returned: get my driver's license and get married so I could experience marital relations.

Now I can say, "*Maranatha!* Come, Lord Jesus, come!" Still, I want to plan my future. But Jesus said, "The Son of man is coming at an hour you do not expect" (Matthew 24:44). How inconvenient—it's hard to keep oil in your lamp twenty-four hours a day, seven days a week. If He had just *told* us when He would be coming, we could set our lamps down once in a while and take a break.

When you least expect it, expect it.

Well . . . okay . . . when do I least expect it? But then I shouldn't expect it because then I'm *expecting* it and He comes at an unexpected hour . . . so when is that unexpected hour? I'll expect it *then*. But then I shouldn't expect it, which means I should, then shouldn't, then should, ad infinitum. That's really *confusing!* I want *control* over my life and future. Otherwise, I have to walk by faith(!)

So I need to know . . .

who,

what,

when,

where . . .

I need to know the chronology.

And there are at least four traditional views of chronology in the Revelation.

Preterist. Preterists believe that all of the events in Revelation—or at least most of them, up until chapter 21—have already happened. Oh, no—does that mean all of us have been left behind? Not according to the preterists. They say all the imagery was easily understandable and applicable to the people to whom John the Revelator wrote. It was about them, not us. Most historical-critical Bible scholars today hold this view.

Historist. Historists believe that Revelation is an elaborate map of all church history. They're the ones who usually pegged the pope as the antichrist (it was a really popular view during the Reformation . . . among Protestants). Its adherents were folks like John Wycliffe, John Knox, William Tyndale, Ulrich Zwingli, Phillip Melanchthon, John Calvin, Martin Luther, Isaac Newton, John Wesley, Jonathan Edwards, George Whitefield, Charles Finney, Charles Spurgeon, Matthew Henry . . . *all* the heavyweights. Hardly anybody ascribes to historism anymore, however, because they ran out of time once they established that a day in Revelation equals a year of human history. Not only that . . . nowadays the pope seems to be a pretty good guy.

Futurist. Futurists believe that everything in Revelation after the first three chapters refers to future events. This is the most popular view today among evangelicals and in pop culture. (Movies about bloodthirsty popes with 666 stamped on their heads are just not in vogue.) Understandably, the Catholic Church popularized this futurist view during the Reformation, but most Protestants shunned it until the mid-1900s.

There are different types of futurists. The most popular today are the dispensationalists, who argue the Church won't even be around for most of Revelation, because we'll be raptured . . . in which case Christians won't need canned food and shotguns. Along with the historist position, this view implies that most of the details of Revelation have little to do with the people to whom the book was written.

Idealist/Spiritualist. Idealists, or spiritualists, believe that John didn't intend or believe his message to correspond to any historical events in particular. Instead, it was a visionary expression of timeless truths. This view was popular among the early church fathers. Origen, for instance, taught that the beast with seven heads represented evil and the seven deadly sins.

All of these views would suggest that the precise *who, when,* and *where* of Revelation is pretty hard to nail down. But is it?

Let's read it. Chapter 1, verse 1: *The Revelation* (the word in Greek is *apocalyptus) of Jesus.* Notice it doesn't say "The Revelation of the Antichrist" or "The Revelation of End Times Chronology." The Revelation of Jesus Christ either means it was given to Jesus and comes through Jesus or it was *about* Jesus. It must mean both: For this is the "plan for the fulness of time, to unite all things in him, things in heaven and things on earth" (Ephesians 1:10).

REVELATION 1:1–3: *The revelation of Jesus Christ, which God gave him to show to his servants what must soon take place; and he made it known by sending his angel to his servant John, who bore witness to the word of God and to the testimony of Jesus Christ, even to all that he saw. Blessed is he who reads aloud the words of the prophecy, and blessed are those who hear, and who keep what is written therein; for the time is near.*

Blessed are those who read . . . hear . . . and keep—not just a few Bible scholars locked away in a seminary somewhere. In the early church, most people were probably illiterate, so they would gather to hear one person read the Revelation in one sitting, in the context of worship.

Blessed are those who hear and take it to heart. Blessed. That could be *us.* Why? "For the time is near" (v. 3).

As the Greek implies and the King James Version translates: *The time is at hand.* "At hand" is a common biblical phrase meaning "right where my hand is" . . . what is accessible to me . . . what can be taken hold of. Jesus came preaching, "Repent, for the kingdom of heaven is at hand" (Matthew 4:17). *Whose* hand? Whoever reads and hears and takes it to heart. Think about that.

> *They* read;
>> *they* heard;
>>> *they* took it to heart.
>
> *We* read;
>> *we* hear;
>>> *we* might take it to heart.

That must mean the time has been *at hand* for two thousand years!

For those early Christians in Ephesus, Smyrna, Pergamum, Thyatira, Sardis, Philadelphia, and Laodicea, the time *was* at hand. "Then where was the antichrist?" you might ask. John tells us in 2 John 7 that the antichrist was already in the world. But this also means that for Martin Luther and his historist friends who read Revelation, the time was at hand. Does this mean the pope was the antichrist? No . . . however, according to John, the spirit of the antichrist is in the world and has been, and every spirit that does not confess Christ is the antichrist (see 1 John 4:2-3). That's wild!

But then, this also means that for every believer in the future who reads and hears, the time is at hand. I'm not simply being a spiritualist or talking psychology. I'm talking physics, space, and time, the *real* world—the eternal world—invading this one.

"Fine," you say, "but when *is* Jesus coming?" I know He is coming on a white horse at the end of the age, and all eyes will see Him. But if we take our Bibles seriously, and literally, if that's what you'd like to call it, He has been coming back again and again throughout Scripture . . . throughout the Book of Revelation.

- He may come to the church in Ephesus and remove their lampstand (Revelation 2:5).
- He may come to Pergamum to war against the Nicolaitans (2:15–16).
- If Sardis won't wake up, He may come on them like a thief (3:3).
- He said to suffering Philadelphia, "I am coming soon; hold fast" (3:11). Did he mean 2010? How depressing.
- And He said to those in Laodicea, "If any one hears my voice and opens the door, I will come in to him" (3:20). He comes for each of us.

- And Jesus told His disciples, "I will come again and will take you to myself" (John 14:3). I think Jesus comes to get each of His beloved individually at death. Like He said to that thief on the cross, "Today you will be with me in Paradise" (Luke 23:43).

"The time is at hand." In Greek, "*Kairos* is at hand." Guy Chevreau writes:

In biblical Greek there are two words for "time": the first is *chronos,* from which we get English words such as chronometer and chronology. *Chronos* is clock time, calendar time: 1 o'clock, 2 o'clock, 3 o'clock; January, February, March . . . all marching right along. The second Greek word, *kairos,* means " special time." [Mothers] know the difference between *chronos* and *kairos.* About nine months or so into a pregnancy—*chronos* time—many soon-to-be mothers shake their husband by the shoulder and say . . . "It's time!" He opens a bleary eye, looks at the clock, and says, "It's 3:17 in the morning; go back to sleep!" She's on *kairos* time, he's talking *chronos.* So he gets shaken again: *"It's time!!"* This time he gets it. "IT'S TIME!!!"[6]

All reality is now pregnant with "the time," with "eternity." All *chronos* is pregnant with *kairos.* All times are pregnant with meaning. All reality is pregnant with the Plot, the meaning, the Word, the Logos . . . Jesus.

Revelation isn't a chronology; it's a *kairology.* It isn't just about some seven historical churches in the preterist past . . . or some ten-nation confederacy in the futurist future . . . or just some series of events in the Middle Ages involving the popes . . . or just some spiritual ideals floating in space.

It may be about *all* those things, but it is at least about . . . *you!*

The *who* is Jesus and you;

 the *where* is here;

  the *when* is now.

   The *Revelation* is Jesus.

Their eyes got big in youth group ten years ago, because they thought the Revelation was about *them,* and they had met the antichrist, and Jesus was coming soon. Your eyes should get big too . . . because the Revelation is about *you* and where you are, and you *have* met the antichrist, or at least the spirit of the antichrist . . . and Jesus *is* coming soon. Apocalypse now. Eternity now.

You might say, "Well, that's nice. But I just don't *get* it."

You don't have to *get* it. You don't have to understand it. You have to keep it and believe it in faith.

Time is weird in the Bible. "One day is as a thousand years, and a thousand years as one day" (2 Peter 3:8). Bible time doesn't always travel in a straight line—a chronology. Many Old Testament prophecies seem to refer to something in the time of the prophets. But when we read the New Testament we find they were also referring to Jesus. Multiple fulfillments.

Time shows up in different times—*kairos* in different *chronos,* qualitative time at different chronological times. The story of Jesus shows up again and again in Old Testament chronology. In Revelation 13:8, John writes of the lamb slain from the foundation of the world. That's Jesus—but wait; He was slain in A.D. 30 outside Jerusalem! How can that be?

But it gets even weirder. Jesus says, "Before Abraham was, I AM." Not I *was,* but I *am.* God told Moses His name was "I AM THAT I AM." In Revelation 1:4, John calls the Lord "him who is and who was and who is to come." And Paul says we "have been crucified with Christ," and are already seated "with him in the heavenly places" (Ephesians 2:6).

People who believe the Word of God know that the distinction between past, present, and future is a stubbornly persistent illusion. Time is weird in Scripture.

Time is also weird in physics. At Niels Bohr's funeral, Albert Einstein reportedly said, "People like us who believe in physics know the distinction between past, present, and future is a stubbornly persistent illusion."[7] Physics has demonstrated that the faster you go, relatively speaking, the slower time goes. At the speed of light, all time is present . . . *was, is,* and *is to come* are all present. There is no chronology, only eternity. And in the beginning God said, "Let there be light," and there was light.

God is bigger than time! His eternal *kairos* is pressing in on our temporal *chronos.* His light enlightens all men. His light entered our time in Jesus, the light of the world.

He came that we might have eternal life.

Eternal life is knowing Him.

We can know Him now.

Now is the day of salvation!

But what is *now?* As soon as we see it in our chronology, it's no longer *now.* It's already gone. *Now,* the present moment, is when we step out of time—our chronology—reflect on our history, and ask, "Does my time have meaning? Does my *chronos* have *kairos?*—love, joy, peace, patience, kindness, goodness . . . eternal meaning?"

And Jesus (the Logos, Word, Plot, Meaning . . . the light of the world), gives us meaning now. Eternity presses in on our temporality. God's *kairos* invades our *chronos.* Apocalypse now. Eternity now. Revelation now. Jesus now.

Sorry to get so philosophical. You might say, "Well, what does that mean?"

It means that when you're surfing the Web alone in your room, and you're tempted to sexual immorality, like they were in Thyatira, you'll see the truth: It's not just about biology. It's about an ancient harlot drunk with the blood of the saints, who rides a beast with seven heads drunk with the blood of the saints. The time is at hand, you call out to the Lamb . . . and you may end up changing Web sites. That's what it means.

When your life is falling apart in poverty, suffering, and tears, like the church in Smyrna, the preterist-futurist debate won't help much. But if you read about the New Jerusalem and streets of gold and believe the One on the throne who says, "I make all things new," that will help.

If they put a knife to your throat saying, "Renounce your faith or die!" like they did in Pergamum, like they've been doing in Indonesia, theories of the numeric acuity of the seven bowls won't help. But it will make all the difference in the world if you put your faith in the rider on the white horse: "Then I saw heaven opened, and behold, a white horse! He who sat upon it is called Faithful and True, and in righteousness he judges and makes war" (Revelation 19:11). That will make a difference.

Recently our church received an e-mail from an Australian pastor working with Christian refugees in Indonesia. Islamic extremists had declared a jihad on the island of Maluku and slaughtered more than ten thousand men, women, and children. Half a million fled their homes. The pastor (a friend of my friend) described the incredible suffering the Christians were under and then he shared this:

> We have heard on several occasions from different sources the story of jihad warriors attempting to land their boats in order to attack another Christian village. There is a mysterious figure dressed in white with a beard, riding a white horse, which repels the attackers. There is total confusion, and in the confusion a number of Muslims are killed. This is without Christians firing a shot! The Christians did not know this was happening until they started being visited by the military that were looking for an Australian (can you believe that?!) who was fighting for the Christians. They sent out investigative teams to look for this "Australian." Christians asked them to describe what he looked like and then responded, "That's not an Australian; that is the Lord Jesus Christ." Isn't that cool? And I've heard it from enough credible sources to believe it is not an "urban myth."[8]

I don't believe it's an urban myth. I believe the rider on the white horse went riding through that Indonesian village. And they recognized Him because

11

they'd read, heard, and taken it to heart. The time is *at hand*. "Then I saw heaven opened, and behold, a white horse! He who sat upon it is called Faithful and True, and in righteousness he judges and makes war" (Revelation 19:11).

If you say, "Oh, that can't happen until after the ten-nation confederacy!" then *stop trying to control your future*. Let God's future—God's eternity—control you. The time is at hand.

In fact, the end of your time is as close as your next heartbeat. He's coming back on the clouds of heaven at the end of the age. I really believe that. But I also believe that you may get hit by a truck on your way home. And behold, you will see Him—the *kairos* overtakes your *chronos*. The time is at hand.

REVELATION 1:4–8: *John to the seven churches that are in Asia:*

Grace to you and peace from him who is and who was and who is to come, and from the seven spirits who are before his throne, and from Jesus Christ the faithful witness, the first-born of the dead, and the ruler of kings on earth.

To him who loves us and has freed us from our sins by his blood and made us a kingdom, priests to his God and Father, to him be glory and dominion for ever and ever. Amen. Behold, he is coming with the clouds, and every eye will see him, every one who pierced him; and all tribes of the earth will wail on account of him. Even so. Amen.

"I am the Alpha and the Omega," says the Lord God, who is and who was and who is to come, the Almighty.

"Behold, he is coming." That's present tense.

TWO

DREAMING GOD'S DREAMS

(Revelation 1:9–20)

REVELATION 1:9–20: *I John, your brother, who share with you in Jesus the tribulation and the kingdom and the patient endurance, was on the island called Patmos on account of the word of God and the testimony of Jesus. I was in the Spirit on the Lord's day, and I heard behind me a loud voice like a trumpet saying, "Write what you see in a book and send it to the seven churches, to Ephesus and to Smyrna and to Pergamum and to Thyatira and to Sardis and to Philadelphia and to Laodicea."*

Then I turned to see the voice that was speaking to me, and on turning I saw seven golden lampstands, and in the midst of the lampstands one like a son of man, clothed with a long robe and with a golden girdle round his breast; his head and his hair were white as white wool, white as snow; his eyes were like a flame of fire, his feet were like burnished bronze, refined as in a furnace, and his voice was like the sound of many waters; in his right hand he held seven stars, from his mouth issued a sharp two-edged sword, and his face was like the sun shining in full strength.

When I saw him, I fell at his feet as though dead. But he laid his right hand upon me, saying, "Fear not, I am the first and the last, and the living one; I died, and behold I am alive for evermore, and I have the keys of Death and Hades. Now write what you see, what is and what is to take place hereafter. As for the mystery of the seven stars which you saw in my right hand, and the seven golden lampstands, the seven stars are the angels of the seven churches and the seven lampstands are the seven churches.

WOW! THAT'S PRETTY INCREDIBLE.
 Do you believe it? Do you?
  You believe it as a metaphor, right?
   Because you don't *actually* believe

Jesus had a sharp, two-edged sword
coming out of His mouth!
How could He talk?

Do you *actually* believe He had seven stars in His hand? Do you *actually* believe that your church is a *lampstand?* Was Jesus actually on Patmos? He is at the right hand of the Father on high . . . so was He actually at Patmos or was it more like a *dream?*

Psychologists say dreams are critical—metaphors that help us work through realities. But dreams are not real . . . are they?

In a *Rocky Mountain News* article on people's belief in the paranormal, Professor Robert Baker was quoted as saying, "Modern Americans aren't so different than primitive humans who thought that when lightning struck it was God throwing thunderbolts. So many things about the world and nature are absolutely mysterious to them. The desire to find supernatural explanations for natural events is still with us, and will be until more people get good basic scientific educations."[1]

This last century was the pinnacle of modernism. People argued that the only things that are real or true are those that can be verified by the scientific method. That is: Only hypotheses that can be tested in a controlled environment in space and time are true. Well . . . how do we know even that is true?

What if truth is bigger than space and time?

Satan took Jesus to the top of the temple and said, "Let's run a little test. Throw yourself down, and we will see if Scripture is true, if angels will come and bear you up." And Jesus said, "Thou shalt not put the Lord your God to the test!" (see Luke 4:9–12).

This last century argued that the only things you *can* believe are things you can put to the test. And Satan smiles, for that means we cannot believe in God, who is truth. We may know more facts than anyone in the world . . . but none of them have any meaning or truth, for meaning and truth themselves (Himself) can't be scientifically proven.

"Thou shalt not put the Lord your God to the test."

Why? I suppose it's because it is insanely arrogant to act as if God were a laboratory mouse. Yet even more than that, it's profoundly stupid. If God *were* to submit to our test, we wouldn't believe it was *God.* What would we do? Probably crucify Him. And if He rose from the dead, we still wouldn't believe, because it wasn't a controlled environment or a repeatable event.

Anything really good can't be proven by science anyway. What laboratory has ever discovered *goodness?* Or justice? Or truth? Or beauty? Or love? For that matter, the scientific method cannot even be proven by the scientific method! Any real scientist knows that.

In the last hundred years, science has shown that there is so much more to our universe than science (repeatable events in space and time). Science tells us that the universe had a beginning—a big bang. It sprang into existence, seemingly out of nothing (no space or time). Even more shocking is Einstein's theory of relativity: that time is relative to the speed of light. Time is not the constant; light is . . . (hey, Jesus is the Light). Our experience of time changes with gravity and the velocity at which we travel. According to science, the world is 15.75 billion years old from earth's viewpoint. Yet if you stood at the big bang looking out at the earth, the world would be not quite seven days old (not because the Bible says so but because MIT physicist Gerald Schroeder says so).[2]

Even more bizarre, quantum physics implies that at the subatomic level, the quantum state of matter is mysteriously dependent on an observer, not a "what" but a "who." As if spirit is more real than matter. Isn't God spirit? (John 4:24) And doesn't He observe all things and uphold all things by His word of power? He isn't a "what" but a "who."

It must be hard to be a materialist when science itself shows that matter is like a dream. Reality is a very persistent illusion, remarked Einstein. He also observed that imagination is more important than knowledge—as if dreams are more real than fact!

Have you ever had a dream that you were dreaming, but the dream within your dream was actually a person in the waking world trying to wake you up? What if this entire world is like a dream, and we're in the process of being awakened?

When we are awakened from a dream, the thing that wakes us is a reality that won't fit in our dream. My dream can all be explained by *me.* Some dreams are very weird, but they all emanate from me. They are all about *me.* But when someone or something wakes me, my mind can't fit that reality from the outside waking world into the interior reality of my dream world.

If you wake someone too quickly from a dream, you can kill him from the shock. Did you notice that in Revelation 1:17 John fell down as though dead until Jesus touched him and said, "Fear not"? The loving thing to do when rousing someone from a dream is to wake them up slowly, whispering, "Sweetheart . . . you're having a bad dream. Wake up. It's just a bad dream."

To the dreamer in her dream, there is a gradual realization that the whisper in her ear can't be explained by the dream. But for a while it's like the whisper is a part of the dream—an incongruous part of the dream.

Are there things in your world that are incongruent? That don't fit? That can't be explained by this world? Paradoxes, mysteries, things you can't comprehend?

Maybe *they* are real, and this entire world is the dream. Maybe those things are somebody whispering in your ear, "Sweetheart . . . wake up."

About those people who believe God is actually somehow behind thunder, Professor Baker said, "So many things about the world and nature are absolutely mysterious to them."[3] Maybe that's because *they* are waking up . . . and Professor Baker is enchanted by his own self-centered dream.

No mystery . . . meaning . . . paradox . . . wonder . . . because he's entirely asleep.

John records in his Gospel that at one point in Jesus' ministry a voice from the sky said, "I have glorified it [His name], and I will glorify it again" (John 12:28–29). Some standing there said, "It thundered." Others said, "That was *more* than thunder!" Who was dreaming and who was awake?

Maybe Jesus really *did* appear to John. Maybe Jesus really *did* have a sharp, two-edged sword coming out of His mouth. Maybe your church really *is* a lampstand. Maybe it's not just a metaphor, and maybe mystery . . . paradox . . . wonder . . . aren't *less* real than this world, but *more* real than this world.

In 1880 a preacher and schoolmaster named Edwin Abbot published a book called *Flatland: A Romance in Many Dimensions*.[4] It was adapted as a film to explain geometry concepts, although Abbot's purpose was to help people believe in God. The movie featured an entirely two-dimensional world called Flatland, whose inhabitants can perceive only two dimensions. One day, one of them has a revelation. For a few moments, he is lifted out of Flatland and experiences three dimensions. When he returns to Flatland, he tries to explain what he saw: "It's not simply a square, it's a *cube!*" he exclaims. "That's not just a circle, it's a *sphere!*" The other Flatlanders think he's dreaming.

Jesus reveals: "You're not just a church, you're a lampstand!" We say, "Nice metaphor . . . interesting dream." If we were Flatlanders, we'd understand our world as a piece of poster board. With our scientific method we could perceive two-dimensional realities such as squares, circles, and triangles. But suppose that a three-dimensional object entered our world and passed through it, like a sphere. (See figure 1.) What would we see? A circle. What would we call it? A miracle. Why? Because all at once a point appeared in our world, then grew into a circle, then shrank back to a point, and then was gone.

What if three-dimensional objects (spheres, cubes, cones) intersected our flat world all the time and stayed? We'd be surrounded by miracles all the time but probably wouldn't know it.

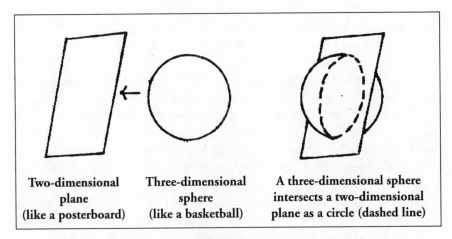

| Two-dimensional plane (like a posterboard) | Three-dimensional sphere (like a basketball) | A three-dimensional sphere intersects a two-dimensional plane as a circle (dashed line) |

Figure 1

- We'd say, "Oh, that's a square." But the one who received the revelation would say, "That's more than a square. That's a cube!"

- We'd say, "Hey, that guy over there is reading the Bible." But the guy with a revelation would say, "No! The sword of the living Christ is piercing a human heart."

- We'd say, "Look—a church." He'd say, "It's a lampstand."

- We'd say, "Look—that woman is giving a cup of cold water to a little kid in Jesus' name. What a nice thought." He would say, "Behold, Jesus the Christ is drinking His own love."

- We'd say, "Hey, look—a baby in a manger." And he would start singing with the angels.

Why? His world would be full of miracle and meaning. He couldn't explain paradox, but he could believe it.

If I took three fingers, stuck them through Flatland, and proclaimed, "Behold: all three circles are one. They are all me. Three yet one. I am trinity." Flatlanders would say, "Inconceivable." The guy with the revelation would say, "It's true!" Would it be a metaphor? No. It would be truth more real than Flatland.

Maybe you came to Jesus at a junior high camp. Did you know you were chosen before the foundation of the world? Predestined, chosen in Him, yet chosen to choose. That's a paradox—I can't comprehend it! But it's *true*.

Now suppose time is one of the dimensions of Flatland. Imagine its breadth across a piece of poster board. On the left it's A.D. 30; on the right it's two thousand years later. If I took that piece of poster board and held it a millimeter in front of me, saying, "Behold, Flatland! The kingdom of Peter is at hand!" in every place in Flatland that would be true. In every *time* in Flatland that would be true. And every place I intersected Flatland I would have come to that place in the space and time of Flatland.

Where *I* intersected Flatland, I would be *present* at all those points in their space and time. Now let's say I intersected Flatland at *every* point in their space and time, because Flatland was a two-dimensional plane inside of *me*. Then what could I say to Flatlanders? "Behold, in me you live and move and have your being." And they wouldn't even know it . . . unless they believed.

In fact, you could say I was a *reality* in Flatland, that I was present in Flatland wherever people *believed* . . . wherever they *saw*, not with their eyes, because their eyes can see only two dimensions, but with their *hearts*.

What would *really* be cool is if I could somehow *enter* Flatland as a two-dimensional being. I don't have that capability. Wouldn't it be cool if someone did? But suppose I could, and I came back to Flatland to end its space and time. What if I revealed myself to all of Flatland at once? All eyes would see me coming. Maybe they'd say, "Behold! He comes on the clouds of heaven." A thief on a cross in A.D. 33 might say it, and an old lady dying on a nursing home bed in A.D. 2003 might say it. Every person might say it—but each in a different space and time on the board. And they'd all be right, all at once (not *their* once, but *my* once).

I'm not sure what all this means for the timing of Christ's return at the end of the age, but it does mean I'll believe what Jesus said to that thief on the cross in A.D. 33: "Truly . . . today you will be with me in Paradise" (Luke 23:43). And I'll believe what Jesus said to His disciples, including those in nursing home beds in the twenty-first century: "I will come again and will take you to myself that where I am you may be also" (John 14:3). And I'll believe Him when He says, "Behold, the time is at hand."

Mystery, meaning, paradox, *miracle*—all would seem like dreams in Flatland. Yet those dreams would be *more real* than anybody in Flatland could comprehend. Here's an interesting question: Do you ever experience paradox in *this* world of four dimensions (breadth, length, height, and time)? Do you ever sense mystery? Or perceive meaning (truth, beauty, justice, love)? These things cannot be isolated, tested, and comprehended in the three or four dimensions of this world.

Did you know that in order for physicists to make their calculations work for the big bang and the first few moments afterward, they have postulated *at least* nine dimensions of space and time? Those are physicists! Christians are the ones who believe God made all those things and is bigger and better, before and after, smaller and larger, outside and inside *all* of them.

Stop taking these three or four dimensions so seriously! Ironically, it's many Christians who take space and time—this world—so *seriously!* We spend our time arguing about the timing of the great tribulation and never stop to ask, "What does it *mean?*"

If you believe the Revelation is *literally* true, that's great! I think *I* do, if I understand what you mean by that: It's more than a metaphor. But it's also more than literally true; it's about far more than space and time in this world —and your life had better be about far more than space and time in this world.

Not every glass of water given to a child is an encounter with the living God. It must be given in Jesus' name . . . in faith and in love.

For on that day many will say to Him, "Did we not . . . do many mighty works in your name?" And He will look at them and say, "I never knew you; depart from me, you evildoers" (Matthew 7:22–23).

You might do all the two-dimensional works of a Christian and look good to everybody in Flatland, but God would know you never knew Him. Maybe you just went around drawing squares, acting as if you believed in cubes. Not every square in Flatland is really a cube. And there is more to being a Christian than just being square.

You might own every graph mapping the Revelation. You might know every detail. You might comprehend the science of a bloodred moon and still not know its meaning.

Jesus reveals its meaning. Jesus *is* meaning . . . Logos . . . Word . . . Truth . . . Plot.

Right here in the first chapter of the Revelation, Jesus reveals the meaning of the stars: "John, I'll tell you what the stars are." And right here in chapter 1, Jesus reveals the meaning of the lampstands: "John, I'll tell you what the lamp-stands are." But we have to trust Jesus to reveal His meaning for the rest of the book as well.

Jesus is the uncreated Creator,
> from beyond and before space and time,
>> who enters our four-dimensional world,
>> and reveals meaning.

He is the Lamb who opens the scroll. He entered this world, limiting Himself in our four dimensions in order to reveal truth. He purchased us with His blood, from principalities and powers that kept us in darkness and bondage, and He's waking us up to life in *His* world—the kingdom of God.

In order to wake up, you must dream His dreams. His dreams are more real than this world. One day you'll see they *aren't* dreams; they're reality.

How can we know *anything* truly real? Only through revelation. Even science depends on revelation; that is, faith that there is such a thing as truth or meaning. How can we encounter anything truly real? Only through revelation. And in this world, that looks like worship.

Did you notice that John was "in the Spirit on the Lord's day"? (1:10). The Lord's day probably refers to Sunday. When the church worshiped God they gathered together on Sunday. He was in the Spirit on the Lord's day *when* he received the revelation. Receiving the revelation was not being in the Spirit. So what *was* being in the Spirit? I think it must have been worship!

Prayer, praise, wonder, sacrament, worship . . . in God, in Christ. Worship is the opposite of the scientific method. It's not conquest but surrender. In an experiment, a scientist tests things to comprehend them. In worship God tests us and comprehends us. A scientist masters his subject. A worshiper is the subject that is mastered. In worship we surrender to God, and God in His grace reveals His glory. Do you want to know God? Then worship Him, in spirit and in truth.

"The hour is coming, and now is, when the true worshipers will worship the Father in spirit and in truth, for such the Father seeks to worship him. God is spirit" (John 4:23–24). Worship *in* truth: Worship Jesus and surrender to the dreams He gives you. *God* is more than you know, and *you* are more than you know. He is waking you up from the bad dream of a fallen world.

- Have you ever felt love in worship? John wrote, "He who loves is born of God and knows God" (1 John 4:7). That's more than you know.

- Have you ever felt joy, peace, patience, kindness, gentleness, goodness in worship? In one dimension they may be chemicals in the blood responding to a good song. But Paul tells us they're fruit from the Spirit of God (see Galatians 5:22).

- Have you ever felt grateful in worship? Every good and perfect gift comes from God (see James 1:17).

Worship and pay attention to the dreams that come. God has already given you this dream—the Revelation. It only seems like a dream because this world is asleep.

"Awake, O sleeper, and arise from the dead, and Christ shall give you light." (Ephesians 5:14)

THREE

AWAKENING TO JESUS

(Revelation 1:12–18)

ONE EVENING OVER DINNER, a friend and I had a conversation about government and "the kings of the earth"—specifically, politics and power. "Peter," he said, "I think where you and I see things differently is that I'm not *sure* that God is always in control. This idea of omnipotence is a Greek idea—*all power.* I believe Jesus won at Calvary. I believe He will win in the end. But I'm not sure He's *always* in control."

Then he said, "Go to Auschwitz and stand there as I did, and tell me God's in control. Such suffering? Under His sovereignty?" In other words, my friend argued God has control at the beginning and the end, but maybe He's not in control of every little battle in your life. He'd like to help, but He can't. Therefore, we have to be pragmatic about winning, especially in politics, as we battle the "kings of the earth."

"It sounds like you're saying God *needs* you," I observed.

"Of course!" he responded. You need the people you love, don't you? You *need* them. God *needs* me."

You know, that is a really exhilarating thought . . . God *needs* me.

And it's absolutely horrifying.

THE BIBLE ENDS WITH A GREAT UNVEILING—the *Revelation* of Jesus. *Apocalypto* means "to unveil." The Bible begins with a great *veiling—katacalypto.* The great dragon is conquered in the Revelation. But the great dragon (the serpent) shows up in the garden at the beginning of Scripture and tempts the man and the woman. He seduces them with the dream of their own absolute sovereignty. The serpent says to them, "Hey—eat the fruit. Make yourself like God."

So they eat, they know shame, and God casts them out of the garden. God had told them, "The day you eat the fruit of the tree you die." Adam and Eve become the walking dead, asleep in the illusion of their own sovereignty. They can no longer see God; all His glory is veiled.

Adam and Eve are blind, dead, and enslaved to the dragon. The dream turns into a nightmare that turns into hell: to be alone forever in the insane self-centered dream of your own sovereignty.

Reread Revelation 1:1–8. It begins the "unveiling of Jesus" and is addressed to the seven little churches facing immense persecution at the hands of the "kings of the earth." In verse 5 we read that Jesus is ruler of the "kings of the earth," and that Jesus had "freed us [the seven little churches] from our sins" and "made us to be a kingdom and priests" (KJV "hath made us kings and priests) (v. 6). We are already kings and priests (see 1 Peter 2:9).

These seven little churches under persecution have already become kings and priests—what a weird picture this is—it's like a God joke on the kings of the earth. Despite their illusion of power, the "kings of the earth" are not where the action is in the Revelation.

The action is with a baby: the Lamb that was slain, who turns out to be born of a woman (in Revelation 12) who is clothed in the sun and wears twelve stars on her head. I believe that woman is us—the people of God, "the Israel of God," who gives birth to the child. The child caught up to heaven is Jesus. Jesus is born of *us*. He is fully human as well as fully divine. He is born of us and saves us— His mother, and His brothers, and His sisters—the Church. He even said it: "Who is my mother and who is my brother and who is my sister? All those who do the will of my Father in heaven (see Matthew 12:48–49).

Who is that? Us! The Church.

So the action is with the Church. The action is with some baby believers in Asia Minor. They, in fact, are the real kings and priests, while the kings of this world are only pawns in the hands of Jesus the Christ in the service of His Father and His brothers and sisters. For He is King of kings and Lord of lords.

"Behold, he is coming with the clouds, and every eye will see him, every one who pierced him; and all tribes of the earth will [mourn] on account of him. Even so. Amen. 'I am the Alpha and the Omega,' says the Lord God, who is and who was and who is to come, the Almighty" (Revelation 1:7–8).

Sounds like Jesus is pretty much in control. In fact, that word "Almighty"— *pantokrator* in Greek—can be translated "omnipotent, all powerful." This isn't some abstract, philosophical concept; it means actual control over everything. The Lord God "who is and who was and who is to come, the Almighty" (v. 8) is a reference to the Hebrew *Yahweh Sabaot*—absolute and unrivaled power and control over . . . all time, all space, all history; for every time, every place, and every*how.*

He accomplishes all things according to the counsel of His will (Ephesians 1:11). He never loses control; He only *surrenders* it—and even then, He only surrenders it to Himself, the Son surrendering it to the Father. It is according to plan, and what appears to be His greatest loss—crucified in shame on a Friday—we find out is His greatest victory come Sunday.

In the Book of Revelation . . .

- there is never any question of God's victory, every*where,* every*when,* and every*how.*

- there is never any question about the dragon and what the dragon will do.

- there is never any question about what the *beast* will do.

- there is never any question about what the *harlot* will do.

- there is never any question about what the kings of the earth will do, or whether or not there will be famines and plagues and earthquakes and natural disasters.

They *will* all happen according to plan. None of that is in question.

The only question in the Book of Revelation is . . . *you.* This is a paradox of time and eternity; sovereignty and freedom; predestination and free will. The question is, *Will you conquer?*

In Ephesus, will they repent of dead works and conquer?

In Pergamum, will they renounce idols and conquer?

In Thyatira, will they repent of immorality and conquer?

In Philadelphia, will they hold fast and conquer?

In Laodicea, will they humble themselves and conquer?

Will *they,* will *you*—the Church—conquer?

How are we going to find the strength to conquer? *I think that's what this whole vision is about.* It's not as if John wrote seven letters to these churches and then said, "Oh, by the way, I had this vision." They must read it, hear it, and surrender to it. That is, they must surrender their *dream* of sovereignty to the reality of God's sovereignty in Jesus the Christ. And *Jesus always conquers.*

Even when Jesus bleeds, He wins.

Even when He dies, He wins.

If you surrender sovereignty to Jesus, *you always win.*

Every*where,*
  every*when,* and
    every*how.*

"Thanks be to God," writes Paul, "who in Christ *always* leads us in triumph" (2 Corinthians 2:14, emphasis added). God has put *all things* under Jesus' sovereignty—He has made Him head over all things. Why? For the Church, which is His body, the fullness of Him "who fills all in all" (Ephesians 1:20–22).

All creation, the kings of the earth, the plagues, the famines, the dragons, the sufferings . . . become instruments in the hands of Jesus, for loving you. All time and space become an instrument in His hands for loving you. He literally transforms past, present, and future, for love of you. When you repent, even your past sins are transformed into a means of unveiling for you the wonders of His mercy.

Think of it . . . the kings of the earth . . . dragons and demons . . . space and time—no big challenge for Jesus.

But He died for you
  that you would surrender
    your dream of sovereignty
      to Him in love.

Now is the day of salvation, writes Paul. I surrender in the present moment, *now*—the point at which eternity touches time—and *all* time is transformed. How can He *do* that? He's the Lord of time.

Your past . . . transformed; your future . . . sealed and secure. It really doesn't matter what the kings of the earth do or don't do. They are only pawns in your Savior's hand. It matters what *you* do . . . *now.* That *you* walk in the obedience of faith *now.* Let's be honest, I can't win. I can't conquer. I am called to surrender . . . *now.* When we surrender, "thanks be to God who gives us the victory through Christ Jesus" (1 Corinthians 15:57). He conquers . . . in us.

As soon as I think *I'm* in control, as soon as I think Peter Hiett can preach a really great sermon that could save somebody . . . as soon as I think I could enact legislation that would affect the kings of the earth and change the world . . . as soon as *I* think I could bring the kingdom . . . *I'm dreaming—the walking dead enslaved to the dragon and the beast.*

Now, Jesus may do all those things through me . . . save people . . . enact legislation . . . bring the kingdom . . . but without Him I can do nothing. My calling is to surrender sovereignty to Him. In other words, my calling is *faith* . . . *trust* . . . every moment. Surrendering to God's sovereignty is waking from the dream of my own sovereignty, and that is terrifying.

REVELATION 1:12–17: *Then I turned to see the voice that was speaking to me, and on turning I saw seven golden lampstands, and in the midst of the lampstands one like a son of man, clothed with a long robe and with a golden girdle round his breast; his head and his hair were white as white wool, white as snow; his eyes were like a flame of fire, his feet were like burnished bronze, refined as in a furnace, and his voice was like the sound of many waters; in his right hand he held seven stars, from his mouth issued a sharp two-edged sword, and his face was like the sun shining in full strength.*

When I saw him, I fell at his feet as though dead.

In our own dreams, our minds are sovereign—they are in control. The thing that wakes us is something outside our sovereignty and control.

> The children of Adam are dead
> in a dream of their own control.

John *saw* the voice. He *saw* the Word of God, in whom and by whom all things were made, who is before all things, in whom all things hold together (see Colossians 1:17 and John 1:1–3). And John's dream of his own sovereignty was utterly shattered. He fell at the feet of reality as though dead.

Every particle in his body was held together by the express will of this voice.

> Every heartbeat was a gift;
> every breath—entirely dependent on the continuous
> grace of the One before him.

And he could see it.

Your next heartbeat exists solely because of the express will of Jesus Christ our Lord in God His Father. Because He wills it. Do you believe that? Not really. You consent to it, but if you really believed it, you'd be on the floor.

John woke to the sovereignty of God and collapsed in terror.

When Susan and I were newly married, we were living in a dangerous part of Los Angeles. I came home unexpectedly from a great distance at "an hour she did not expect." She was sound asleep, dreaming her dreams. I had been driving all night. I had been through a crisis and *missed* her so very much. I *wanted* her.

I tried desperately not to startle her, for she thought she was alone and wasn't expecting me. But trying not to startle a person at 3:00 A.M. is all the more entering like a thief in the night. I remember thinking if only I could enter her dreams and whisper, "Honey, it's me. I'm coming home. And I'm coming like a thief in the night, but it's *me* and I'll be waking you soon." But I couldn't do that. I wiggled the lock; the keys jiggled in my hand. And I heard a voice of absolute terror from the other room. "Is somebody there? Who is it! Oh my God, who is it?" In that instant I knew she believed that whoever I was, I was in absolute control, and so she expected me to hurt her, to rape her. Rape is stolen sovereignty.

In that instant I so wished that I could have entered her dreams and told her, "Sweetheart . . . I will never rape you. However, if you wish, my greatest desire is to make love to you. I am your husband. So awake, O sleeper. And I will give you life."

The only "if" in all the Book of Revelation belongs to the bride of Christ. Don't you see it? He says, "I will not rape you, but I long to love you. If you will only surrender, I will impregnate you with life." His love is life.

Well, I didn't have all that figured out at three in the morning when Susan freaked out, but I do remember that after I calmed her down and she realized it was me, I received a pretty great loving that night.

THIS IS A MYSTERY. Jesus has been veiled, for we have sinned and dreamed our own sovereignty. But listen closely: Jesus has also been veiled according to God's sovereign plan that God might unveil to us His glory . . .

- that we might see the road that leads nowhere,
- that we might glimpse over the edge of the abyss,
- that we might taste, or at least smell, the scent of hell,
- that we might dream the insane dream of our own sovereignty . . .

. . . and then *wake up* to His glory with a knowledge that the angels long to look into—the knowledge of the grace of God in Christ Jesus our Lord. "For God has consigned all men to disobedience," writes Paul in Romans 11:32, "that he may have mercy upon all." I believe in the Revelation we will find out that we, the Church, sing a song nobody else knows—not the angels, not the demons, not the creatures around the throne; but *we* know it.

It's the song of the Lamb, and it infuriates the ancient dragon, for it is the grace of God in Christ Jesus our Lord. By it the dragon is defeated. That's why the dragon hates all the children of the woman in chapter 12. It's why human life is so sacred, for we can know the glory of God in Christ Jesus our Lord, and we can become vessels for that very glory, which is Christ in us. In Christ we conquer. He *gives* the victory to us in grace.

It's not that He *needs* us. He *wants* us, so thoroughly and completely that He emptied Himself, became small and weak, and entered the insane little dream of our own sovereignty in order to whisper to us His Bride, "Awaken to my love and live." He was born into our world as a baby, crucified, then resurrected in glory. He is born into our lives and our churches like a whisper from beyond, so we may waken to His glory without being utterly destroyed.

REVELATION 1:17–18: *But he laid his right hand upon me, saying, "Fear not, I am the first and the last, and the living one; I died, and behold I am alive for evermore, and I have the keys of Death and Hades."*

"John! John! It's Me—Jesus. I was born in Bethlehem. And I met you that day you were fishing in Galilee, remember? John, it's Me—Jesus. You laid your head on My chest at supper, you listened to My heartbeat and I whispered in your ear of this day, John.

"John, I asked you to come pray with Me, and you were so sleepy. I was praying about this day, John, sleepy-head John. You saw Me die. John, *I* am the living one. *I* hold the keys of death and hell. I am in control; I always win. So don't fear, John. Get up."

One day I think you'll feel a hand on your shoulder, and you'll hear the voice that created the worlds and the galaxies say something like this: "Hey, it's *Me*. I was singing to you through your mom, remember? You met Me at camp, remember? I was with you on the couch those nights when you were so scared. So don't be afraid. Because I hold the keys of death and hell, and now it's time to get up. It's time to live."

Four

Awakening to Ecstasy

(Revelation 2:1–7)

In 1978 I WENT ON MY FIRST DATE with my Susan Coleman, who is now Susan Hiett. We went to see *Close Encounters of the Third Kind.* It was sold out, so we went next door and saw another movie that turned out to be terrible. After that we went back and saw the late showing of *Close Encounters of the Third Kind.*

During the first movie I had managed to get my arm around my date. I was so enamored with her that I would not move it. She asked, "Doesn't your arm hurt?"

"Oh, no," I said, "it's fine." By the second movie my arm was screaming in pain, but still I wouldn't move it. Finally, it was utterly paralyzed . . . from my neck all the way to my fingertips. At last I had to excuse myself, reach around her head, pick my arm up, set it on my lap, and slap it until it came to.

On our second date, I worked like crazy cleaning my car and making plans. I prepared a picnic and took her up to a mountain pasture where my family kept our horse. But we couldn't catch the horse, so we picnicked on a rock under a pine tree, and we talked about death. My friend Bobby had died that week in a car accident. We talked, and talked, and talked . . . and I was stricken with her.

On our third date, I arranged for another picnic. We drove to the top of Loveland Pass, parked the car, and hiked up a thirteen-thousand-foot mountain in our tennis shoes in midwinter. I remember looking at her and thinking, *Wow! What a woman!*

Of course, I was being conned. I found out later that my wife would rather scrub a million toilets than climb a frozen mountain in midwinter. But, you see, it was a *beautiful* con. She didn't climb it because she loved frozen mountains; she wanted to be with *me.* She disciplined herself for me.

After that we snowshoed to my Uncle Chuck's cabin in the woods, and we had a picnic in the treehouse that I played in as a little boy. Having picnics in treehouses doesn't especially float my boat, but I thought that maybe it would float hers. And it *did*. It *worked*. I was in *love*.

On our fourth date, we went to a dance. In a James Bond-like, romance-induced fog, I drove my dad's car over a median on South Broadway in Littleton, Colorado, and bent the frame. It was *bad*. And she still liked me!

I was feeling pretty secure in our relationship, so on the fifth date . . . we just went to a movie. And on the sixth date we went to a movie . . . on the seventh date we went to a movie . . . eighth, ninth, tenth, eleventh, twelfth, thirteenth . . . went to a movie.

It was about then that I said, "You know, maybe we ought to date other people too."

REVELATION 2:1–7: *To the angel of the church in Ephesus write: "The words of him who holds the seven stars in his right hand, who walks among the seven golden lampstands.*

"I know your works, your toil and your patient endurance, and how you cannot bear evil men but have tested those who call themselves apostles but are not, and found them to be false; I know you are enduring patiently and bearing up for my name's sake, and you have not grown weary. But I have this against you, that you have abandoned the love you had at first. Remember then from what you have fallen, repent and do the works you did at first. If not, I will come to you and remove your lampstand from its place, unless you repent. Yet this you have, you hate the works of the Nicolaitans, which I also hate. He who has an ear, let him hear what the Spirit says to the churches. To him who conquers I will grant to eat of the tree of life, which is in the paradise of God."

Can you imagine how Jesus felt, writing to His Bride in Ephesus? "You've abandoned the love you had at first." That must have been a very *painful* letter for Jesus, for He was being spurned by the one He loved.

In the last chapter, I shared with you how I came home and woke my wife at an unexpected hour. I said I wished I could have entered her dreams and whispered to her so she wouldn't die in shock. "Don't be afraid, honey. I won't rape you. But if you desire, if you wish, my greatest longing is to make love to you. I'm your *husband!* Don't be afraid. Awake, O sleepy one, and I will impregnate you with life."

Did that offend you? I've found that some people get offended when a pastor preaches about sex in church. I think that's strange, for we are the Bride of Christ, bound to Him in a covenant, communing with Him in the sanctuary, receiving His body and blood, receiving the Word, which is seed, that we would bear His life in us.

You see, I was making a very serious point: One day, Bride of Christ, you will awaken to ecstasy, and the joy will be that much deeper and that much stronger because you have been to the edge of hell, in bondage to the dragon who steals your sovereignty and rapes your soul. But now you are being awakened by the Bridegroom, who is the lover of souls. He does not force Himself; He romances your soul into the ecstasy of surrender—surrendered sovereignty. His goal is *ecstasy.* Joy! Deeper than this entire, fallen world—and it is not cheap.

- "For the *joy* that was set before him [he] endured the cross, despising the shame" (Hebrews 12:2). And what was that joy, Bride of Christ? *You!*
- *The Lord delights in you,* says Isaiah. "As the bridegroom rejoices over the bride, so shall your God rejoice over you" (Isaiah 62:5). How does a bridegroom take delight in his bride?
- The psalmist wrote that the sun declares the glory of God. It comes forth "like a bridegroom leaving his chamber" (19:5). *The bridegroom is radiant with delight.*

The great Bridegroom longs to take delight in His Bride. But He will *not* take delight unless she surrenders it, because His delight is *her* delight. And that communion of delight gives birth to life, fruit, babies.

But Satan steals,
> and the dragon rapes,
>> and gives birth
>>> to death and fear.

Several years ago I sat in a car with a man who was planning to leave his wife. I was pleading with him to stay. Finally he said, "Peter, do you know that on our wedding night she wouldn't let me touch her? She wouldn't let me make love to her for three days, because she wasn't interested."

No doubt this man's divorcing his wife was a great sin. But my friend's wife was also guilty of a great sin. Both believed the dragon.

We may be married to Christ, and Satan can't prevent that now; however, with lies he can keep us from bearing fruit. Roommates bear no fruit. Only lovers bear fruit.

God doesn't want a roommate. He pursues a lover.

The dragon tempts us to immorality *and* morality: that is, to shame, so we would eventually just become roommates with hearts sealed off to the great Bridegroom, so that the *seed*—the Word of God, Jesus Himself—could not be implanted in the fertile, open soil of our hearts.

Through immorality the dragon tempts us to offer our hearts to idols that end up raping us to our shame. Then we associate passionate, intimate communion . . . with shame.

We watch television and laugh at sexual innuendos. We talk openly about these things with friends. We tell sexual jokes in the parking lot after church. But if the preacher mentions sex in the sanctuary, we're offended. How strange. That's the one place we should not be offended: In the sanctuary experiencing communion (a sacramental union of the physical and spiritual) all bound by an unbreakable covenant.

Paul wrote to the Ephesians, about thirty years before John: "'For this reason a man shall leave his father and his mother and be joined to his wife, and the two shall become one flesh.' This mystery is a profound one, and I am saying that it refers to Christ and the church" (5:31–32).

Maybe the ancient dragon is lying to us about far more than just sex. He is lying to us about Jesus. He lies through immorality, but he also lies to us through morality—sin and law. Immorality is the door to morality—the law. Satan whispers, "Since your heart was raped, never surrender your heart again. Guard your naked heart. Guard it . . . with morality . . . with law . . . everything in its proper place! Maintain control over the sovereign little kingdom of your heart. This is what Jesus is for—to guard the borders and keep your little kingdom secure."

We are the Bride of Christ. Why are you betrothed to Christ? So He will guard the border of your prim and proper little kingdom, keeping you safe inside? Are you betrothed to Him for security—eternal fire insurance? "What a great provider!" Jesus may want to come and scatter the kingdom of your primness and draw you into a wild, passionate romance in which you lose everything and gain Him. He did not hang on a cross and bear the pain of hell so you would be regular in your devotions, go on one mission project a year, and be a faithful tither. He suffered, died, and endured hell in order to win your heart . . .

> that you would surrender your sovereignty to His sovereignty;
>
> that you would surrender to ecstasy.

But Satan has made you fear the deepest longing of your soul so you would spurn the Lord's advances and turn Him into a roommate and a border guard.

Jesus says to the Ephesians, "Ephesus, I see your works. I see your faithful endurance. I see your orthodoxy. And you hate the work of the Nicolaitans. I hate their works too." (The Nicolaitans may have been a group that taught sexual immorality was just fine.) I think Jesus is saying, *Thank you, Ephesus, for hating immorality—passion out of bounds. But, my dear, you have come to hate passion in bounds! You cook, you clean, you take care of the children, and I'm absolutely convinced you'd never give your passion to another. But what's the point? You never give it to Me.*

"You have forsaken the love you had at first."

We can philosophize and theologize all we want about what "love" means . . . *agape, storge, phileo, eros* . . . but *you know* what Jesus means. "You've lost that loving feeling." And we say, "Lost the loving *feeling?! I* can't control my feelings!" *Wrong.* If you're a Christian, that is basically psycho-bull-ony. How do I know that? Because the living Lord says, "Repent. Remember. And do those things you did at first, Ephesus."

People have commented to me that my wife and I seem to have a pretty passionate relationship—as if that just kind of *happens.* It is a gift, but let me tell you: We've had to *fight* for it, beginning twenty-four years ago, after our thirteenth date, when I remember praying, "Oh, God, I think the problem is with me. Every time I win a girl's heart, I get tired of her and lose passion for her. God, I don't think I understand love. Help me."

We've had to discipline ourselves for passion. While we were dating it meant abstaining in hope of greater passion when we were married. Once married, it meant disciplining ourselves even *more* for passion. Four little children, a wife that gets no sleep, a job that can consume every waking moment, a culture that constantly invites us to be unfaithful, the middle-aged spread on my gut and on my wife's whatever—and most of all, the frightened little insecure, painful hearts that we each carry into the sanctuary of our bedroom, where God calls us to celebrate the sacrament of our marriage covenant.

It's been a fight for passion. And it has cost me energy and, mostly, pride.

Can you imagine how Jesus—the Word that was with God and was God— felt writing to His Bride in Ephesus? I think *I* can . . .

Years ago when my wife was nursing our last child, she didn't have much energy for me. And I was desperate for her affection . . . *any* affection—a hug, a kiss, a smile. She would say, "I grew up in a family that didn't express itself that much. I cook, I clean, I take care of the children . . . *that's* how I say I love you."

But I knew the truth. She was growing tired of fighting for passion. And it *was* a fight for her, because, unlike Jesus, I can be very critical and self-centered and insensitive . . . not easy to love.

During that time I would stay awake all night sometimes, angry and frustrated, not knowing what to do with my feelings. Sexual immorality—movies, the Entertainment Channel—was especially *tempting!* I could demand sexuality, but I couldn't demand delight. For her delight is my delight: a communion of delight. Yet to tell her how I felt was utterly humiliating. Some nights I remember thinking to myself, *Peter, just give up! Give up on being lovers, and settle for being roommates.*

That temptation came from hell.

By the grace of God, one of those late nights I wrote my wife a letter. I bared my soul: "Susan, this is my heart. Remember how you were when we were dating? When we were first married? I *remember* the things you did at first. Do those things." That letter gave her hope, and it became a new beginning for us.

God has written His sleeping Bride a letter. The name of the letter is "Jesus"—the Word of God. I'm hard to love, but look at Jesus: beaten, bloody, humiliated, exposed . . . the heart of the Living God hanging on an old Roman cross for the love of you—His Bride.

Ephesus, Ephesus . . . oh, Ephesus, remember what we had? Repent! And do those things you did at first.

And we say, "What *were* those things that they did at first in Ephesus?" Because if we *knew* them, we could *do* them, and everything would be okay: our kingdom in order, prim and proper. We would establish a new denomination: First Church of the Things They Did First in Ephesus. And we would be as dead as ever.

We don't know exactly what they did in Ephesus, but whatever it was, they did it out of that first love. God doesn't want us to be simply stuck in first love, such that it never matures; He's always drawing us into the deeper things of love. But that doesn't mean He wants us to *lose* that first love.

So the question is, when Jesus says to Ephesus, "Remember, repent, and do the things you did at first," what is Jesus saying to *you?*

- "Remember those hikes we used to take? And *you* probably didn't even think of them as your devotional, but remember those hikes? You thought of *Me* the whole time! Would you go hiking again?"

- "Remember how you used to stay up late and *devour* My Word? You *memorized* it. Could you do that again?"

- "Remember how you sang songs to Me? Would you sing Me a song now?"

- "Peter, remember how you used to see Me in your kids every time you looked at them? You've forgotten to *look*. Take another look . . . I'm still there."

In a few weeks He may call you to something else. When Susan and I did the same thing we did on our first date, over and over and over again, we got tired of each other. If we went snowshoeing and ate picnics in treehouses for thirty years, we would *still* get tired of each other!

The point is, *work* at your relationship. Do the things that nurture your affections—your *first love*. That's what Christian disciplines are about. Discipline yourself for affection.

When Susan and I turn into cold fish, I know there are things I need to *do*, whether I *feel* like it or not. I need to discipline myself to call a baby-sitter, arrange a dinner, buy some flowers, stop criticizing her, do some dishes, make a date. Those things are disciplines.

You may say, "How do I get the strength for those disciplines? Aren't they just new laws and dead works? No! Not if you discipline yourself in *hope* of that first love.

Satan whispers, "Discipline yourself in shame. In fact, discipline all your desires away."

Jesus whispers, "My beloved, discipline yourself in *hope*. Hope of communion with Me, your desire for Me."

Ephesus means "desired one." *My desired one, do the things you did at first.* "To him who [overcomes] I will grant to eat of the tree of life which is in the paradise [lit. the 'pleasure garden'] of God" (Revelation 2:7). *Would you dream of that day? Believe in that day? You will overcome.*

The victory that overcomes the world is our faith, and faith is the assurance of things hoped for, and hope does not disappoint us (1 John 5:4; Hebrews 11:1; Romans 5:5). Believe *that!*

That Jesus *saves* you;

that He *washes* you;

that He *forgives* you;

that He *died* for you, cleansing you.

Surrender to Him, and He will bear life in you. He doesn't want a roommate; He wants the communion of delight. He romanced you all the way to that cross outside Jerusalem and even from the depths of hell. So, in the name of Jesus, do a little romancing yourself.

FIVE

RICH CHURCH, POOR CHURCH

(Revelation 2:8–11)

REVELATION 2:8–11: *And to the angel of the church in Smyrna write: "The words of the first and the last, who died and came to life.*

"I know your tribulation and your poverty (but you are rich) and the slander of those who say that they are Jews and are not, but are a synagogue of Satan. Do not fear what you are about to suffer. Behold, the devil is about to throw some of you into prison, that you may be tested, and for ten days you will have tribulation. Be faithful unto death, and I will give you the crown of life. He who has an ear, let him hear what the Spirit says to the churches. He who conquers shall not be hurt by the second death."

SOME THIRTY-FIVE MILES NORTH of Ephesus was the ancient city of Smryna, a wealthy and beautiful place with large, glorious boulevards. We know quite a bit about Smyrna from ancient history, the writings of Polycarp, and because the city is still there. Its most famous boulevard was called the "Golden Street."

That street was not very golden for Christians, however, because Smyrna was one of the most dangerous places for a Christian to live in all the Roman Empire. In A.D. 26 Smyrna won the right to erect a temple to the Emperor Tiberius. It was a center for Caesar worship. But Smyrna was also the center of a large Jewish population with a strong influence on the Roman authorities. Because Judaism was a recognized and official religion, Jews were exempt from emperor worship. The early Christians considered themselves Jews— "heirs of the promise." However, if the Jews wanted the Christians out of their synagogues or felt threatened by their influence, they could turn them over to the Romans, saying, "They say they are Jews, but they're not"—subjecting the Christians to the confiscation of property, persecution, and death.

Jesus said to Smyrna, "I know your tribulation and poverty, and the slander you suffer. But *you* are rich." It appears they had great spiritual qualities, so we would expect God to bless them. Because they had been faithful in Philadelphia, Jesus told them He would keep them from the hour of trial coming upon the whole world.

Most American, evangelical Christians believe that God will deliver us from the hour of trial that is coming on the whole world. We like to cite Jeremiah 29:11: "I know the plans I have for you," declares the LORD, "plans to prosper you" (NIV). God's plan *is* prosperity. God *will* make His faithful Church *rich*. Yet Smyrna is the most faithful of all the churches, and they get suffering, prison, and death. Yikes! Is *that* prosperity?

Notice that Jesus didn't say, "You are poor but you *are going* to be rich," He said, "You are *already* rich." Do you ever get the feeling while reading the Bible that we really don't know what riches are? If we do, we're not so sure we want them! "To him who has will more be given" (Matthew 13:12). Ouch. Sorry, Smyrna. But meet in Laodicea and we'll have a slide show on the sufferings in Smyrna, take a collection, say a prayer . . . "Oh, Lord, help those poor people." *Poor people.* Who is poor? Who is rich?

Maybe we're born not knowing what is and isn't valuable. When my son Coleman was a toddler he was constantly getting disciplined for eating dirt. I can picture his precious, little face streaked with tears, dirt caked around his lips, suffering immensely because he got another spanking for eating dirt. A house full of great food, and he was outside eating dirt!

Maybe we're like that—born again, even as babies, sticking anything in our mouths (an inherited problem), as if somewhere in our family tree someone got addicted to bad fruit . . . an entire garden full of great and wonderful fruit, and someone had to go and eat that one problem fruit. Ever since then, we've been outside the garden eating dirt.

Maybe our Father wants us to come inside and stop eating dirt. Maybe we don't know what's good . . . what's rich . . . where everything really is. In Smyrna Jesus said, "You are rich." In Laodicea, where they claim to be rich, Jesus said, "You are wretched, pitiable, poor, blind, and naked."

What *are* riches? Why did Jesus say they were rich in Smyrna?

- Tribulation and poverty expose need, which forces the disciplines of relationship.

- Relationship opens the door for love and communion (great riches).
- Tribulation and poverty force us to rely on people.
- People are like a field of dirt that contains treasure.
- Storms wash away the dirt and expose the treasure.

Philip Yancey writes about a poll of senior citizens in London.[1] They were asked, "What was the happiest period of your life?" Sixty percent answered, "The blitz"—the period during World War II when German bombers dumped tons of explosives on the city of London every night. These people huddled together in bomb shelters in small groups while Nazis destroyed all their earthly possessions with fire from the sky. In those shelters . . .

they learned faith;
they experienced hope;
they knew the pain and joy of love.
They were rich.

The tribulation and the poverty weren't the riches. They *exposed* the riches: faith, hope, and love. Although this world burns away, writes the apostle Paul, these three will remain.

Faith in Jesus,
hope in Jesus,
love that *is* Jesus—
     this is treasure.
The jewel exposed by the fire,
the gold refined by the furnace,
the treasure unearthed by the storm—
     treasure is found in people, and it is exposed by suffering.

Jesus said, "Trials will come, but woe to him by whom they come." In Smyrna the devil *will* throw them into prison. *Woe* to the devil, but *glory* to the Church. For God has the devil on a leash. God uses him to uncover His treasure in Job . . . in Joseph . . . in Smyrna. His glory in Christ is faith, hope, and love.

Our faith is "more precious than gold, which though perishable is tested by fire," writes Peter (1 Peter 1:7). "The crucible is for silver and the furnace is for gold, and the LORD tries hearts," declares the writer of Proverbs (17:3).

To the lukewarm, rich, and very poor church in Laodicea, Jesus says, "Buy from me gold refined by fire, that you may be rich, and white garments . . . and salve to anoint your eyes" (Revelation 3:18). How do they get gold in Laodicea? The same way they do in Smyrna: Invite Him in.

To the church at Laodicea, Jesus says, "Behold, I stand at the door and knock; if anyone hears my voice and opens the door, I will come in to him and eat with him and him with me" (3:20). In Laodicea they had just as much treasure as Smyrna; they just weren't letting Him in. Why?

They thought they had no need. They were blind to the treasure, deaf to His voice; so they would not say, "Blessed is he who comes in the name of the Lord." They couldn't see Him.

If you want to be rich, join a church and thank God for the storms. Storms wash away dirt. Maybe that's what God is weaning us from.

At the end of the Revelation there is the strangest picture: an eternal city, which is also a bride. The "gates of the city shall never be shut by day—and there shall be no night there" (21:25). The gates are *always open.*

Then in Revelation 22:15, Jesus says, "Outside are the dogs and sorcerers and fornicators and murderers and idolaters, and every one who loves and practices falsehood"—that is, everyone who loves to eat dirt.

Just think of it: Doors *wide open* to riches beyond belief, the richest food and wine, the great banquet, but they don't go in. Why? Maybe they don't *want* to. They *like* eating dirt. Maybe the kingdom is an acquired taste.

So now God in His grace and mercy is weaning us from dirt, bad apples, gold watches, big houses, the riches of this world . . . and trying to show us real treasure. You say, "What's *wrong* with dirt, apples, gold watches, and big houses?" Actually, nothing! It's just that we are addicted to them. Gold watches aren't evil; it's that we love them more than we love hungry people. Things and riches of this world aren't evil in themselves; what is evil is that we *use* people to love *things* instead of using *things* to love *people.*

Use dirt to grow food, but eat the food. Use money to grow people, and love the people. Dirt isn't evil. We would all die without it; we just shouldn't *eat* it!

My son Coleman is now eight years old, so last Christmas morning I woke him up early. (His eyes were wide with anticipation.) I took him downstairs and out back behind our house, and I said, "Coleman, this morning I'm giving you what you've always wanted! All the dirt in the backyard belongs to you! Chow down!"

Actually I didn't do that. Why? Because through my discipline Coleman has acquired a taste for . . .

prime rib,
cherry pie,
rich food;
electric trains,
pogo sticks,
and Nintendo games under the tree.

What a living hell if my son Coleman spent all Christmas morning out back eating dirt while his family feasted inside! I would lay aside my feast, my kingdom, and my house, and go sit in the dirt with him. (That would *really* be Christmas.) I'd suffer with him until he came inside. (That would be Easter.)

Well, now it's safe to give Coleman dirt. He still *likes* dirt; he just no longer wants to *eat* it.

On your Easter morning, your heavenly Father will say something like this to you: "My church from Smyrna, remember that street in your town called 'the Golden Street'? Do you remember how you longed to strut down that street but had to fear your life? Look, My beloved! *This* street is made of gold, and you own it!"

But you won't be looking at the streets;

> you will have acquired a taste for Jesus—
> > the Lamb who was slain.

You'll be dancing on those streets but looking at Him! And He won't be entirely unfamiliar to you, because you acquired a taste for Him *here* . . . in Smyrna.

I went to visit an eighty-two-year-old man in the hospital. An hour earlier, he had received some very bad medical news about his heart problem. I said, "Are you ready to meet Jesus?" He answered, "Oh yeah. He'll heal me or He'll take me home." We prayed, and I felt rich. What faith! It was *Jesus.*

I met with a woman who had been on death's door the night before. This day, all she could talk about were some visions and the Book of Revelation. I thought, *What hope!* I then talked to a friend who'd just been widowed with two small children. She hugged me and said, "I'm so thankful for the twenty years I had with my husband." Such faith, hope, and love. Treasure in an earthen vessel. It was *Jesus.*

Smyrna, you are rich—

> not just that you *have* riches;
> you *are* riches.

There was a letter written around A.D. 160 by the church in Smyrna to circulate among the churches in Asia Minor. It expressed great joy and gratitude for all that God had done recently in Smyrna: Twelve believers had been martyred, eleven scourged and devoured by beasts in the coliseum—it was so obvious that Christ was with them.

Paul wrote, "All things are yours, . . . and you are Christ's; and Christ is God's" (1 Corinthians 3:21–23). Where is everything?—In Smyrna, where Christ suffers.

The letter went on to describe the death of the twelfth martyr, the eighty-six-year-old bishop of Smyrna, who knew John as a young man and no doubt had read the Revelation aloud many times to that small church.

They decided to burn the eighty-six-year-old Polycarp. Jews from the synagogue gathered the wood for the fire and tied him to the post. He prayed, thanking God that he was counted worthy to suffer—to share—in the cup of Christ *with* Christ.

When they lit the fire, witnesses say it encompassed Polycarp like a sail in the wind, and it would not consume him. Finally, in desperation, the executioner thrust a spear in Polycarp's side. But while the fire raged around him, witnesses said he appeared "not as flesh that is burnt but as bread that is baked, as gold and silver glowing in a furnace."[2]

He *was* gold. He *was* rich. Smyrna is rich.

Jesus said, "The kingdom is like a treasure buried in a field, and a man stumbles upon it and sells everything for the field." The people of God are that field! And then He said, "The kingdom is like a pearl merchant [not a *pearl* but a *pearl merchant*], and when he finds the pearl of great price, he gives up everything" (see Matthew 13:44–45). He gives up his kingdom for the pearl.

Jesus gives up His kingdom for His pearl, the Church—His inheritance, His riches. A pearl is formed in suffering. It is riches wrapped around a wound. The Church is faith, hope, and love wrapped around the wounded body of Christ.

Lord Jesus, make us rich for you—
>your pearl of great price,
>>your gold purified by fire,
>>>your city decked with jewels,
>>>>your city in which you dwell.

And the twelve gates were twelve pearls, each of the gates made of a single pearl, and the street of the city was pure gold, transparent as glass. (Revelation 21:21)

SIX

LET GOD CALL YOU BY NAME

(Revelation 2:12–17)

WHEN SHE WAS YOUNGER, if you asked my daughter Becky her name, she would say, "My name is Pretty Pretty Princess." She knew that was her name because that's what her father called her, and it fit. But she no longer goes by that name. She's older now. In elementary school, they call her by other names.

Jesus commends the church in Pergamum for holding fast His name. Names are really big in the Bible. That's hard for us to understand, because modern people tend to think of names as little more than vibrations in the atmosphere. Ironically, many postmodern people and some physicists think words and meanings, perceptions and beliefs have real power.

In Scripture, everything is *created* just with words and names. In Hebrew, *dabar* is "word," but that word really means "thing." A word is a thing; likewise, a name is an extension of a thing. God makes a place for His name to dwell on the earth. His name is a revelation of Himself, and His name has power.

By the time of Jesus, the Israelites would not even speak the name of God—*Yahweh*—for fear of taking it in vain. We're not even sure *Yahweh* (or Jehovah) is correct, because Hebrews didn't write the vowels and no one said the word.

But God wants us to say His name—to call on Him. Perhaps we're learning His name . . . and ours.

REVELATION 2:12–17: *And to the angel of the church in Pergamum write: "The words of him who has the sharp two-edged sword.*

41

"'I know where you dwell, where Satan's throne is; you hold fast my name and you did not deny my faith even in the days of Antipas my witness, my faithful one, who was killed among you, where Satan dwells. But I have a few things against you: you have some there who hold the teaching of Balaam, who taught Balak to put a stumbling block before the sons of Israel, that they might eat food sacrificed to idols and practice immorality. So you also have some who hold the teaching of the Nicolaitans. Repent then. If not, I will come to you soon and war against them with the sword of my mouth. He who has an ear, let him hear what the Spirit says to the churches. To him who conquers I will give some of the hidden manna, and I will give him a white stone, with a new name written on the stone which no one knows except him who receives it.'"

TO THE ANGEL OF THE CHURCH IN PERGAMUM were written "the words of him who has the sharp two-edged sword" (2:12). That's Jesus. Later in Revelation (19:15), He will smite the nations with this sword. He is the Word, which is a sword—the Word through whom all things were made and through whom all things will be judged or named.

God has given Jesus "the name which is above every name, that at the name of Jesus every knee should bow, in heaven and on earth and under the earth" (Philippians 2:9–10). He's also called the second Adam. When God created the first Adam, He had Adam name all the animals—a way of participating in Creation. Then God made the woman, and Adam named her Eve, or "woman." They had children and named them.

In Scripture, people usually received their formal names from a father or a husband. I know that sounds paternalistic and sexist, but the Bible does sound kind of paternalistic and sexist. (So just consider that perhaps the custom holds a truth that if we really understood, we'd love . . . like a blessed child loves his name, like a beloved bride loves her new name. But as orphans and widows, we mourn.)

Adam is a namer of things before the Fall. He is still a namer of things after the Fall, but his naming is fallen. He does it very poorly; he makes orphans and widows. Today lots of brides don't take their husband's names, and that's understandable. Children renounce the name of their father. But maybe we aren't any better at naming ourselves than our fathers or mothers were. Maybe we can't name ourselves. We long to be known by another.

In Scripture, names work like mirrors that reflect back the essence of a thing. But more than that, they help *create* a thing. "No longer shall you be called Simon, but Peter—Rock." (You are "Rock," and one day three years from now you'll act like one.)

"Abraham," father of nations.

"Sarah," mother of nations.

"Israel," strives with God.

God is always giving new names.

Sometimes the world gives us evil names: *worthless, moron, no good.* Good or bad, names still cut and shape and create and even desecrate. Good or bad, we name and get named and try to make names for ourselves . . . because even a bad name seems more desirable than no name at all. To never hear another call your name would be hell.

Maybe that *is* hell: to be finally and ultimately orphaned or widowed.

At the Fall, humanity was cut off from the Father and from the great Bridegroom. Now we're desperate for a name, and even a bad one seems better than none.

In Genesis 11 all those orphaned and widowed from the Garden get together and say, "Let's make a name for ourselves and build a tower to heaven." God comes down and destroys their tower and their name.

Maybe you've been building a tower called success in order to make a name for yourself. Well, don't be surprised if God comes and knocks it down. Maybe He has another name for you.

Isaiah prophesied of the day that the towers of Jerusalem would be torn down. It happened in 586 B.C. at the hands of the Babylonians, and it happened in A.D. 70 at the hands of the Romans. Isaiah prophesied, "Instead of perfume there will be rottenness. . . . Your men shall fall by the sword. . . . Ravaged she shall sit on the ground, and seven women shall take hold of one man in that day saying, 'We will eat our own bread and wear our own clothes, only let us be called by your name; take away our reproach'" (3:24–4:1). God takes away their arrogant name, the name they made for themselves, but they are so desperate for a name they will sleep with any man who comes along.

But in Isaiah 62:1–2, God says, "For Jerusalem's sake I will not rest. . . . The nations shall see your vindication, and all the kings your glory; and you shall be called by a new name, which the mouth of the LORD will give."

Maybe God is stripping us of arrogant names and evil names that don't fit so we can hear Him call our real name. Yet in that process we're desperate for any name, like the women of Jerusalem who would go to bed with any man just to get a name, bow down to *any* god in order to have a name—*any* name. That must have been tempting in Pergamum.

The people of Pergamum were dwelling "where Satan's throne is" (2:13). In Revelation 13:2 Satan gives his throne to the beast—Pergamum was the capital of the Roman province of Asia. Caesar was to be worshiped as a god. In the midst of this empirical pagan culture, Antipas was a "faithful witness" (2:13 NIV). We don't know how he died, but it must have been because he would not renounce the name of Jesus and worship the name of Caesar. When he died, undoubtedly there were many spectators, probably in the coliseum, chanting names at Antipas. To control the mob, Rome gave out white stones as tickets to the coliseum to get free bread and watch people die.

Although the church in Pergamum held fast Jesus' name, they had allowed pagan teaching to slip into their midst, as the Israelites had done when the pagan prophet Balaam encouraged King Balak of Moab and the Midianite elders to intermarry with the Israelites. This way, Israel would be enticed into worshiping their gods and would not pose a military threat to Midian and Moab. They wouldn't attack Moab, for part of their own name would be Moab. (See Numbers 22–25.)

It appears that some in Pergamum were teaching that a little sex outside your marriage covenant won't hurt; a little worship of Caesar or Zeus won't hurt. In the Revelation it is hard to tell sometimes whether the text refers to sexual immorality or idolatry. That's because idolatry *is* adultery—going after another bridegroom in search of a name. Some in Pergamum may have been sleeping with pagan temple prostitutes; others were "marrying" Caesar—i.e. the powers of this world. They were doing things to fit in, to be accepted, to have a name and reputation.

If you get your name by marrying yourself to the ways of this world— whether through sex and drugs, the Republicans or Democrats, the stock market and the Fortune 500, *Vogue* or *GQ*—you're in trouble, trapped by old King Balak and the ancient dragon.

To name something is to exert power over it: to judge, divide, quantify, bring under control, categorize. The world and its beast and dragon want to name you: "Oh, he's one of those conservative, fundamentalist, evangelical, homophobic, early-potty-trained, religious types."

We use psychology, sociology, and anthropology to name people:

"Those tribal, animistic Bronze Age thinkers . . ."

"The Black Voter"

"The Proletariat"

"The Bourgeoisie" (Middle Class)

"The Introvert"

"The Extrovert"

Did you ever notice that when someone's a threat, we love to name them? "Oh, she's a borderline schizophrenic." Since we named her, we don't have to listen to her.

God told us to name animals (biology). But we had better not get too cocky with anthropology, psychology, and sociology—naming people; for God seems to really get uptight about how we name people—*judge* people.

What names has this world given you? What names has the crowd given you?

Success?

Failure?

Rich?

Poor?

Satan loves to name you, because names catch people, control people, and shape people. This world and the beast and the ancient dragon love to name us. We're susceptible to names because we're orphaned and widowed—we're so desperate, we believe them. *But the one we let name us is our idol . . . our god, our father and groom.*

PERGAMUM WAS ALSO TO REPENT of the teaching of the "Nicolaitans" (Revelation 2:15). We don't really know who they were, but it's interesting to note that "Nicolaitan" is two Greek words: *nicos*, meaning "superior, conqueror," and *laity*, meaning "people." Together they mean "conqueror of the people" or "superior to the people." Some have speculated that this group was the beginning of the clergy–laity split: two classes of Christians in which one judges and defines the other by telling them their name. Clearly God calls people into places of authority in His Church, but never as despots or judges of persons. What I mean is, I can't tell you the name God gives you. I can help you find it, but I don't know it.

When I was in college I went on a retreat at which colored folders were handed out: red for new Christians, blue for medium Christians, green for advanced Christians. I had been a Christian a long time, but because it was my first retreat, I was given a red folder. I was so ashamed that I snuck into the staff area with a friend and we stole green folders . . . to prove our maturity in Christ; that is to make ourselves a name. Yes, it was wrong to reduce our relationships with Christ to red, blue, or green folders. But what was *really* wrong was that I coveted the green folder—I let them *name* me "red" or "green."

The world can't name me; even religion can't name me, but . . . listen closely:

REVELATION 2:17: *He who has an ear, let him hear what the Spirit says to the churches. To him who conquers I will give some of the hidden manna, and I will give him a white stone, with a new name written on the stone which no one knows except him who receives it.*

Scholars debate whether the new name in 2:17 is a name for God or Jesus or an individual name for each person. There is great evidence for both views, and I'm convinced both views are correct. The new name will be your name *and* Jesus' name. Dare I even say it?—*God's* name is the same name. We are the children of God, and we are the Bride of Christ. We're even His body—His city, the New Jerusalem.

The name "faithful witness" is given to only two people in all of Scripture. Jesus calls Antipas of Pergamum "my faithful witness" (NIV), and in 1:5, Jesus is called "the faithful witness." But Antipas has another name he shares with Jesus (that we don't know), and for eternity Antipas will be trying to tell you that name, and for all eternity you will be trying to tell Antipas another name: the one Jesus shares with you. That is, you will each be telling the other something utterly unique and wonderful about Jesus: your story, your song, your name. You are part of His body, His song of grace. You, Antipas, and all the saints sing the same song, the song of the Lamb. But you each have different parts. It's a symphony.

I believe Jesus is beginning to tell you your name in this world so you'll recognize it on that great day when you first hear it. He may use other people to help name you, but they can never finally name you. Do not let them! They do not know your name. It's unique.

Believe the name your Father gives you in the grace of Christ Jesus our Lord. How will you know it when you hear it? Well, it will fit on Jesus—the resurrected Jesus. You share it, and if you belong to Christ, He's been everywhere you have been and in every situation. He wants to tell you your name in each place. You've been to some awful places in this life—perhaps to hell and back. So has Jesus. Your story is His story and your name, His name. He changes your old name through the power of His blood. It's a story of His grace on you.

When I was a child, I got named almost every day on the bus coming home from school: "Fatso," "Wussy," "Chicken," and another name I thought was worst of all. I never wanted to fight; I didn't know how. I was scared, really cowardly. To this day, when I finish preaching, I have to fight the urge to curl up in a ball in shame and fear, like a coward. But that's not a name that fits on Jesus.

Recently I had some friends pray for me about my struggle with shame and fear. They asked me where I thought the fear came from. I told them about the bus in second grade and about the other name—"Mr. Decent." You see, I was a minister's kid, I didn't cuss, and I had a hard time being "indecent." The guys on the bus would chant "Decent, decent . . . Mr. Decent." I was utterly intimidated and entirely ashamed of that name. (Bizarre, yes, but put yourself in the mind of a second grader.)

My friends then prayed that I could picture Jesus on that bus with me. I imagined Him there as best I could. (To imagine what is true is faith. It's true that Jesus will never leave me or forsake me.) They asked me what Jesus was doing. I said, "I think He's laughing. Not at me, but for me, like all those names don't matter."

When I told my friends that the kids called me "Decent," my friend DeeDee said, "I think Jesus is proud of you. . . . Decent isn't bad." When she said that, I broke. I had never occurred to me that "Decent" could be a good name. I realized it was even a name for Jesus, and I had been decent (in my own childish way, at least, because I liked Jesus). Jesus suffered for being decent and He was being decent in me. Our name was "Decent," not "Coward." In fact, it was Peter—the Rock. Even then Jesus was shaping me into the Rock . . . by His grace. Though there's still a great deal of cowardice in me, that's not who I am. He's taken all my fear to the cross and is revealing Himself, "Courage," in me. I must believe His names for me.

This may seem a silly little story, compared to some of yours, and I can't ultimately name you, but by God's grace, I can help. In Christ you are no longer "the Liar," but Israel; no longer illegitimate, but daughter or son; no longer the forsaken, but the chosen; no longer "Mother of Death," but Eve, "the Mother of the Living"; no longer "the harlot," but the Bride. That's only the beginning of your name, and He is telling you your name all the time.

Do not listen to the chanting mob in the coliseum of Pergamum. Do not listen to the dragon and his beasts and this world. Maybe you have been called names that fill you with fear, shame, and self-hatred, names spoken by the enemy, and you have cursed yourself. Give them to Jesus and let Him take them to His cross. He will change the meaning of those names or give new ones. Believe that Jesus names you, or you'll hop in the sack with any demon that comes along.

One day you'll get a white stone—a ticket—and you'll enter the coliseum of God with the great cloud of witnesses and eat the bread of life and the hidden manna (2:17). Jesus will say, "Read the stone," and you'll hear your *true* name, your full name, for the first time, and you'll know you're home at last.

SEVEN

NAKED BODIES, INTIMATE SECRETS

(Revelation 2:18–29)

I FIRST THOUGHT of asking my wife Susan on a date in high school while walking behind her on the stairs between the second and third floors. She was wearing very nicely fitting pants. I remember thinking, *Wow! A goddess . . . Venus in white polyester pants.*

On our first date I was thinking, *Wow . . . she's gorgeous!* I think she was thinking, *Wow . . . he's* listening *to me! That's really nice.*

I loved dating Susan, not only because she was pretty but also because she did most of the talking. I was too nervous to say much, and I wasn't always sure what she said, but it came out of that *beautiful body.* We had a symbiotic relationship: my admiration of Susan's tight, white pants, and her desire to tell me everything. We didn't realize it was the beginning of the greatest lesson we'd ever learn.

Whether you are single or married, whether you are male or female, if you are a Christian, God is teaching you the very same message—a lesson built into the nature of reality and you: In the beginning God created man in His own image—male and female He created them. Together in His image. And He said, "I like it. It's good."

Man is born from woman, and woman is created from man, out of his side. God brought them together in the covenant of marriage, a communion in which two persons become one flesh and in that communion bear fruit. They are *commanded* to bear fruit, but soon they steal fruit. They fall and cover their nakedness.

They cover the part where they are incomplete without the other.

He covers the part that is to penetrate the female with life.

She covers the part that is to invite the seed of the male, which she is to

48

receive in ecstasy as a gift of grace, in order that her body would nurture that seed and bear life.

They cover those parts where they are joined in communion . . . those parts they *long to* join but now are *ashamed* to join . . . those parts that not only join body but connect spirit and soul.

And in the place of ecstasy, life, and joy,
>there is fear, shame, and pain.

Instead of love that brings life,
>there is lust that brings death.

So they cover *those parts* from each other, and they hide them*selves* from the author of life.

In Ephesians Paul tells us that God made us this way—male and female— to be joined together as one flesh, as a way of illustrating Christ and His Church. He designed us this way *before* the Fall, as if He knew even then that He would need a way to tell us, while we were in exile, of His love and life *and* of our sin and His redemption.

More than love as a concept, He could say to us, "I *long* for you like a groom longs for his bride," and "You are only complete in *Me* and with Me *in you*."

More than the words "salvation by grace through faith," He could say, "You can only bear life—fruit, my Bride—when you surrender to My love and receive My joy in your place of shame."

Sin hurts, not like some law that is broken, but like . . . when you find your wife with another man . . . when you long for your lover's embrace and he's in another room gratifying himself with pornography or she's whispering intimate secrets to another . . . when you love someone *so much* yet you are so wounded by them you want to kill them in a rage precisely because you so desperately long to be loved by them. Finally, torn, you choose to die for them.

Marriage is a covenant to depict the eternal covenant. Sex is a sacrament of that covenant, as communion is a sacrament of the new eternal covenant. *Sacrament* is a theologian's word to describe the "sign and seal of a covenant," a *physical* act that is far more than physical. It's spiritual. Sacrament is a covenant that bears fruit . . . *life*.

Little did Susan and I know in 1978 that God was beginning to teach us the deep things of His love. He was sucking us in—He does that, you know.

At the start of John's Gospel, Jesus turns water into wine at a marriage feast, and everybody wants to follow. Who wouldn't? Then in John 6 Jesus says His followers are to drink His blood (not *wine* but *blood*). By John 19 Jesus hangs naked on a cross on a hill outside Jerusalem. Almost everyone is gone, but John is there to watch as a Roman soldier plunges a spear into the side of

Jesus—the second Adam. A river of blood flows out, and the Church is born—the Bride of Christ—the second Eve.

In a kindergarten Sunday school class, the teacher was explaining how God formed Eve out of Adam's rib. Little Tommy was mesmerized by the lesson. Later in the week, his mother noticed him lying down holding his side. She asked, "Tommy, what's wrong?" He said, "I have a pain in my side. I think I'm going to have a wife."

I know it hurts,
what Christ is showing you,
but don't throw in the towel.
There are no shortcuts that bypass Calvary.

REVELATION 2:18–25: *And to the angel of the church in Thyatira write: "The words of the Son of God, who has eyes like a flame of fire, and whose feet are like burnished bronze.*

"I know your works, your love and faith and service and patient endurance, and that your latter works exceed the first. But I have this against you, that you tolerate the woman Jezebel, who calls herself a prophetess and is teaching and beguiling my servants to practice immorality and to eat food sacrificed to idols. I gave her time to repent, but she refuses to repent of her immorality. Behold, I will throw her on a sickbed, and those who commit adultery with her I will throw into great tribulation, unless they repent of her doings; and I will strike her children dead. And all the churches shall know that I am he who searches mind and heart, and I will give to each of you as your works deserve. But to the rest of you in Thyatira, who do not hold this teaching, who have not learned what some call the deep things of Satan, to you I say, I do not lay upon you any other burden; only hold fast what you have, until I come."

THYATIRA WAS THE SMALLEST AND LEAST CONSEQUENTIAL of the seven cities to which the Revelation was written. It lay at the juncture of two valleys along a critical trade route. I think of it as a truck stop. Do you remember, guys, that as a kid it was in truck stops on vacation where you first encountered porn or condom dispensers in the restrooms? There was something about being out on the road hidden . . . unseen. Jesus has eyes like a flame of fire (Revelation 2:18). He sees everything hidden. He knows Thyatira. It's the smallest town but gets the longest letter.

Jesus intimately cares about the secret places and the private parts.

He commends the church but then says, "I have this against you, that you tolerate that woman Jezebel" (2:20). In the Old Testament, Jezebel was the pagan queen of wicked King Ahab. She enticed Israel into worshiping Baal, the Canaanite fertility god, and Asherah, his consort. This worship included feasting and ritual prostitution.

Evidently a woman in leadership in Thyatira was enticing folks into idolatry and *porneuo,* translated "sexual immorality" or just "immorality." Thyatira was a Greek city with Greek gods. Across the Aegean Sea in Corinth stood the great temple to Aphrodite (Venus, in Latin), the goddess of love. The temple contained a thousand cult prostitutes. In Thyatira they would have had similar practices, even a mingling of Greek gods and Canaanite gods. We wonder how they could ever be enticed into such sins, but for the Greeks it wasn't such a stretch, because in health class at school they taught that sex was mostly just sperm, egg, and biology. (You know . . . like we teach today.)

Paul wrote to the church at Corinth saying, "Do you not know that your bodies are members of Christ? Shall I therefore take the members of Christ and make them members of a prostitute? Never! . . . For, as it is written, 'The two shall become one flesh.' But he who is united with the Lord becomes one spirit with Him. Shun *porneuo.* . . . Do you not know that your body is a temple of the Holy Spirit within you . . . ?" (1 Corinthians 6:15–19).

You see the lie of Satan, don't you? *What you do with your body really doesn't matter.* But then he uses your body as a door for demonic spirits and all the lies of hell. In places like Thyatira and Corinth, they visited cult prostitutes, yet with the underlying belief that one's body doesn't really matter—like Vegas or Hollywood. It's no wonder that in Corinth they also abused the communion table, acting as if it were only bread and wine. Paul had to tell them that anyone who eats and drinks without discerning the body of Christ drinks judgment on himself (1 Corinthians 11:29).

Our communion table is laid with food and *spirit.* It's a sacrament.

The marriage bed is made with biology and *spirit.* It's a sacrament.

I'm not only one *body* with my wife, but if Paul is right, I commune with my Lord who resides within her: one *spirit* with Jesus. I had better discern *His* body or I defile *His* temple. But in a culture such as ours, we may no longer even have a category for understanding the ecstasy that God plans in marriage to a spouse or to Him.

Either willingly or unwillingly, your temple has been defiled without ever having been cleansed, and that is the tragedy.

You not only cover your private parts from your marriage partner but you hide your naked heart from the lover of your soul, our Lord Jesus. So religion for you is not a communion of *delight* but of fear and shame.

Jezebel was seducing believers in Thyatira to *porneuo*. That means sex outside marriage, sacrament outside covenant. *Porneuo* gives us our word *pornography*. And *porne* in Greek is translated "harlot."

In Revelation 17 an angel takes John and shows him the great *porne* who has seduced the kings of the earth and the nations of the world. The merchants of the earth have grown rich with the wealth of her wantonness. The great harlot is fallen, and she is the abode of demons.

John hears a voice issuing from heaven saying, "Come out of her, my people, lest you take part in her sins" (18:4). The woman rides the beast, which seems to be the entity or power behind the fallen governments and economies of this world. She is drunk with the blood of Christians.

The U.S. is the world's leading producer of porn. No wonder it's tough for you guys, because you're sinners living in a fallen world, and the harlot rides the beast. She knows your deepest hungers and so does the beast. Our economy is built on seducing you. It goes beyond what we call porno—it's an entire advertising industry. God made you to be the initiator in the image of Jesus. He *made* you to be aroused by the sight of your naked bride. The dragon, the beast, and the harlot *know* it, so they lure you to other temples, especially when *your* temple requires sacrifice and grace.

But Jesus says that to worship at other temples, even in your own mind, is adultery. It opens the door to the evil one—to his lies, to his demonic spirits, and to shame that deadens your heart and makes you unable to experience communion as God intended.

You long even more for communion,
> but you are unable to experience it.

The hunger is stronger than ever,
> but you can't feel it,
>> for your heart is encased in shame.

You go back for more and more and more and receive less and less and less, and the great harlot laughs and drinks your blood while you pay her to ride the beast. You are defiling your temple, you are probably defiling a young woman's temple, *and* you are defiling your wife's temple. You're spitting on your heart and the heart of Jesus.

How can you expect your wife to receive your love when it's not her that you're loving in your mind? You say, "It's just another *body*." No. It's a temple.

And it's at your wife's body alone—no matter how broken or bloodied; old, out of shape, or frigid; no matter how she emasculates you and rejects you—that you're to seek to worship the living God with your sexuality. Your seed—your "sperma"—belongs to her, not to a magazine.

You may have noticed that I have been preaching to men. But I believe men and women are equally fallen. Men are fallen pursuers—corrupted masculinity. Women are fallen receivers—corrupted femininity.

Jesus says to Thyatira that Jezebel, a woman, beguiled and seduced His servants. We don't know exactly what that means, but apparently she taught what Jesus calls the "deep things of Satan" (v. 24). Probably that means she taught "deep truths," truths that others just wouldn't understand . . . mystical, prophetic, intimate secrets . . . perhaps the idea that something is found in idolatry or fornication that others aren't ready for or can't see. Whatever the case, it was justification for keeping their communion of intimate secrets entirely in the dark.

A friend of mine who does a lot of Christian marriage counseling commented to me, "It's weird. When a man gives up on a marriage and throws in the towel, he turns to porn. When a woman gives up on a marriage and throws in the towel, she turns to gossip."

Paul told the Corinthians that if they couldn't control their burning passions, they should get married. I think he was talking mostly to guys. He tells Timothy to refuse to "enroll" young widows. He says they will want to marry. Then he says, "Besides that, they learn to be idlers, gadding about from house to house, and not only idlers but gossips, and busybodies, saying what they should not" (1 Timothy 5:13). Apparently, Paul saw marriage as a cure for gossip in women in the same way he saw marriage as a cure for burning lust in men . . . kind of like what God was saying back in 1978 to two immature high school kids:

> "Hey, Peter and Susan, there's a place for that burning passion, young man. There's a place for that desire to tell someone everything, young woman. It's marriage. I'm sucking you in, and you will learn the deep lessons of love, and it will hurt. So I'm binding you in a covenant. Don't you go looking for fulfillment in any other naked bodies. Don't go seeking communion by sharing intimate secrets with another."

You know, the harlot rides the beast for women as well as for men. We get upset about pornography at the checkout stand, but what about all those magazines that are devoted to nothing other than exposing the intimate secrets of other people's covenants?

Remember this: Jezebel was part of the church. I have been surprised at women emotionally communing with women, sharing all their intimate secrets with other Christian women, and them being *cold* to their husbands, saying, "He just *doesn't get it.*" I think Jesus may call that "the deep things of Satan."

I'm not saying that if you're the perfect wife, he'll be a perfect husband. He may be *wretched*. And he may divorce you. Then Jesus says, "Turn your passion toward Me. No man could ever fulfill it. Turn it to Me."

I'm not saying that if you're the perfect husband, she'll be the perfect bride. She may be *wretched*. She may emasculate you, degrade you, and refuse you. But then you may learn the *deepest* lesson of love: grace. You may then learn forgiveness.

Grace, forgiveness, body broken, blood shed . . . these are the deep things of God. He was crucified for all to see.

Robertson McQuilkin was the president of Columbia Bible College. Several years ago his wife was diagnosed with Alzheimer's disease. He resigned his post as president in order to care for his failing wife. He now spends his time changing Muriel's diapers, spoon-feeding her meals, and holding her as she sleeps. She hardly has the youthful body of a goddess, but he still washes her naked body. She cannot speak to him intimate secrets anymore, yet their touch *is* an intimate secret.

A young man asked Robertson one day, "Do you ever miss being president?" "No," he said. He enjoyed loving Muriel. But that night he couldn't sleep. He prayed, "God, I like my assignment, but if a coach puts a man on the bench, he must not want him in the game. You don't have to tell me, but why don't You want me in the game?"

The next day on their walk around the block, a familiar, old drunk stopped the couple and slurred, "I like it. That's good . . . that's really good . . . I like it." Then he headed off down the street mumbling to himself over and over, "That's good . . . I like it."

The McQuilkins finished their walk and sat down, and Robertson realized with a start, "God, it's You. It's You whispering to my spirit, 'I like it . . . it's good.'" Later he wrote to God: "I may be on the bench, but if You like it and say it's good, that's all that counts."

Robertson McQuilkin may be hesitant to say it about himself, but *I* will say it: He's not *on* the bench; he's at the absolute center of the game with Jesus.

Women, every powerful man is becoming weak until he dies. Men, every beautiful woman is becoming less beautiful until she dies. Yet there is a deeper beauty and a deeper power and a deeper love. In marriage, God covenants you to a dying sinner and teaches you to love like Himself. Marriage is to be a picture of Christ's love for dying sinners. A lesson for all, married or unmarried, in fulfillment or longing. The lesson is this: body broken and blood shed.

He has loved us at our absolute worst. Will you love Him at His absolute worst?

Naked?

    Weak?

        Ugly?

            On a cross?

                His worst and yet His best.

Can you see it? Nothing is more beautiful; nothing is more powerful.

At the Lord's table Christ gives us His body and blood . . .

We find the communion we most desperately desire.

We find the power to be single or to be married to His glory.

At the Lord's table, we surrender naked shame and He impregnates us with His life.

The sweet wedding wine of Cana turns into the blood of the covenant on Calvary. But it turns back into wine at the marriage supper of the Lamb, and this wine is better than the first: He always saves the best for last.

Good Friday turns into Easter.

Your wife will soon look like a goddess.

Your husband will soon listen and move with power.

You will have a new body.

You will *be* a new body . . . Christ's body.

Jesus says to Thyatira:

REVELATION 2:26–29: *He who conquers and who keeps my works until the end, I will give him power over the nations, and he shall rule them with a rod of iron, as when earthen pots are broken in pieces, even as I myself have received power from my Father; and I will give him the morning star. He who has an ear, let him hear what the Spirit says to the churches.*

My wife told me women tell secrets to get power. Well, men want sex to *feel* power. Pornography is evil, destructive power. Gossip is evil, destructive power.

"He who [endures] . . . I will give him power over the nations" (Revelation 2:26). What power? *His* power (Psalm 2) . . . a *communion* of power. You are His body. Marriage refers to this. "And the two shall become one flesh" (Genesis 2:24; Ephesians 5:3). And He says, "I will give him the morning star" (v. 28). In Revelation 22:16 Jesus says, "I am . . . the bright morning star." I don't know exactly what to make of this, but to those Greeks in Thyatira, the morning star had yet *another* name: Venus.

Every desire created in you by God will be fulfilled in glory. Be patient and endure. *Right now* learn the deepest lesson: the love of God that hangs on a cross and gives birth to a new world, even through us, His Bride. The Morning Star hangs on a cross and says to you, "Would you love Me? For I have loved you all the way to hell." Give to Jesus your deepest shame, fear, and anxiety, and let His love enter into those places so that you might receive His grace.

EIGHT

WAKING THE DEAD

(Revelation 3:1–6)

REVELATION 3:1: *"I know your works; you have the name of being alive, and you are dead."*

Have you ever been to a dead church? My wife and I once attended an evensong service at Westminster Abbey in London. Beautiful ceremony, impeccable music, magnificent words . . . and astounding boredom.

We sat in the chancel for all to see, and *three times* Susan fell asleep, hitting the wood with a loud thud that reverberated through the cathedral.

Have you ever been to an alive church? Growing? Changing? Vital? Awake?

When I was a youth pastor, Susan *never* fell asleep in church, because the senior pastor was such a dynamic preacher. People would say, "Wow! The Holy Spirit is moving!"

Yet at that church the place that most affected me was out back, hidden where few could see: the dumpster. You can learn a lot about people by hanging around a dumpster. It smelled, but it was where the action was . . . secret pastor meetings between services; grooms and groomsmen sneaking beer before the wedding.

Sometimes babies are found by dumpsters. The dumpster is metaphorical in a way. It smells like death, but it can teach a lot about life.

One week I ran into our senior pastor by the dumpster, sitting back there in his car. It was his first day back from a sabbatical. I had heard some rumors, and now he had called an emergency special meeting. I walked up to his window and said, "Hey, what's up?"

He told me he was resigning because he had been so stressed and busy. He wanted time to speak and write. Before I could catch myself I said, "Oh good!"—then, trying to recover, "I mean, good that it's not something *bad.*"

He looked at me, chuckled, and said, "Oh you mean like a *divorce* or something? Oh no. Nothing like that." He got out of his car, and together we walked past the dumpster up to the special meeting, where he shared the same story.

A few days later I found out that his story was a lie, covering a series of illicit relationships in his congregations.

Then I found out the same thing had happened at a church where I had worked before coming to this one. *Another* pastor at a church with an incredible "name" for being alive.

I'm not so sure we're all that good at telling whether something is dead or alive. Maybe we confuse alive with lots of noise, emotion, and zeal. Maybe we confuse growth with something getting bigger. Maybe we confuse a great name with life.

Maybe we are just not good at telling what's alive and what's dead.

We see lots of excited people, activities, mighty works, maybe even miracles and demons fleeing, and it all smells good. "Wow, that church is *alive!*" we say.

We see just a few people weeping, numbers shrinking, no miracles, some not even sure they believe, and the place smells of demons. "Man, look at that guy on the middle cross," we say. "He's *dead!*"

Maybe we don't know alive and dead so well.

"Sardis, you have the name of being alive, but you're dead." Other folks *called* them "alive." But sometimes just being *named* "alive" can kill you.

The letter to the seven churches has a chiastic Hebrew construction. That means the last three letters mirror the first three. Sardis is parallel to Pergamum. We learned from the letter to the angel in Pergamum that even a *good* name can kill you.

The senior pastor told me later it was the pressure of ministry. Well, it wasn't the pressure of any ministry *God* gave him; it was the pressure of living up to a name. It had become an idol. I've heard that pastors sometimes fall into sin just to get out from under the pressure of a *good name.* I'm talking about pastors because I am one. But the same is true with business executives, government officials, teachers, salesmen, cops, actors, and parents . . . anybody who wants to have a *good public name.*

You have built a name, and you're working to live up to the name. But inside you're tired, lonely, empty, dying, and desperate. You want someone—

anyone—to know you, but you think . . . *what if they really knew? What if the kids knew?*

The evil one is extorting you: "Pay, work, struggle, strive for your name, because what if they found out who you *really* are?" So you strive for your name, but deep inside you long for the dumpster. "The power of sin is the law." Yet Satan's extortion is powerless without an addiction to a good public name.

REVELATION 3:1–6: *And to the angel of the church in Sardis write: "The words of him who has the seven spirits of God and the seven stars.*

"I know your works; you have the name of being alive, and you are dead. Awake, and strengthen what remains and is on the point of death, for I have not found your works perfect in the sight of my God. Remember then what you received and heard; keep that, and repent. If you will not awake, I will come like a thief, and you will not know at what hour I will come upon you. Yet you have still a few names in Sardis, people who have not soiled their garments; and they shall walk with me in white, for they are worthy. He who conquers shall be clad thus in white garments, and I will not blot his name out of the book of life; I will confess his name before my Father and before his angels. He who has an ear, let him hear what the Spirit says to the churches."

Wake up! "Strengthen what remains and is on the point of death, for I have not found your works perfect in the sight of my God" (Revelation 3:2). Jesus calls us to perfection! Are your works *perfect?* We represent the author of life . . . love, joy, peace, patience, kindness, goodness, gentleness, faithfulness, and self-control.

Do people look at you and say, "Wow! That's life!"?

When was the last time *you* danced before the Lord in joy?

When was the last time *you* led someone to the living Christ?

When was the last time someone stopped *you* on the street and asked, "Why are you so happy? How can you be so alive?"

Look alive! . . . like Mother Teresa; like Billy Graham; like Ann Kiemel singing, "God loves you, and I love you, and that's the way it should be."

Do you *want* the white garments? Do you *want* your name in the Book of Life? Then look alive! *Live! Live! Live!* . . . Or am I just screaming at dead things?

Now do you feel more alive? Or do you feel more dead, imprisoned to the *name* of being alive? A lot of yelling outside, but inside more death. The more I scream, "Live!" the more you are reminded how dead you actually are. The more you're reminded how dead you are, the more self-conscious you become. The more self-conscious you become, the more dead you become!

Jesus was very clear: Lose your life and you'll find it. That means stop thinking about *yourself*. Are you thinking about yourself right now? The power of sin is the law. The law *makes* us dead. On top of that, we are not even very good at knowing what dead *is!* (Dead doesn't know dead.)

But if we're dead, somebody telling us to look alive won't do any good. We won't be joyful just because someone is trying to shame us into being like Mother Teresa. Try saying to a dead thing, "Get up!" It doesn't do any good. And how could a dead thing conquer?

Each letter to the seven churches ends with a similar phrase: "To him who conquers I will give . . . I'll do . . . such and such." So I read them and wonder,

Will *I* conquer?

Will *I* revive that first love?

Will *I* be faithful unto death?

Will *I* renounce false teaching?

Will *I* tolerate that Jezebel woman?

Will *I* wake up and live?

Will God blot *my* name out of the Book of Life?

It can scare you to death! We know faith is exhibited in works. But this sounds like *law* . . . works righteousness. That's weird, considering it was John who wrote this down.

When I preached through the Gospel of John a couple of years ago, time and time again I was struck by the fact that Jesus does *everything!* He calls people, He chooses people, He saves people, He sanctifies people, He lives His life through people. But here in these letters to the seven churches He's saying: repent, endure, don't tolerate, get living! Are we going to conquer? What is Jesus saying to us?

Technically, He's not actually talking to us. We are overhearing Him communicate with someone else, the way John overheard Jesus talking to God the Father in the Garden of Gethsemane. John is writing down what Jesus is saying to someone *else*.

Notice that each of the letters to the seven churches is addressed to the angel of each church. "Angel" means "messenger." Each letter ends with this phrase: "He who has an ear, let him hear what the Spirit says to the churches," as if the angel is some kind of counselor or advocate, as if the angel is this spirit (small s), or somehow the Spirit (capital S), that gives the message to the church.

Most of the pronouns in the letters are second person *singular* pronouns that get lost in translation. When Jesus says, "I have not found your works perfect," He is talking to the *angel*. Now that's really weird . . . because in Scripture, angels (the spirit kind) are good or bad, but this angel gets rebuked for bad things and commended for good. Not only that, but the rest of the New Testament teaches that we don't need some angel telling us stuff or representing us *to* God.

Some have postulated the angel is a bishop or a prophet or some person in the local church. (An *angelos* can be a spirit or a person.) But *bishop* hardly fits the biblical usage. And it puts a whole lot of pressure on these seven guys to save the churches. Neither "angel" nor "man" works, so some see it as simply an unprecedented, bizarre literary device. Yet Jesus seems to make a very big deal of these seven star messengers held tightly in His hand (1:16).

Seven messengers, yet one. Seven is the number of God's manifold fullness. In Revelation 5, the lamb has seven eyes, which are the seven spirits of God sent out into all the earth. Seven spirits, yet we know that it is *one* spirit—the Holy Spirit—the Spirit of Jesus. The seven angels are the seven stars in Revelation 1:20. Then in our text we read, "The words of him [Jesus] who *has* the seven spirits of God *and* the seven stars" (3:1, emphasis added). Some commentators say that the "and" is epexegetical, meaning "namely," or "that is," and that the seven spirits of God *are* the seven stars, and the seven stars *are* the seven angels.

Are these seven spirits the very same seven spirits that are the seven eyes of the lamb, which is the Spirit of the Living God, which would mean Jesus is writing to His own Spirit resident in each individual church?[1]

So *of course* He knows their works. And *of course* Jesus says to His spirit, "Let him with ears hear what the Spirit says to the churches."

The *Spirit* is the Counselor. He is the Advocate.

Now, we should be asking: If the angels are the Spirit . . .

- how could the Spirit be dead?
- how could the Spirit be accused of having tolerated Jezebel and having lost His first love?
- how could the Advocate—the *Paracletos*—be accused of sin?

Remember what Paul wrote: "In Christ God was reconciling the world to himself, not counting [imputing] their trespasses against them" (2 Corinthians 5:19). He must have been imputing them somewhere else. . . . "For our sake he made him [Jesus] to be sin who knew no sin, so that in him we might become the righteousness of God" (v. 21).

Some might say, "That's Paul; this is John." In 1 John, John says, "If any one does sin, we have an advocate with the Father, Jesus Christ the righteous" (1 John 2:1). John also calls the Holy Spirit "advocate"—*paracletos*. It means "one who pleads another's case before a judge."

In the Gospel of John, Jesus says He is sending another advocate. "You know him, for he dwells with you, and will be in you" (14:17). Then He tells the disciples that the advocate will teach you all things. "He will not speak on his own authority, but whatever he hears he will speak." (He gets direction.) "And he will declare to you the things that are to come." (That sounds familiar.) "He will take what is mine and declare it to you" (16:13–14).

The letter goes to the churches. A church is all those indwelt by the Spirit of Jesus. *They* are the ones who will hear the Spirit. So when Jesus says, "You're dead," could He be speaking to His own Spirit in those He chose to be alive? His Spirit can hear, "You are dead. Now live!"

Could it be that Jesus is so identified with His Bride—His own body—His beloved, even in her wretched garbage, that her sin is imputed to Him and His righteousness imputed to her?

So He takes his own rebuke for us and answers His own call *in* us;

So He not only *saves* us, He also *sanctifies* us; that is, he does good works *in* us;

So in these letters we hear our Lord speaking His directions to the Advocate—His Spirit—calling, "Live . . . live . . . live!" until "it is no longer I who live, but Christ who lives in me; and the life I now live in the flesh I live by faith in the Son of God, who loved me and gave himself for me" (Galatians 2:20).

WE ARE LIKE A PATIENT ON AN OPERATING TABLE overhearing the Great Physician talk to Himself about our surgery. If that is the case, what should we do? *Hold still.* Surrender, especially whatever is sick or rotten. Don't hide the gangrene.

Surrender,

trust,

hold still,

and see the salvation of your God.

Conquering then depends on surrendering deadness and sickness to the Physician. "Will the Physician conquer? Will the Advocate conquer? Will *Jesus* conquer?"

Well, that's what the rest of the book is about! "The Lamb will conquer . . . for he is Lord of lords and King of kings, and those with him are called and chosen and faithful" (17:14).

So will He conquer? Absolutely!

Will His name (a name He shares with you) be blotted from the Book of Life? *No way!*

The question then is, "Am I with Him, surrendering all to Him? For if you are "united with him in a death like his, [you] shall certainly be united with him in a resurrection like his" (Romans 6:5).

The saints conquer by the blood of the Lamb and the word of their testimony. That Word is Jesus. So even if I'm wrong about interpreting who the angel of the Church is, I'm right about how we conquer. For John wrote in 1 John 5:4, "This is the victory that overcomes the world, our faith." Jesus said we can do nothing apart from Him.

Overhearing the seven letters makes us call out, "Help! I can't conquer!" Then *the Lamb* conquers.

In Revelation 3:3 Jesus says, "Remember then what you received and heard." Amazingly enough, we know what the Sardisians (or the Spirit even then enlightening them) received and heard. They had heard Paul in Ephesus, a day's journey away. You can read about it in Acts 19. For two years Paul taught in the hall of Tyrannus, and all the residents of Asia heard the Word of the Lord.

We know what Paul said in Ephesus and *to* Ephesus—things like, "You he made alive when you were dead . . . for you have been saved by grace through faith, and this is not of yourselves lest any man should boast. No, not by works . . . for you are *his* workmanship, created in Christ Jesus for good works, which God prepared beforehand that you would walk in them" (see Ephesians 2:5–10).

Later he says, "Anything . . . exposed by the light . . . is light. . . . Awake, O sleeper, arise from the dead, and Christ shall give you light" (5:13–14).

> The key is complete surrender, exposing things to the light.
> Sardis, stop trying to make a name for yourself.
> Stop trying to hide garbage.
> Surrender the garbage, confess your sin one to another, and the Author of Life will be born in your stable.

He will give us His name; He will clothe us in white garments, which are the righteous deeds of the saints; He will get all the glory, for He conquers.

> And when you get a good look at Him,
> you'll forget about yourself,
> and that is life.

SHORTLY AFTER THE CONVERSATION AT THE DUMPSTER with my former senior pastor, I went for a walk with an old man. He was a pastor. His last ten years had been hard . . . a struggle with some difficult churches and difficult people. He hadn't published a book; his last church was no mega-church; he didn't have a big name.

Yet I'd have to say that it was in him more than in anyone else in my life that I had seen . . .

love,
joy,
peace,
patience,
kindness,
goodness,
gentleness,
faithfulness,
self-control.

I don't mean he was perfect, but those things were *real*.

We sat down by the dumpster on the steps out behind the church where I worked. He said, "Peter, I want you to know I haven't been very on fire for Jesus lately . . . not really alive like I should be [dead]. I want to recommit my life to Jesus [surrender], and I'd like you to pray for me."

Feeling pretty small and pretty dead myself, I did. I prayed for my dad with fumbling words, or I should say the Spirit in me called to the Spirit in him, "Live! Live! Live!" He did and he does. For about forty years now the Spirit in him has been calling to the Spirit in me, "Live! Live! Live!"

Whatever is good in me is a product of the Spirit of Jesus mostly working through my dad, because he is so alive he freely admits being dead.

Sardis had a reputation
for being alive,
but they were dead.
Jesus had a reputation
for being dead,
but He is life.
Entrust everything to Him.

NINE

HOLDING ON

(Revelation 3:7–13)

SISTER MARY ROSE MCGEADY helps homeless kids with nowhere to go. She tells the story of finding a dazed little boy in a sixteen-year-old body on a street corner. At first she thought he had a drug problem but soon realized he had a mental challenge. He had been wandering around looking for his father, who had told him to wait; he would be right back. Then he disappeared. Eric had been living under a bridge in a cement pipe ever since, waiting for his daddy to come back. "Eric, what's your last name?" she asked him.

"Eric."

"No, your other name," she persisted. "Do you have another name? Like, I'm Mary Rose, but my last name is McGeady. Do you have another name?"

"Just Eric."[1]

I wonder how many people there are in this world like Just Eric . . .

- people with little power, who find a closed door at every turn.
- people who feel shut out while the world passes them by.
- people who have a confused but belligerent hope that "somebody is coming back for me, because I belong somewhere else."

Whether we like it or not, to other street kids and most of the world, Just Eric is rather ordinary. In Africa, there are millions of orphans due to AIDS. Throughout the world, hundreds of millions are desperately hungry. Hundreds of millions would be thankful for a good cement pipe. Hundreds of millions . . . and their struggles are *not* extraordinary.

But American POWs, the families of Oklahoma bombing victims, Columbine High School . . . now *that's* extraordinary (we think): huge publicity and incredible stories of courage . . . like the recent story of the *Andrea Gail*, in the book and movie *The Perfect Storm*. Tragic, but it's a glorious picture: Man pitted against the raging sea.

In Scripture the sea is the abode of demons and the dragon, as well as an instrument of God's judgment. The *Andrea Gail's* heroic struggle against the perfect storm at sea is glorious. But what about all those simply lost at sea? What about all those whose stories are never heard?

Maybe you feel like "Just Eric." Doors keep shutting in your face. It feels like the world is passing you by, and you are powerless to prevent it. You are a Christian and you profess, "Jesus is coming back," but in your honest moments you have your doubts. So you serve on a church committee, you help out on a church mission, but you wonder, "Do I really matter? Do I count?" For most of your life you've felt as if you are just treading water . . . entirely ordinary . . . maybe *less* than ordinary.

REVELATION 3:7–10: *And to the angel of the church in Philadelphia write: "The words of the holy one, the true one, who has the key of David, who opens and no one shall shut, who shuts and no one opens.*

"I know your works. Behold, I have set before you an open door, which no one is able to shut; I know that you have but little power, and yet you have kept my word and have not denied my name. Behold, I will make those of the synagogue of Satan who say that they are Jews and are not, but lie—behold, I will make them come and bow down before your feet, and learn that I have loved you. Because you have kept my word of patient endurance, I will keep you from the hour of trial which is coming on the whole world, to try those who dwell upon the earth."

A GREAT STORM IS COMING—the perfect storm—to test those who live upon the earth. But Jesus is going to keep the Philadelphians from the storm. Some say that storm is strictly a seven-year period some time after the year 2001. So Jesus would be saying, "Guys, cheer up! You won't be around for the seven years of tribulation two thousand years from now! Hang on; I'm coming soon . . . actually, some time after 2008. Of course you'll be dead, but if you were alive, I'd rapture you and take you out of this world!"

Is *that* what He is saying? I don't think so. Persecution will intensify in their lifetime, and He will keep them. In the Gospel of John, Jesus prays this to His Father: "I have given them thy word; and the world has hated them because they are not of the world, even as I am not of the world. I do not pray that thou shouldst take them out of the world, but that thou shouldst keep them from the evil one" (John 17:14–15).

Maybe the storm will intensify right before Jesus comes back. But if we would step out of our rich, powerful, American mind-set for a little while and take a good look at this world, I think we would see that for *most* Christians in *most* of the world, things are pretty stormy and have been stormy for quite some time.

I think that we might also see something else:
Jesus still walks in storms on the raging sea;
behold, He is still coming soon.

PHILADELPHIA, twenty-three miles southeast of Sardis, was plagued with earthquakes. It was a rather young city established as an outpost of Greek culture, a frontier town. Jesus says, "You have little strength"—the Greek word is *dunamis,* from which we get "dynamite." There weren't many fireworks in Philadelphia; they were ordinary or less than ordinary. But because they were faithful Jesus will keep them from the storm.

Over in Smyrna they are also faithful, and they get thrown in prison and some get martyred. In Smyrna we met Polycarp. Incredible suffering; incredible heroes of faith.

But here in Philadelphia, "Keep treading water."

It appears the Philadelphians were going through ordinary kinds of suffering. Folks from the synagogue (to which many undoubtedly belonged) were ridiculing them saying, "God doesn't love you. You're no longer part of the people of God!" Rejected, ridiculed, and excluded by old family and friends, through whom the evil one whispered, "Unloved . . . unworthy . . . rejected."

Ordinary church, ordinary bride . . .
I imagine she was feeling kind of frumpy . . .
housecoat, slippers . . .
one more day of doing the laundry . . .
and what does it matter?

And Jesus says, "Yes. I know. But look! I place before you an open door" (see Revelation 3:8). He also told them he had the key of David (v. 7). Isaiah 22:22 refers to the key of the *house* of David, and the one who wields it can open doors that nobody can shut, and can close doors that no one will open. It's the key to a kingdom!

This key in Revelation 3 is not just to the *house* of David; it is the key *of* David. I think that's interesting, for David had little power. He was an ordinary shepherd boy, smaller than all his brothers, yet God called *him*. As a *weak* boy, David had incredible *power*. He conquered Goliath and spread the kingdom of Israel. He conquered evil spirits in Saul and sent them running with his music. Everywhere he turned there were open doors.

And then he became king, no longer small, but immense—Israel's *greatest* king. Ironically, it was then that he seemed most weak. When he saw himself as strong he sank . . . into adultery, murder, betrayal by his own children.

Jesus says, "I place before you, Philadelphia, an open door" (v. 8). There's debate over the meaning of that open door. Many say it's the door of evangelism, because in both Corinthian letters Paul refers to open doors of spreading the gospel. Paul also wrote, "We have this treasure in earthen vessels, to show that the transcendent power belongs to God" (2 Corinthians 4:7).

That is, "Philadelphia, your very weakness allows you to show forth the kingdom to those who haven't heard." That makes some sense, especially to rich Americans like us living in a commercial society where everybody is trying to sell us something. We are highly suspicious of commercials. They almost always lie. Powerful people can afford to live their lives like commercials . . .

always striking a pose,

wearing the right clothes,

saying the right things,

every word carefully scripted.

So we have learned it is what comes out in the unguarded moments of life that is most convincing.

A little boy watched a minister as he did some carpentry out in his yard. He wouldn't leave but watched intently. Pleased with the thought of being admired, the minister said, "Son, are you looking for some pointers in carpentry?" The little boy said, "No. I'm waiting to hear what a preacher says when he hits his thumb with a hammer." That was a smart kid.

JESUS WAS A CARPENTER in a little frontier town called Nazareth. He never wrote a book, held public office, or earned a degree. He never traveled more than two hundred miles from His place of birth. Sure, there were miracles, but He *hid* them from people. No dynamite unless they had faith first. To the world, it looked like a rather ordinary life. But He said to a few folks, "Come walk with Me awhile." They watched Him do ordinary things in an extraordinary way . . .

hold children.

talk to a woman by a well alone at midday.

sleep on a boat in a storm.

He died between two ordinary thieves, crucified like hundreds of thousands of others in Rome. But His ordinary life exposed extraordinary faith, hope, and love in a way that our powerful, scripted, and together lives do not.

He chose weakness to expose the glory of God. On the cross, where the hammer drives nails through His flesh into wood, He exposes the heart of God. There He draws all men to Himself (John 12:32).

Most people come to Christ because they saw Him in some ordinary person at some unscripted moment. Sure—they may come forward at the Billy Graham Crusade, but it is because they saw faith, hope, and love in people like you—their neighbor.

Live your ordinary life in faith, and you wield supreme power. Faith . . . shining through the cracks in an ordinary clay pot.

At the last judgment the sheep say, "Lord, when did we see you hungry or thirsty, sick and in prison?" That is, "Jesus, we don't remember you there . . . it was just an ordinary day . . . I was just helping out at the nursing home . . . *that* was *You?*"

When Peter walked on the water in that raging storm, I don't think he knew what he was doing. He hadn't been sitting in the boat psyching himself up for great and mighty works. He just *loved* Jesus and *believed* Jesus. Jesus said, "Come," and he did. Only when he noticed how extraordinary his situation was, and how extraordinary *he* was, did he sink.

Maybe you don't know when you're walking on water. Maybe something is good about that, because the moment you notice, it becomes about *you,* and you sink. Then the people watching you sink, because *they* think it's about you too.

"Philadelphia, you have little power. But before you I have placed an open door." Maybe the open door is the door of people's hearts won to Christ. In the next letter Jesus says, "Behold, I stand at the door and knock; if any one hears my voice and opens the door, I will come in to him and eat with him, and he with me" (3:20). *Maybe* the door is evangelism—the door to people's hearts.

But *maybe* it's much bigger than that, because in chapter 4 John writes, "After this I looked, and behold, a door was opened in heaven" (v. 1).

Little David had power over demons and giants, and little David had a key to the kingdom of Israel, but he also had a key to something much bigger than that: the heart of *God.*

Faith, hope, and love in weakness; a man after God's own heart.

This is hard for us Americans to believe, but maybe God isn't in short supply of dynamite, miracles, and power. But just maybe He would die for a little faith, hope, and love from His children.

ETERNITY NOW

IN OCTOBER 1991, weather fronts over New England combined with the remains of a hurricane coming up the eastern seaboard. Together they formed what we've called the Perfect Storm. To the north, the *Andrea Gail* battled with all her expertise, power, and might. To the south, a six-year-old little girl practiced her ordinary back float.

My friend Gary from Philadelphia told me her story. He was the girl and her father's pastor. Her father John had not checked the weather report when he took his young daughter sailing off the Jersey shore. Six miles out, he was shocked at how fast the winds changed and a storm came up. Soon the boat capsized and they were in the water. The life preservers were still tied to the boat while the boat was being swept out to sea.

John realized there was no way he could swim the six miles back to shore while holding his little girl; to save them, he would have to swim alone. "Mary, you can float on your back as long as you want," he told her. They had practiced in the pool at home. "Float on your back, Mary. I'll swim to shore, and I will be back for you."

Three hours later the Coast Guard found John. For the next hour and a half as darkness came on, they looked for the little girl amid twenty- to thirty-foot swells. Then, miraculously, the spotlight found her. She had been floating nearly five hours.

The guardsmen later asker her, "Mary, how did you *do* that?" She said, "Well, my daddy said I could float on my back as long as I wanted to, and that he would come back for me. My daddy *always* does what he says."

The *Andrea Gail* fought with courage and power, and she sank. There is glory in that. Mary just practiced her back float, and she didn't even know she beat the storm of the century. You could say that faith in her daddy kept her from the great storm that came down on the whole east coast.

"I know you're small and weak, Philadelphia, but keep on keeping My Word. Hold on, Philadelphia, and I will be back. I'll keep you from the hour of trial. I'm coming soon."

And Jesus said to His struggling disciples, "Where I am going you cannot follow." He was swimming into the heart of the perfect storm—hell itself. But He said to them, "I will be back, and My Spirit will keep you. Patiently endure in faith."

Maybe, just maybe, *you* are walking on water, and you don't even know it. You're just hanging on . . . one more day. Angels watch in wonder from the deck of the boat. They say, "Look! She's floating in the storm of the century!"

Maybe you *are* walking on water, but that's not my main point. My point is this: Faith in weakness ravishes the Father's heart. What father could resist faith, hope, and love like Mary's? Certainly not *God* the Father, so it is . . .

Mary who has the key to the Father's heart;

David who has the key to God's heart;

Just Eric who has the key to the Father's heart;

Jesus the Christ (the perfect child) who trusted His Father from the pit of hell and bore the perfect storm of God's judgment in faith.

Now, what is Christ's is declared to Philadelphia, and the Spirit says, "Look!—A door." In Revelation 4:1 we begin to look through that door, and what do we see? The throne of God, and in the midst of the throne is someone we know—a Lamb! . . . weak and powerless, slain for us . . . bleeding (5:6).

John tells us Jesus is "from the bosom of the Father"—the heart of God. And we see He is worthy to open the scroll and receive . . .

power and

wealth and

wisdom and

might and

honor and

glory forever and ever.

For He, the root of David, has conquered! He has even conquered our *dead hearts* with His own blood. He has the key to our hearts. He opens the scroll and history happens: four riders and storms, conquest, warfare, famine, death, martyrs, signs and wonders, the consummation of this creation. But right before He opens the scroll and gives meaning to all history, a scent rises from the throne: incense. It's the prayers of His saints. They ascend to the heart of God, like Mary murmuring, "He said he would be back."

Prayers of the saints, not building projects, crusades, mighty works, wonderful mission programs, sermons. *Prayers,* rising from prisons, hospital beds, lonely apartments, boring church services, frumpy wives in housecoats.

You see, there is an open door between the boring little frontier town of Philadelphia and the heart of God Almighty. So nothing is more powerful in *all* created reality, including kings, famines, earthquakes, dragons, storms.

Nothing is more powerful than the frumpy little church in Philadelphia. They are given the key to the Creator's heart as they do their back float in the midst of the raging storm.

What father could resist faith, hope, and love like that?

Like David's,

like Mary's,

like Eric's, the kid in the Bronx?

When you read about Eric, you stopped thinking about yourself. Eric's faith, hope, and love opened your heart. That's the power of God in Christ Jesus our Lord.

In Jesus, God opened the door to your heart.

Jesus *in* you has opened the door to *God's* heart;

Jesus *through* you opens the door to other people's hearts.

Faith, hope, and love—displayed in weakness. And *Jesus* does it! To Him be all glory, honor, and praise for evermore! Amen.

Eric's earthly father didn't come back. I suspect he was evil. But God the Father is not. I believe He came to Eric in the form of Sister Mary Rose McGeady. And He is the one who created in Eric the longing—"faith, hope, and love." I imagine Eric is not "Just Eric," but that his surname is "God," and he has a new name: "Jesus." His home is not the Bronx but the New Jerusalem. I believe God will move *all creation* for Just Eric.

Bride of Christ, no matter how frumpy, ordinary, and dull you may feel, your faith exists in the great storm of a fallen world. Your faith is the power that ravishes the heart of God Almighty. Keep holding on.

REVELATION 3:11–13: *"I am coming soon. Hold on to what you have, so that no one will take your crown. Him who overcomes I will make a pillar in the temple of my God. Never again will he leave it. I will write on him the name of my God and the name of the city of my God, the new Jerusalem which is coming down our of heaven from my God; and I will also write on him my new name. He who has an ear, let him hear what the Spirit says to the churches."*

TEN

DISGUSTINGLY NICE CHRISTIANS

(Revelation 3:14–22)

TIME MAGAZINE ran a cover story proclaiming good news about how "science is offering new hope for treating all our fears."[1] On the title page in big, bold letters was the phrase, "FEAR NOT."[2]

In the margins of the article they list hundreds of phobias now known to science. Phobias like . . .

- *alektorophobia*—fear of chickens.
- *arachibutyrophobia*—fear of peanut butter sticking to the roof of the mouth.
- *homilophobia*—fear of sermons.
- *ophidiophobia*—fear of snakes.

The article goes on to talk about how all these fears may have been helpful at one point in our ancient past, but not now, of course. They're *silly*. We live in the United States of America! This is a *nice place*.

So scientists have therapies and powerful medication to squelch all these irrational fears. Here are some more from the same list:

- *satanophobia*—fear of Satan.
- *pecatophobia*—fear of sinning.
- *hadephobia*—fear of hell.
- *zeusophobia*—fear of God.
- *staurophobia*—fear of Jesus hanging on a cross.
- *thanatophobia*—fear of death.

Don't worry. They can medicate all these fears away. How about this one?

- *emetophobia*—fear of vomiting.

REVELATION 3:14–17: *And to the angel of the church in Laodicea write: "The words of the Amen, the faithful and true witness, the beginning of God's creation. I know your works: you are neither cold nor hot. Would that you were cold or hot! So, because you are lukewarm, and neither cold nor hot, I will spew you out of my mouth. For you say, I am rich, I have prospered, and I need nothing; not knowing that you are wretched, pitiable, poor, blind, and naked."*

Ouch . . .

Poor? But Laodicea was a center of commercial prosperity!

Blind? They manufactured a world famous eye salve!

Naked? They were known for their black woolen textiles!

They were so prosperous that when a devastating earthquake struck the region in A.D. 60, they refused to accept financial assistance from the Roman Empire, saying, "We have prospered and need nothing."

The only thing anyone could really complain about in Laodicea was the water supply. Nearby Colossae was known for cold, pure, drinking water. Hieropolos, six miles to the north, was known for hot, therapeutic mineral springs. Because Laodicea had no water supply of its own, an aqueduct was built from Hieropolos to Laodicea. But by the time the water got to Laodicea, it became lukewarm and distasteful.

Just as the town viewed themselves, so did the Church: spiritually rich. The Laodiceans knew the apostle Paul! And the famous Epaphras was a hometown boy!

Their faith was organized, categorized, certified, franchised, homogenized.

But Jesus says, "You are wretched, pitiable, poor, blind, and naked." Wow! Laodicea kind of reminds me of the United States of America.

I've been thinking about that list of phobias . . . thanatophobia, for instance: fear of death. Pretty much everybody *dies.* Yet we call thanatophobia a form of insanity?

Maybe the thanatobes are the most sane.

Maybe the people crouching under beds and hiding in closets are most in touch with reality.

Maybe we really *will* die one day.

Maybe great tribulations are always at hand.

Maybe there is a God, and we ought to fear Him somehow (zeusophobia).

Maybe there really is sin (pecatophobia), Satan (satanophobia), and a hell (hadephobia). Maybe ophidiophobia (fear of snakes) is about more than just reptiles in our ancient past but one hellacious snake in our ancient past . . . and present.

Maybe the *in*sane are the most sane.

The only way we could really function well as this productive American society is to pretend that our fears are irrational phobias. If we didn't deny fears, death, and our consciences, we would be *paralyzed* with fear, hiding in closets, and crouching under beds, ice cold with terror. Or, worse yet, we would all freak out and become fiery hot religious zealots who didn't care about the economy, Volvos, or the stock market. Fear could totally *screw up* this incredible economy of conspicuous consumption!

So if *I* were in control of the economy, wanted to control all the people in the economy, and was evil (working for some ancient snake), I would try to get people to *ignore* their greatest fears and dreams. Even better, I'd attach my *merchandise* to their greatest fears and dreams. That way I could sell my merchandise and, better yet, keep them enslaved in bondage to me.

I would come up with slogans like these:

"Volvo—It can save your soul."

"Diamonds last forever."

"Levi's—because you are what you wear."

So then they would live with a vague dissatisfaction, a confused hope, and an unexamined fear . . . this idea that something's wrong.

"But I bet that next year's *Volvo* will do the trick!"

"If I only had a *diamond* I would be set!"

"If I had a pair of *Levi's,* I would *be* somebody."

Addicted, intoxicated, blinded . . . it would work like magic.

Well, that's just a crazy thought. But when was the last time you saw a commercial that said something like, "We have Volvos, diamonds, and jeans to sell, but we had a meeting and realized: We're all going to die! We don't know how to save your soul or why we even exist! So we were thinking . . . cars, rocks, and pants don't seem like much of a priority." Of course we wouldn't see a commercial like that—because it's the truth. We do a good job with our illusions here in America. We can afford to. We even dress up dead people so they look nice. We spend thousands of dollars on embalming, nice suits, and beautiful caskets, so dead people look alive.

My friend Gary told me about a very nice funeral he did in a wealthy part of town. They had gone out to the graveside . . . Gary in his robes . . . beautiful liturgy . . . deceased in an expensive casket. . . . At the start of the ceremony, Gary somehow slipped and fell in the grave! And he couldn't get out! They had to pull him out of the grave. Everyone kind of *woke up*. It kind of broke the spell for a moment. Maybe the pastor ought to always fall in the grave: the new liturgy.

Just as the town of Laodicea rubbed off on the church in Laodicea, maybe the U.S. is rubbing off on *us*. We're rich, we've obtained prosperity, and we need nothing . . . nice church. And if we *do* need something we know exactly what to do: Ask the pastor, get a counselor, go to the Christian bookstore, attend a seminar, or take a class on the victorious Christian life—how to conquer this or that. We have it all worked out like a science—even the Revelation. So we have nice churches and nice people. "Don't worry, Jesus. We've got it all figured out. We don't need any help. We've got You covered."

When I think I have my wife all figured out and what I need to do to make this marriage thing work very nicely, I'm in trouble. You know those *very* nice couples who get along so well—and then one day they just split up? They don't need each other. They've stopped caring.

The thing I fear most in my wife is when she gets lukewarm, gives up the fight and settles for the status quo—a *nice* marriage. She smiles and acts nice, but I can't get her to look at me. If she's screaming in anger or hot with passion, she's looking at me. Lukewarm—she won't. It's worse than hatred. Unconsciously she's trying to convince herself I don't matter and she doesn't need me. Invariably I have to pick a fight and press the issue until she cracks. We each lose control, fight, and then heal.

Apathy is blindness.

"Would that you were cold or hot," says Jesus. "At least then you would look at Me. Looking at Me is life, abiding in Me, is life. But lukewarm—you make Me want to *em-eh'-o* [spew]."

I think perhaps the American church is full of blind people, and I can't make them see. No book can do that, no class can do that. No program can do that. Worse than this, the blind Laodiceans don't even *know* they're blind. I may not even know where *I'm* blind. Let alone make anyone else see.

The blind leading the blind.

I take it on faith that we're all at least a *bit* blind, for we are all at least a *bit* lukewarm. Nobody can truly see Jesus in His glory and just stay lukewarm.

So we're all at least a bit blind, a bit asleep, and a bit intoxicated; maybe that's because we want to be. Lukewarm can be pretty comfortable. Sometimes it's nice to be in the dark—but then we become blind to being blind. What should we do?

In the Chronicles of Narnia book *The Silver Chair,* the Marsh-wiggle Puddleglum and the children they find themselves in the dark underground kingdom of the evil witch, who is really the great serpent. But she doesn't look or act like a witch—she lures them in with sweet talk. They were being enchanted, Lewis writes, "and of course, the more enchanted you get the more certain you feel that you are not enchanted at all."[3]

When they tell the witch about the real world, including the sun and Aslan the Lion, she coos at them that they just made up those ideas after seeing her lamps and one of her housecats. So the children mumble, "I suppose the other world must be a dream."

"Yes, it's a dream," coos the witch.[4]

Their hopes are a dream; their fears are obviously a dream, because this woman is lovely. She is making them comfortable . . .

fireplace . . . music . . . food . . . wine . . . sweet smells . . . maybe Volvos, diamonds, and designer jeans. In*toxicating.*

She says: "There is no Narnia, no Overworld, no sky, no sun, no Aslan. And now, to bed all. And let us begin a wiser life tomorrow. But first, to bed; to sleep; deep sleep, soft pillows, sleep without foolish dreams."[5]

And Jesus says, "You're lukewarm. You think you're rich and prosperous, but you're wretched, pitiable, poor, blind, and naked."

How could that *be?* In Revelation 18 we see how it could be. The great harlot rides the beast under the authority of the great serpent. The economies of the governments of this world are under the dominion of Satan. "All the nations have drunk the maddening wine of her adulteries. The kings of the earth committed adultery with her, and the merchants of the earth grew rich from her excessive luxuries. . . . By [her] magic spell all the nations were led astray" (18:3, 23 NIV).

Even the *Church—*

> intoxicated, lukewarm, dead.

So what are we to do? Print more T-shirts and sing "Get all excited"?

Here's what Puddleglum did, just as the enchantment was almost complete—a brave thing. In a daze he walked over to the fire and plunged his bare foot into the coals. The pain was clear, but now so was his mind. Lewis writes, "There is nothing like a good shock of pain for dissolving certain kinds of magic."[6] At the smell of burnt Marsh-wiggle feet, the enchantment was broken for all—eyes opened, they saw the witch for the serpent she was, and they escaped to Narnia and Aslan.

ETERNITY NOW

REVELATION 3:18–22: *"Therefore I counsel you to buy from me gold refined by fire, that you may be rich, and white garments to clothe you and to keep the shame of your nakedness from being seen, and salve to anoint your eyes, that you may see. Those whom I love, I reprove and chasten; so be zealous and repent. Behold, I stand at the door and knock; if any one hears my voice and opens the door, I will come in to him and eat with him, and he with me. He who conquers, I will grant him to sit with me on my throne, as I myself conquered and sat down with my Father on his throne. He who has an ear, let him hear what the Spirit says to the churches."*

WHAT ARE WE TO DO? Perhaps like Puddleglum, Jesus is saying, "Buy gold from me, refined by fire." Where will they find that gold in Laodicea? How will they get it?

Remember that over in Smyrna they thought they were wretched, pitiable, and poor? But Jesus said, "You're *rich*, Smyrna!" There were few illusions in Smyrna as Polycarp burned at a stake in the Roman coliseum and appeared like gold, together with Jesus.

"Laodicea, maybe you could get some gold in Smyrna . . . share in their sufferings, and when you see their sufferings, you will realize this *is* a fallen, God-cursed world, and you need a savior.

Not a book,

not a class,

not a program;

but a Savior

to reach into the grave

and pull you out.

"Maybe you'll see what this world is and you'll call out in need, and He will cover you in His righteousness; He will anoint your eyes with salve. Jesus makes blind eyes see Him. Then you will believe in *Him* . . . not in 'Christianity.'"

Peter writes that our faith is more precious than gold which is refined by fire (1 Peter 1:7). Where do we buy gold refined by fire? Look around . . .

I have a friend who is very successful in business—a prince by Laodicean standards. He and his wife adopt hurting children from around the world. He goes to Africa to "buy gold" by supplying power to remote, impoverished villages. He *could* be content with his power and wealth, but he has chosen to share in other's sufferings and go places where he has to call out in need, "Jesus, help me!"

I know a woman who could be the queen of Laodicea, if she chose. But she spends her weeks in downtown Denver ministering to homeless people, single mothers, kids stranded in poverty. She doesn't have to, but she goes there—to buy gold, and to meet Jesus.

Where do you buy gold, Laodicea? In the next verse . . .

John sees a door in heaven and the Revelation opens up before him—the throne of God Almighty. The Lamb that was slain opens a scroll, four horsemen bringing . . .

> conquest,
>> warfare,
>>> famine,
>>>> pestilence.

The rider of the pale horse is death, and there is a serpent and beasts and a great harlot . . . it's all to help us see Jesus in all His glory. It's salve for the blind eyes of Laodicea.

"Laodicea, how dare you say, 'I am rich, I have prospered, and I need nothing!' You are seduced by the great harlot riding the beast under the dominion of Satan! You need *Jesus!*

"Laodicea, the horsemen are riding right *now:*

> conquest,
>> warfare,
>>> famine,
>>>> pestilence.
> Death,
>> martyrs . . .

"Don't you read the paper? Stop retreating into your nice, comfortable American churches, hiding behind you watertight Bible studies and your charts of the end times. The *time* is at *hand.*"

NOW I MUST CONFESS that the interpretation of the Revelation I find most unbiblical is the most popular interpretation in America right now. It is peculiarly American and peculiarly recent: the idea that we get *raptured* in the next verse (3:21), so the rest of the Revelation really isn't *about* us, but those left behind who have to go through the great tribulation. It makes most of the book irrelevant to us and an insult to suffering Christians around the world. It makes us voyeurs of suffering. I can see why it's so popular in the U.S. I'm sure it would have been popular in Laodicea too. But the tribulation was their medicine . . . and *our* medicine.

Jesus said, "In this world you *will* have tribulation, but be of good cheer, for *I* have overcome the world." In tribulation our eyes are opened, and we see He *has* overcome the world. We have cheer!

Quit trying to manage your fears, and *face* them. Walk right into them—and realize that your control has been an illusion all along. *You need Jesus every second.*

Behold, He has been standing, knocking, all along. Invite Him in. He's with you in the fire and the storm. He's courage in the fire and storm.

If you're thinking, "I just don't have courage to plunge my foot into the fire, to buy gold refined by fire," well, you're right. You don't. But He does and He did. He went to hell and back to get you—His golden treasure

One day they will drop you in a grave . . .

thanatophobia,
zeusophobia,
satanophovia,
hadephobia,
pecatophobia,
staurophobia.

They'll drop you in a grave and you'll feel a touch—you're not insane. Now you're sane. A voice will say, "Friend, let's get out of here! I *beat* this place!" And you'll see Him.

ELEVEN

CASTING CROWNS

(Revelation 4)

REVELATION 4:1 (NIV): *After this I looked, and there before me was a door standing open in heaven. And the voice I had first heard speaking to me like a trumpet said, "Come up here, and I will show you what must take place after this."*

For THE LAST TWO CHAPTERS, John has been dictating for the angels of the seven churches what he has *heard*. Nevertheless, the seven churches are clearly expected to overhear what is said to the angels. They overhear that they have some real needs and each one common challenge: to conquer. Real and multiple and varying needs such as:

- Some need to restore their first love.
- Some are facing persecution and death.
- There is false doctrine and idolatry.
- There is sexual immorality and a need for church discipline.
- Some are dead even though everybody else thinks they're alive.
- Some are doing well but don't know it.
- Some are "wretched, pitiable, poor, blind, and naked," although they think they're rich and wise.

All of them are called to "conquer."

There is a huge variety of need in my congregation, just like those seven churches. And *I'm* supposed to *preach* to it all?! What do I say "after this"— after they see their need?

Now, let's have a little sympathy for John. John sees himself as their pastor. And what is he supposed to say now, after all of this *need?*

After the legalism of the Jews, the first great cultural enemy of the early Church was gnosticism. *Gnostic* means "one who knows." The gnostics were the first major illegitimate offspring of the early church, sired by the philosophy of Greece. The Greeks thought our highest function was the ability to think. They loved *gnosis*—knowledge. Education was savior. Those early believers wanted something worthwhile "after this."

We're not as distant from those believers as we might think. Thanks to the eighteenth-century revival of Greek thought in the Enlightenment, which valued rational thought above all, we have inherited the assumption that knowledge is salvation. And the Enlightenment believed that man was the measure of all things—kind of like my daughter's T-shirt that says, "It's all about me."

So after the Revelation points out all our problems, we expect some helpful information. We want some practical advice on how we can *conquer* them.

It seems that God is our chief problem, so how can we comprehend Him? How can we make this whole God thing *work?*

This is hard for us modern people to take, but "after this," Revelation 4:1, we are really not *mentioned* as such in the rest of the book. The seven *churches* are really not mentioned as such in the rest of the book.

No instructions; no understandable, practical advice whatsoever!

So we think it must not be about *us.* In fact, the dominant view in the American church today is that we get raptured out of there at this point. So the rest of the Revelation isn't *about* us. And that's kind of strange, because this is the beginning of the very part of the book that Jesus says is particularly for us. In chapter 1: "[John] write what you see . . ." and send it to the seven churches.

Maybe it isn't *about* us, meaning *dependent* on us, but it is *for* us, because Jesus said so. And the part we think is for us (chapters 2–3), the part we understand—do this, do that, repent here, repent there—is technically not *for* us. It's not addressed to us, but to the seven "angelos."

When I used to teach the Revelation, I would reach this point and then stop, saying, "Sorry. I don't understand past here." Many people have approached me and said, "I've never read the Revelation because I don't understand it."

We think it's *so important* to understand. I guess I'm still not sure I *do* understand, but I'm beginning to understand I'm not *supposed* to understand everything! Maybe if I *did* understand, it wouldn't be God. Because if I *understand* God, I don't know Him.

There are a lot of different ways of knowing. A daughter set out to introduce her elderly mother to the wonders of the Internet. She went to a popular Web site called "Ask Jeeves" and told her mother it could answer any of her questions. Her mother looked skeptical. "It's *true*, Mom," she said. "Think of something to ask it, and it will have the answer."

They sat there for a few moments, and then her mother responded in a very serious voice, "Okay, how is Aunt Helen feeling?"

There is one way to know objects and another way to know subjects, one way to know data and another way to know Aunt Helen.

Maybe God is more like Aunt Helen and less like a computer.

You can conquer, capture, and measure things that are less than you. But you can't really measure things that are greater than you. So if man is the measure of all things, then you must believe that all things are less than you, and that you're the king of all things. Yet all things in your kingdom are dead.

A world of facts, and none of them worth knowing.

I've heard that if a tribal African wants to *know* something, he dances with it. If a *modern* person wants to know something, he captures it, kills it, and cuts it into little bitty pieces. Knowing something means reducing it to its basic parts. To know a tree, cut it down and count its rings. To know a frog, capture it, kill it, and dissect it. If you want to know a wife . . . well, I *could* capture it, kill it, and cut it into little, tiny pieces—and sometimes I think I do, emotionally and spiritually, when we fight. But if I did it *completely*, even *physically*, what would that be?—anatomy and physiology. I would learn *about* my wife—what color her kidneys are, how many ribs in her rib cage—but I would no longer *know* my wife, because she'd be dead! And I'd be a murderer . . . alone.

I wonder if in our lust for understanding God we could murder Him. "That's a crazy idea," you say. "You can't murder God!" But perhaps we murder Him to *us*—make Him so entirely understandable that we render Him dead.

In John 5, John records that Jesus said to the Pharisees and preachers, "You search the scriptures, because you think that in them you have eternal life; and it is they that bear witness to me; yet you refuse to come to me that you may have life" (vv. 39–40). Because they so wanted to comprehend God, because they so thought they understood God according to the book, when God showed up in the flesh in front of them, they could not understand Him; they could not know Him, and they killed Him.

Maybe in our lust for understanding God we *did* murder God. We nailed

Him to a tree; I think it was the tree of knowledge. And wasn't that the sin in the Garden? We wanted the knowledge of God more than we wanted to know God?

If Revelation 4:1 is our first step back into the Garden since we left it back in Genesis 3, maybe we had better be prepared to drop the fruit of knowledge we're clutching so tightly in our hands at the gate . . . in order to know the Maker. Maybe we should give up *having* to understand in order to *know.*

Maybe God doesn't *want* to be "understood" so much as *known,* like my wife, who wants to be known, not captured. If I think I have captured her, comprehended her, understood all of her, she'll do something to make sure I understand differently. She wants to be *known* . . . loved.

When a Hebrew man *knew* his wife, she often got pregnant. There are different ways of knowing and different things to be known.

Maybe this explains most of our modern gnostic problems with God. We constantly ask, "How could bad things happen to good people?" Maybe good people are like murdering Pharisees, who try to set a trap for God and end up pounding the Son of God to their tree of knowledge.

Now, to be sure, practical, understandable ideas are fine—such as, "four understandable things you can do to restore first love"; or "practical advice for the seven churches on how to experience life"; or "how to make the Christian life work for you."

But too much,

in the wrong way,

at the wrong place,

and God begins to look more like a computer

and less like Aunt Helen . . .

more like a *thing* to be captured

and less like a *person* to be known.

I was listening to a tape of sermons, and the host praised the sermon he introduced by saying, "The preacher leaves us with several practical things to do, not just with the sense that God is great."

I thought a lot about that statement. I think *I* believe, in a sense, that "God is great" is pretty much *it.* It's called faith, and it looks like worship.

From here on out in the Revelation, I think John is pretty much going to leave us self-conscious, self-absorbed, needy, sinful, frightened, confused, Gnostic people with an overwhelming sense that God is really great in every possible way we could ever imagine.

I think *that* is what we need most.

Maybe our chief need is to see our needs and then lose them by losing ourselves in His greatness. Then it really isn't *about* us! And that's great news,

because we're the chief problem. Maybe the first step and *only* step in conquering is being conquered. Not to comprehend, but to be comprehended.

REVELATION 4:2–8: *At once I was in the Spirit, and lo, a throne stood in*
heaven, with one seated on the throne! And he who sat there appeared like jasper and
carnelian, and round the throne was a rainbow that looked like an emerald. Round
the throne were twenty-four thrones, and seated on the thrones were twenty-four
elders, clad in white garments, with golden crowns upon their heads. From the throne
issue flashes of lightning, and voices and peals of thunder, and before the throne burn
seven torches of fire, which are the seven spirits of God; and before the throne there is
as it were a sea of glass, like crystal.

And round the throne, on each side of the throne, are four living creatures,
full of eyes in front and behind: the first living creature like a lion, the second
living creature like an ox, the third living creature with the face of a man, and
the fourth living creature like a flying eagle. And the four living creatures, each
of them with six wings, are full of eyes all round and within, and day and night
they never cease to sing,

"Holy, holy, holy, is the Lord God Almighty,
who was and is and is to come!"

"AFTER THIS," John is out-carnated . . . Apocalypse.

In the rest of chapter 4, he sees a rainbow—an Old Testament symbol of
God's covenant of mercy. He sees seven burning torches or lamps (*lampus* in
Greek) that sit on lampstands. Jesus already told us that the lampstands are the
seven churches. He sees four living creatures, cherubim and seraphim it seems,
from Ezekiel and Isaiah. Some ancient rabbis used to say they represented all
creation—the strongest, noblest, the wisest, and the swiftest—but we don't
know for sure. They're not *exactly* like that.

This is *pictures on top of pictures on top of pictures,* all loaded with meaning.
And space and time are different here. We just cannot comprehend it all,
because it's larger and greater than anything we've ever seen.

REVELATION 4:9–11: *And whenever the living creatures give glory and honor*
and thanks to him who is seated on the throne, who lives for ever and ever, the
twenty-four elders fall down before him who is seated on the throne and worship
him who lives for ever and ever; they cast their crowns before the throne, singing,
"Worthy art thou, our Lord and God,

to receive glory and honor and power,
for thou didst create all things,
and by thy will they existed and were created."

JOHN SEES TWENTY-FOUR THRONES and twenty-four elders, like the twenty-four divisions of priests in the Temple. Later we'll read that the New Jerusalem is built with the twelve apostles and the twelve sons of Israel—together, twenty-four.

Everything worships the One on the throne. *Everything*—and they don't *study,* they *worship.* Or if they study, it's somehow a part of worship. Everyone is exclaiming, *Holy, holy, holy.* Loosely translated, "holy" means "incomprehensible glory."

The elders continuously cast their crowns before Him. Jesus taught us to pray this way: "Father, thy will be done, on earth as it is in heaven." What are they *always doing* in heaven? Worshiping—casting crowns before Him.

Faith is trusting God's great love for you, and when you do, it looks like worship. In order to conquer, you must first be conquered. You must first lose your life. You must first surrender your crown.

So what do you do with all of your needs and your confusion and your questions? *Just look at how great God is.* Stop struggling to understand and comprehend and analyze your relationship with God and how to make it work. Stop going to worship to *learn* stuff! Go to worship to worship! Every moment of every day, behold how great your God is, and do some crown casting. Cast your sovereignty before Him: your hurts, fears anxieties, dreams . . . control. Not as a practical action step, but as a disposition of the heart, a surrender of the soul.

I hope you realize that I'm not saying we can't understand anything about God. I mean that we can't understand anything about God unless He chooses to reveal it to us—that's called grace through revelation, and when we get it, it looks like worship. In the same way, we can't *do* any good deed for God except for what God does *in* us by His Spirit—by grace, and that looks like faith.

The only crown Jesus ever wore on the face of this earth was a crown of thorns they pounded into His head while He hung on a cross dying for you and me. And *He* is the one who shows John the throne. When John looks at the throne, he sees somebody he knows: Jesus, bleeding for him; the Lamb, looking as if it had been slain (5:6). At the cross we tried to conquer God, nailing Him to the tree of knowledge, where we belonged. But at the cross, God conquers us with love, and reveals knowledge by grace.

We say, "It's not about you!" That's a good thing to say. It reminds us it's not *dependent* on us. But look! It's *all* about you. For the Lamb on the throne is bleeding for you . . . for us. "It's all about you" . . . in grace. "And he [God] has put all things under his [Christ's] feet and has made him the head over all things for the church [you, us]" writes Paul (Ephesians 1:22).

I believe those seven churches show up all over the Revelation—it's just that they show up by grace, so we don't recognize them. I believe they are somehow in those twenty-four elders on the twenty-four thrones. And what are they doing?—Naturally, automatically, and continuously they cast their crowns before Him, not because some preacher says they ought to do it, but because it's their chief joy in life.

I wonder how they get their crowns back on?

According to Scripture (Psalm 103), God is the one who crowns us, with steadfast love and mercy. So John must have seen an amazing picture. God, the one on the throne, must have been crowning them, and they were casting their crowns before Him.

He crowned them; they cast them before Him; He crowned them; they cast them . . . while the heavenly choir is singing, "Holy, holy, holy. . . ." It must have looked like some wild and crazy dance.

It *is*—the dance of love that lies at the very heart of God's creation, and that dance is life. Do you want to begin living *now,* even *here?* Then begin to worship.

Twelve

Unwrapping the Meaning
of Your Life

(Revelation 5)

REVELATION 5:1–4: *And I saw in the right hand of him who was seated on the throne a scroll written within and on the back, sealed with seven seals; and I saw a strong angel proclaiming with a loud voice, "Who is worthy to open the scroll and break its seals?" And no one in heaven or on earth or under the earth was able to open the scroll or to look into it, and I wept much that no one was found worthy to open the scroll or to look into it.*

Revelation 5 opens with the mystery of the scroll held in the strong right hand of God Almighty. It is completely covered with writing and sealed with seven seals. In John's day, it was the custom to have six or seven witnesses attest to a legal document. Each one would wrap the scroll with string, drop hot wax onto knots in the string and the seam of the scroll, and then press their signet ring into the warm wax, which would quickly harden. Opening the scroll would require the authority to break the seals.

Some have speculated that this heavenly scroll is a last will and testament to those who inherit the kingdom at the death of the testator, God's Son. Perhaps the seven seals are stamped with the sevenfold Spirit of God, the Spirit of truth, who bears witness to Jesus and the Father.

Others have suggested that the scroll comprises the Old and New Testaments—all of Scripture—or that it is the Lamb's Book of Life, containing the names of all the saved. Another theory is that the rest of the Revelation is inscribed on the scroll.

I think it is *all* those things and more.

At the start of chapter 5, all heaven has just worshiped God for all things: creation. Now this scroll seems to pertain to all things. It is loaded with the *logoi* of God. *Logoi* means "meanings"—words—of God. Words give meanings to events. These are the words of the Creator, the author of all things. I believe this scroll describes the meanings of all reality.

And so we have creation with a sealed meaning.

A strong angel cries, "Who is worthy to open the scroll and break its seals?" In other words, *Who is worthy to declare meaning to all reality?* And *no one* in all creation answers. Even God the Father is silent.

John begins weeping ("wailing" in the Greek), the activity of absolute despair. It is the weeping of one who is looking into the abyss of hell.

He's not weeping just because he's curious about what's in the scroll. He's not weeping just because he'll never know about the ten-nation European confederacy, the black helicopters, and who is "left behind." He's weeping because *life* has no meaning. *John* has no meaning. The Church's *struggle* has no meaning. Everything is absurd.

There is no point to the suffering of the seven churches, for there is no conquering. In Smyrna they are devoured by beasts in the coliseum while Romans look on and cheer. They are tied to stakes and burned alive.

Meanwhile John rots on Patmos, and there is *no meaning . . .* no logos.

He weeps the tears
    of a fallen world
    cut off from the light of life.

In the words of Bertrand Russell at the end of his life, "I have nothing to hang onto but grim, unyielding despair."[1] Creation without meaning. All things without meaning. Pictures without words. Events without story. No Plot.

A WONDERFUL FRIEND OF MINE came to see my wife, Susan, and me. At one point, the woman shared some pictures from her life—horrifying pictures. She was an abused child raised by a wicked father. I won't share all the pictures with you, but one picture was this: One Halloween night long ago, her mother dressed her up as an angel in a little white robe, wings, and a halo. My friend was thrilled because she had always wanted to be an angel on Halloween. Her father saw her and was furious. After trick-or-treating, he took her to a meeting where people performed rituals . . . stripped her . . . put her on a table . . . molested her.

People come to pastors asking us to give story to the events of their lives. They want us to attach meaning to their suffering and put words to their pictures. I can't unwrap that scroll. Peter Hiett cannot tell her her story. I'm not worthy.

John was weeping and I've tasted his tears. They were tears of despair.

REVELATION 5:6–10: *Then one of the elders said to me, "Weep not; lo, the Lion of the tribe of Judah, the Root of David, has conquered, so that he can open the scroll and its seven seals." And between* ["in the midst of" KJV; "in the center of" NIV] *the throne and the four living creatures and among the elders, I saw a Lamb standing, as though it had been slain, with seven horns and with seven eyes, which are the seven spirits of God sent out into all the earth; and he went and took the scroll from the right hand of him who was seated on the throne. And when he had taken the scroll, the four living creatures and the twenty-four elders fell down before the Lamb, each holding a harp, and with golden bowls full of incense, which are the prayers of the saints; and they sang a new song, saying,*

"Worthy art thou to take the scroll and to open its seals,
for thou wast slain and by thy blood didst ransom men for God
from every tribe and tongue and people and nation,
and hast made them a kingdom and priests to our God,
and they shall reign on earth."

I CAN'T UNWRAP MY FRIEND'S SCROLL, but I know who can.

As John looks up from his tears, guided by the voice of an elder, he sees a little lamb. But this lamb has seven horns and seven eyes. It is all-powerful, all-seeing, all-knowing. The eyes *are* the sevenfold Spirit of God sent out into all the earth, and all heaven is worshiping the lamb, just as they worship God.

God the Father is there, worthy through creation. God the Son—the Lamb— is worthy to open the scroll and break its seals because He has conquered. God the Spirit is sevenfold, emanating from the Father and the Son. The Trinity is *all there!*

After all the confusion of the seven churches,
after the sevenfold are called to conquer,
and after John weeps before
the sevenfold Spirit of God,
the elder says to John,
"Weep not! Stop weeping!"
This is how the elder's announcement appears in the Greek: "*Conquered has the Lion*": perfect tense, completed action with continuing impact.

Conquered has the Lion of the tribe of Judah. John sees a slain little lamb that he knows. He is Messiah, Son of Man, suffering servant, the Lion of the tribe of Judah, the Lamb of God. All these confusing, irreconcilable, mysterious, transcendent figures that the Jews had wondered about for thousands of years are all at once imploded into this one little lamb bleeding on the throne, among the twenty-four elders.

The little lamb is worthy to unwrap the scroll. "For he [God] has made known to us in all wisdom and insight the mystery of his will, according to his purpose which he set forth in Christ as a plan for the fulness of time, to unite all things in him, things in heaven and things on earth" (Ephesians 1:9–10). "In him all things hold together" (Colossians 1:17). And through Him God reconciles "to himself all things, whether on earth or in heaven, making peace by the blood of his cross" (Colossians 1:20).

In Revelation 19 we will find out that His name is the Word—the *Logos*—of God. John writes first in his Gospel, "In the beginning was the Word, and the Word was with God, and the Word was God. He was in the beginning with God; all things were made through him, and without him was not anything made that was made" (John 1:1–3).

The Word—

the *Logos*—

the Meaning—

. . . takes hold of the *Logoi* of God and prepares to declare meaning to all creation. *All things.*

The Revelation is about all things and every creature. That means it's about you.

Remember that. We get caught up in the trivialities—nuclear war, global economy, world history—and we miss what's *truly* great. For *all* power and *all* knowledge belong to the little Lamb on the throne who conquers *all* things by His death.

He died in love.

He is the one who opens the scrolls of history.

He is the one who opens the scroll of your life.

He is worthy to open that scroll.

If you were to line me up with George Bush and Albert Einstein (power and knowledge), and ask my kids, "Which one do you want to be your daddy?" do you know who they'd pick every time? Me. Why? Because I've bled for them. I'm the one worthy to give their lives meaning and tell them who they are. When they were little, they came running to me to kiss their "owies." One night a friend of mine who had no children was in our house. One of my kids came running to me saying, "Kiss it, kiss it." Once I did, they ran away laughing, happy. My friend turned to me and commented, "It's like you *actually heal* their wounds." And I *did:* same pain, but with an entirely different meaning. In a little way, and with an entirely different meaning, Christ uses me to unwrap their scrolls, to declare to my children the knowledge of good and evil. I say, "Elizabeth, you're fine." And she runs off happy.

Jesus is worthy to open your scroll, a scroll of knowledge and understanding. In the Garden we stole fruit from the tree of knowledge because we wanted to understand all things more than we wanted to know the Maker of all things.

Now, knowing Jesus, to walk back into the Paradise Garden we must be willing to surrender that stolen fruit. Knowing Jesus, we discover that He *feeds* us with that fruit of knowledge in grace. We must surrender our meanings and receive His meanings by grace. The fruit that once worked death because we stole it—knowledge of ourselves without God—that fruit now is life—knowledge of all things as gifts through Christ and in Christ. He unwraps the scroll. Then all our understanding is no longer pride but worship. We can't unwrap the scroll, but we know the one who does.

My friend sat in my office after we prayed against some horrific spiritual entities and saw God's incredible powers. "I'm still haunted by the pictures in my dreams," she said. For her they meant shame, fear, and despair. We prayed again, having battled a long time.

I must tell you her pictures confused me. I feel such compassion and love for my friend, yet I am entirely unable to explain or comprehend. I'm unworthy. I've hardly ever suffered. Who am *I* to unwrap her scroll? In my confusion I get angry with Jesus. Yet I feel like Peter when Jesus asked him if he'd leave like the others and Peter replied, "To whom shall we go? You have the words of eternal life" (John 6:68).

As she has before, my friend had a vision—a revelation, an *apocalypse* of Jesus—while we were praying. It was very clear: *all her sufferings are His. He cries her tears. He wears her blood. He aches her aches.* He is worthy to unwrap her scroll.

Then she asked, "Jesus, hold me." I had been thinking, *Jesus, please hold her!* But He wouldn't. That confused me. He said to her, "You have to give Me those pictures." She was ashamed to show them to the glorious Lion of Judah. I prayed, "Jesus, please show her who she is and how You see her."

Jesus said to her, "Those pictures are part of who you are."

I thought to myself, *Jesus wouldn't say that those pictures were part of who she is! Surely Jesus would hold her. Is this really Him?*

But we kept praying, and she began surrendering pictures. Each time she gave the picture to Jesus and we prayed He would reveal truth, she would have another vision. Jesus would appear in that very picture, and His presence in the picture would be like light shining in the darkness, entirely changing its meaning. Lies would vanish in the light of eternity . . . the presence of the Truth.

I hope you caught this: Right before the Lamb opens the scroll and declares meaning to all reality, Logos to all history, story to all events, He smells something—our prayers. They are your prayers and mine and my friend's, our prayers spoken in faith, in space and time, and in the confusion of this world. These prayers rise before the eternal throne of God as He gives meaning to all reality. When God the Father spoke words into the darkness and said, "Let there be light," I believe He was smelling your prayers.

When God the Son unwrapped the scroll declaring meaning to all past, present, and future, He was smelling your prayers. You saints of God reign on earth, whether you know it or not. For He always, writes Paul, "leads us in triumph" (2 Corinthians 2:14).

As my friend and I prayed, she gave one final picture to Jesus: the angel outfit on Halloween night, her wicked father, and the coven. Then she saw reality: Jesus entered the picture. She said He was furious, like a rider with eyes of fire on a white horse. He went over to that wretched table, picked her up, and began to dress her in a white robe. He put the angel costume back on her, sat her on His lap, and held her tightly. He rocked her back and forth and said, "I'm sorry this had to happen." He told her how He hurt for her, how He had fought *so hard* for her. Then He said, "You are and you will always be My little angel."

She told me all this, and then it hit me. "Hey," I exclaimed to her, "He *is* holding you! And He *is* telling you who you are!" She began weeping for joy. Jesus told her, "Your pictures are My pictures."

Those pictures are *their* pictures. When He holds my friend, He holds *all* of her. When He saved her, He saved *all* of her. When He gives meaning to the scroll, He gives meaning to *all* the scroll: past, present, and future. But my friend's scroll is only a glimpse of what all children of God are to believe right now in faith before we see it. That Jesus is gospel meaning to every breath you take.

My friend looked at me after a while and with tears in her eyes, she said, "How do you think it makes God feel when we are ashamed of those pictures?" I answered, "I guess that means we're ashamed of Him."

If you gave your life to Jesus, your life is *His* life. Actually, *His* life is *your* life, because He suffered first. We are His body, and our scroll is His scroll. He is unwrapping the scroll of history, certainly. But when we surrender our lives to Him in worship, He also unwraps the scroll of our lives . . . or should I say the scroll of His life?

"To live is Christ," wrote Paul. And maybe he actually *meant* this: "It is no longer I who live, but Christ who lives in me" (Galatians 2:20).

Logos in me.

Meaning in me.

Glory in me.

Your life is a storybook in the strong right hand of God Almighty as He sits on the throne. God the Son has taken hold of that scroll and is beginning to read that book to you. *Your story.* Child of God, you are waking up to the glories of the Great Lion of the tribe of Judah, Son of God. Behold that Lion: He is the Lamb slain for love, working everywhere in this world.

The Lion gives meaning to your past. "I forget what lies behind," wrote Paul, but he didn't forget past *events,* because he had just listed them. He forgot their *meaning.* They no longer meant shame; they meant glory and wonder. The Lion changes the meaning of your present: from confusion to wonder and obedient faith. The Lion changes the meaning of your future: from anxiety to delirious hope.

My friend in the angel outfit, in reality, is and will always be the Bride of Christ, clothed in white. But now, because she has glimpsed the abyss of hell, she understands the Lamb of God and the love of God and the glory of God in a way that no one else in all creation does. She has an entirely new song.

Paul writes that God works for good with those who love Him and are called according to His purpose in *all* things. "And in all these things I am convinced," he writes, "that through him who loved us we are more than conquerors"— *hypernika*—(see Romans 8:28, 37). We are superconquerors! Hyperconquerors!

The little girl in the angel outfit conquers! Through her, the Lion of the great tribe of Judah is proclaiming to the principalities and powers the glory of the kingdom of God (Ephesians 3:10). Jesus said to my friend in her vision, "I want to use these pictures for My purposes."

At our Saturday evening worship service, I had prepared a sermon on this text, and I was going to tell some stories about my friend, just as I have here. Through the windows of our sanctuary we can see the foothills surrounding us. My wife and I were sitting with the congregation, and as we were singing just before the sermon, my wife whispered to me, *"Peter,* there is an *angel* standing on that little hill out there." She was shaken up.

My wife sees visions; I don't.

We sang some more, and then she said, *"Peter,* the angel is holding a little lamb!"

I got up and preached, and when I came back and took my seat next to her, she was really messed up. "Peter, while you were preaching," she said, *"angels were walking through the walls and standing all around the sanctuary*—especially right around you!"

Whatever, I thought. *That's my wife.*

Sunday morning, she talked to someone who had also been at the service the night before. "Did you see what I saw?" she asked. Yes, they both saw it. They said to me, "We think all those angels were sent because the enemy was so mad about what you were saying."

I have another theory. I think all those angels came to listen to the story of the little girl in the angel outfit, because she declares the glory of the Lamb of God. Angels long to look into our salvation, and they listen with wonder while the principalities and powers, the evil ones, shudder with fear. For the little Lamb who bleeds on the throne is the One who breaks down the doors of hell and conquers everything. "Behold," He declares, "I make all things new."

I dare you to believe what John sees next. I cannot explain it, but it's the truth:

REVELATION 5:11–14: *Then I looked, and I heard around the throne and the living creatures and the elders the voice of many angels, numbering myriads of myriads and thousands of thousands, saying with a loud voice, "Worthy is the Lamb who was slain, to receive power and wealth and wisdom and might and honor and glory and blessing!" And I heard every creature in heaven and on earth and under the earth and in the sea, and all therein, saying, "To him who sits upon the throne and to the Lamb be blessing and honor and glory and might for ever and ever!" And the four living creatures said, "Amen!" and the elders fell down and worshiped.*

The new song conquers everything! If it has already conquered you, you can begin to sing it right now. *Worthy is the Lamb.*

THIRTEEN

SOUNDTRACK TO THE
END OF THE WORLD

(Revelation 6)

REVELATION 6:1–17: *Now I saw when the Lamb opened one of the seven seals, and I heard one of the four living creatures say, as with a voice of thunder, "Come!" And I saw, and behold, a white horse, and its rider had a bow; and a crown was given to him, and he went out conquering and to conquer.*

When he opened the second seal, I heard the second living creature say, "Come!" And out came another horse, bright red; its rider was permitted to take peace from the earth, so that men should slay one another; and he was given a great sword.

When he opened the third seal, I heard the third living creature say, "Come!" And I saw, and behold, a black horse, and its rider had a balance in his hand; and I heard what seemed to be a voice in the midst of the four living creatures saying, "A quart of wheat for a denarius, and three quarts of barley for a denarius, but do not harm oil and wine!"

When he opened the fourth seal, I heard the voice of the fourth living creature say, "Come!" And I saw, and behold, a pale horse, and its rider's name was Death, and Hades followed him; and they were given power over a fourth of the earth, to kill with sword and with famine and with pestilence and by wild beasts of the earth.

When he opened the fifth seal, I saw under the altar the souls of those who had been slain for the word of God and for the witness they had borne; they cried out with a loud voice, "O Sovereign Lord, holy and true, how long before thou wilt judge and avenge our blood on those who dwell upon the earth?" Then they were each given a white robe and told to rest a little longer, until the number of their fellow servants and their brethren should be complete, who were to be killed as they themselves had been.

When he opened the sixth seal, I looked, and behold, there was a great earthquake; and the sun became black as sackcloth, the full moon became like blood, and the stars of the sky fell to the earth as the fig tree sheds its winter fruit when shaken by a gale; the sky vanished like a scroll that is rolled up, and every mountain and island was removed from its place. Then the kings of the earth and the great men and the generals and the rich and the strong, and every one, slave and free, hid in the caves and among the rocks of the mountains, calling to the mountains and rocks, "Fall on us and hide us from the face of him who is seated on the throne, and from the wrath of the Lamb; for the great day of their wrath has come, and who can stand before it?"

REVELATION 8:1–2: *When the Lamb opened the seventh seal, there was silence in heaven for about half an hour. Then I saw the seven angels who stand before God and seven trumpets were given to them.*

I TOOK MY KIDS TO SEE ONE OF THOSE SUMMER MOVIES they release just when school lets out. *The Mummy Returns* was just like all the others—full of deception, warfare, pestilence, death, and demons. It was downright apocalyptic!

Imagine sitting down with your children to read Revelation chapters 6–8 as their Bible story for the day. The seals on the scroll are opened, and after the seventh seal is opened, seven angels blow their trumpets after another angel throws the fire of heaven down upon the earth, igniting a great storm. When they blow those trumpets, a bloody storm begins to devour the world. Wow! The Revelation makes *The Mummy Returns* look like *Thomas the Tank Engine.* How do we make sense of such incredible violence?

Some view it as judgment on bad people, because Christians have been raptured out of there. Almost all the commentaries refer to the seals as judgment or wrath. The only problem with that idea is that Scripture doesn't say that. When the fifth seal is opened, the martyrs cry out from under the altar, "How long, O Lord, before you will judge?" That seems to imply that the first four seals—the four horseman—weren't judgment, or else we have some stupid martyrs. It's finally at the sixth seal that they cry, "Hide us from the wrath of the Lamb." But that's *after* the sky rolls up and the stars fall to earth. Only at the seventh trumpet of the seventh seal in chapter 11 do they sing, "Thy wrath has come."

So what are we to make of the horsemen of the apocalypse? *Deception, warfare, famine, and death.* In some other dimension, they may be some type of judgment or satanic emissaries, but they are not portrayed that way here. In fact, they are called forth by the cherubim and the seraphim as Jesus breaks the seal.

Why on earth would He do such a thing?

Well, technically, because we asked Him to. John wept with all of creation, wailing, "Who is worthy to open the scroll?" We wanted to see what was inside. We wanted the meaning, the *Logos*. But why are these *horsemen* necessary? And when is this going to happen?

Did you notice that chapter 4 begins with creation and chapter 5 ends with all creatures on earth and in heaven worshiping the Lamb on the throne? Sounds like the end.

At the end of chapter 6, once again we're at the end of the world. The sky rolls up, the stars fall to earth, the mountains and hills are removed from their places . . . that's big! And get ready, because we will experience the end over and over again in Revelation. So if we put our end-times charts aside for a moment and let the Revelation speak for itself, I think we'll find there are . . .

patterns on top of patterns,
    times on top of times,
        histories on top of histories,
            sevens on top of sevens.

It's *one* vision of reality, shifting perspective from one angle to another, seeing from one dimension and then another dimension. Revelation is like a great symphony, beginning with the overture of the seven little churches in Asia Minor. As the symphony progresses, new themes are added on top of themes, meanings on top of meanings, until it all crescendos at the end of all things, the new heaven and new earth, the New Jerusalem—the people of God.

There is singing throughout the entire book. The four living creatures around the throne *never stop* singing, "Holy, holy, holy, is the Lord God Almighty." All the other songs must build on that theme harmoniously—and so do events. Everything John sees is true; he just can't say it all at once. This is not an excuse for taking the Revelation less literally; it's a reason for taking our modernistic, scientific mind-set less literally and the Revelation *more* literally. Our God was, is, and is to come, so wondrous that more than one thing can happen for Him at once.

Numbers aren't just for counting. They reveal deep meanings and patterns. Seven is the number of Creation. It is also the number of God's manifold fullness. In seven days He created and on the seventh day He rested. There are seven seals.

Four is often the number that refers to this world: four seasons, four directions, four winds. The first four seals are four horsemen, reminiscent of the four horsemen sent out in Zechariah to patrol the face of the earth (see

Zechariah 6). The first horseman is crowned and sitting on a white horse, which has caused some to speculate that this is Christ, meaning that before all, He conquers. That's a beautiful and true meaning.

But because this horseman is grouped with the other three horsemen, I think this horseman is probably deception, the spirit of the antichrist, or false Christ. John told us it is already in the world (1 John 4:3).

The next three horsemen are warfare, famine, and death. They have power over a quarter of the earth. If you're not an American living in Laodicea, you would probably say, "Oh, yeah. I know those guys. They rode into my village last year."

At the opening of the fifth seal, John sees martyrs under the altar where the priests threw the blood of sacrifice. These people have been sacrificed to the glory of God like slain lambs. They cry out, "How long, O Lord?" Well, if they had one of those end-times charts they would know *exactly* how long. Maybe they don't know.

At the sixth seal, they begin to get their answer. The sky rolls up and the stars fall.

At the seventh seal, like the edge of a great crescendo, there is an awesome silence. The seven angels are handed trumpets. Seals hide mysteries; trumpets proclaim things. These seven seals, I believe, span all of history, but they are *not* the content of the scroll. Anybody in that day would know that you can't read a scroll until you break all the seals.

What is released when the seals are broken are realities necessary for understanding the meaning of the scroll. Whatever is *in* this scroll is *worthy* of all the tribulation of history. We must not see it very clearly yet, because we sure do complain every time a horseman comes riding along. And we don't sing very loudly or very often with those angels and saints around the throne, "Holy, holy, holy" to the one who breaks the seal.

But how *can* we sing when we live in a world of deception, warfare, famine, and death? Now we're back to my first point about our movies laced with warfare, famine, death, and pestilence!

I remember sitting in a movie theater as a young man, watching incredible violence on the screen. There was a man with dark hair and eyes, of Mediterranean descent, nearly naked and covered with blood. An angry mob thirsty for violence cheered as he was beaten beyond recognition, as one from whom men hide their faces. In his pain and agony, he cried out for his beloved. Just when I thought he was dead for sure, a host of trumpets broke in with the theme song: "Growing strong now . . . won't be long now. . . ." Rocky Balboa was making his comeback.

The theme song of the Revelation, "Holy, holy, holy is the Lord God Almighty," is playing the entire time the seals are being opened and the horsemen are riding across the face of the earth. The theme song changes things. It tells us that we are about to receive a revelation of glory.

In the movie, the theme song reveals the glory of Rocky Balboa! That means Apollo Creed, Drago the Russian, and Mr. T are all means by which we can see and know the glory of Rocky. The theme song tells you: Do not be fooled. It's glory time!

Let me translate for you: "Holy, holy, holy is Rocky Balboa." That is, Rocky is different from all other fighters. He loves Adrian his bride *so much* that when she shows up in the coliseum, nothing can stop him. That is, Rocky will endure his fight, despising the shame, for the joy that is set before him: *"Adrian!"*

Without the adversary Apollo Creed, we would never know the glory of Rocky Balboa.

Without the cross, we would never know Easter.

Without the four horsemen, we'd never know the content of the scroll.

Without a great tribulation, we'd never learn the new song.

Our hearts know this; that's why we go to movies. We just don't have the stomach for it in real life. So we become voyeurs of other people's sufferings in movies and in Scripture. Perhaps voyeurs of *suffering* can only be voyeurs of *glory.* Jesus the Rock wants to share His glory with us. Breaking the seals reveals the glory of God. But all the while, the theme song is playing to give us courage. It builds on this one line—"Holy, holy, holy is the Lord God Almighty." *Holy* doesn't mean "pietistic" or "puritanical" or "prudish" or even "wholesome." Holy means "wholly other"—not like other gods, gloriously strange.

The horsemen are not holy. They are the ways of this world: power, pride, conquest, warfare, death, survival of the fittest. We know those guys. We understand them. Right now, they ride the earth. But when we hear the theme song, we know that the horsemen are a setup for the glory of God.

Time for glory. You can see one thing in the darkness better than you can see it in the full light of day—the glory of a single flame.

Jesus is the light. The Light shines in the darkness.

In the last chapter we saw that Jesus reveals the meaning of all history and of our history. Yet all of history is ultimately about revealing Jesus, the bleeding heart of God. Jesus reveals the meaning of our suffering. But in Revelation chapter 6 we see that the horsemen sent out are part of our suffering. Does God create the suffering so that He can then in turn reveal what it means for us? It's *more* than that. Jesus gives meaning, *logoi,* to all our sufferings, but the deeper truth is that all our sufferings reveal Jesus, *Logos,* glory of God: the bleeding heart of God.

We are only beginning to glimpse the glory now, says Paul (see 1 Corinthians 13:12). Our darkened eyes cannot yet handle the full brilliance of Christ. Yet we see something here in the dark that we will sing about forever and ever.

How glorious is the light in the midst of darkness! It is a strange and holy light. See how the Lion of Judah has conquered! Behold a slain little lamb! He opens the scroll. It's Jesus who conquers all.

And when did He conquer? *When He was slain.* That's weird. That's *holy.* He told us, "Now is the judgment of this world, now shall the ruler of this world be cast out; and I, when I am lifted up from the earth, will draw all men to myself" (John 12:31). He was speaking of being lifted from the earth on a cross (John 12:33). The Lion conquers by choosing to be slain in love.

We think that sometimes Jesus is the Lion and other times the Lamb, as if He says, "I'll try that Lion thing for a while, and if it doesn't work I'll do the Lamb thing. If I don't like, I'll go back to the Lion thing." No—the Lion *is* the Lamb.

In the breaking of the sixth seal, the kings and peoples of the earth hide themselves in the mountains and caves crying out, "Hide us from the wrath of the little lamb!" They must look up and say, "Oh God, I slew that little lamb a million times."

The Light of Love judges the darkness like fire.

When He was slain, the world was judged.

When He was slain, Satan was cast out.

When He was slain, He drew all men to Himself.

When He was slain, He revealed the heart of God . . . exalted, glorified, lifted up, crucified, all at once. How strange! How holy!

The title of John's letter is "The Revelation of Jesus." When we get to the end of chapter 11 and the seventh trumpet is blown out of the seventh seal so that the scroll is entirely opened, suddenly we find ourselves reading the Christmas story. A child is born, "one who is to rule all the nations with a rod of iron" (Revelation 12:5; Psalm 2:9). The dragon hates Him. It's Jesus. He is so wholly strange, so different, that even though He is Lord God Almighty, He empties Himself of all worldly power and becomes a baby to die in love, nailed to a cross.

We would never see His glory unless someone nailed Him to that cross: *violence, pride, warfare, horsemen.* In the midst of worldly powers, love is most gloriously displayed. He is not like other fighters. He is not like Rocky Balboa.

He is not like the other gods of this world. He conquers by dying in love, crucified on a cross. The horsemen of the apocalypse reveal Jesus, the heart of God, the grace that is His glory.

There are many meanings to our sufferings: we sinned; we are paying the price of our free choice in the Garden; they shape us and discipline us. There are many explanations for suffering (theologians call them "theodicies"), and they can all be true at once. Only Jesus is worthy to unwrap your theodicy and reveal the particular meanings of your particular sufferings. But if there is one theodicy in Scripture that runs the deepest, the broadest, and the most consistently: *Our world suffers because God wants to show us something.* He wants to show to *us* (not angels)—His Bride, His children—His greatest glory.

True, *we* took the fruit of the tree in the Garden, and we died, blinded to the glory of God. Yet God kicked us out of the Garden and cursed the earth. *He* was the one who subjected the creation to futility in hope, writes Paul (Romans 8:20). He loosed the horsemen for a reason: to wake us up to glory.

Even before the Garden, God knew the plan. He was the one who put that tree right smack dab in the middle of the Garden. He knew we'd eat the fruit, and that one day He would be nailed to that tree.

"God consigned all men to disobedience that he may have mercy upon all. O the depth of the riches and wisdom and knowledge of God! How unsearchable are his judgments and how inscrutable his ways! For who has known the mind of the Lord, or who has been his counselor? Or who has given a gift to him that he might be repaid? For from him and through him and to him are all things. To him alone be glory for ever. Amen" (Romans 11:32–36).

God's plan for the fullness of time was to unite all things in Christ: And He made us alive when we were dead in our sins "that in the coming ages he might show the immeasurable riches of his grace in kindness toward us in Christ Jesus" (Ephesians 2:7).

The horsemen ride so we might know "his grace in kindness"; not just *see* it, but *know* it and *live* it. Eugene Boring writes in his commentary: " 'Conquering' in both cases, that of the Christ and that of Christians, means no more or less than dying."[1]

Those under the altar are witnesses *(marturos),* because they are slain like Christ by the *machiros,* the sword of the horsemen (also used in the temple sacrifice). The saints—"holy ones"—die in love, like Jesus. Without the horsemen there would be no *marturos.*

We Americans tend to forget about *marturos* and focus our energy on passing legislation against the horsemen. We fight power with power. I remember hearing a preacher comment on the parable of the Good Samaritan by saying that being good Samaritans is not enough; we need to care about the social conditions that set the stage for the beating—such as working for better lighting on the road to Jericho and police protection for travelers. I agree with his sentiment, but I think he misses the point. It's very clear in Scripture that the Good Samaritan is Jesus, and He *is* enough, and He *is* the point, and He wants us to see Him. It's when we're beaten, on the side of the road, that He comes to us and we see Him, and He anoints us with oil and wine (cf. Luke 10:34). We see His glory.

The point is not to stop all suffering but to see Jesus in suffering, not to outlaw all crosses but to pick them up. That's what He wants. The *marturos* (witnesses) die like Jesus: sacrifices of love.

It's fascinating that the third horseman is commanded, "Do not harm oil and wine!" (Revelation 6:6). In the midst of the suffering, there is oil and wine. The only other place the phrase "oil and wine" occurs in all the New Testament is in Luke 10, in the hands of the Good Samaritan. In our suffering He anoints us with oil—His Spirit, and He cleanses us with wine—His blood. The blood flows from His body on His cross. Yet we are His body, crucified with Him. And His Spirit is in us. We are called to dispense *His* oil and *His* wine in the midst of a dark and suffering world.

I say this at the risk of being misunderstood: Americans work so hard to eliminate all suffering, *all* crosses, while Jesus just says, "Pick one up and follow." Our brothers and sisters in other countries really don't have much choice on this one. And I imagine that's why it's in places where the horsemen seem to be riding that the gospel seems to be conquering. China, Russia, Africa—lots of crosses there.

The Lamb who opens the seals is also slain by the horsemen. The horsemen are necessary; "in the world you *will* have tribulation" (John 16:33). We must fight the horsemen, but it's an American illusion that we can stop them. In some form, the horsemen will someday ride into your town. What will it mean then?

The horsemen were already riding among the seven churches of Asia Minor. What did this revelation mean to them, when death rode into town—butchering their loved ones, forcing them into starvation and famine?

What does it mean to you, believer, when your body is racked with cancer, and death rides into your home. It means this: It's time for glory. Time to worship. Time to listen for the theme song. For the Lamb, your Lord, who was slain, unwraps the scroll and breaks the seals. It means this: Glory time.

Or have you forgotten just who your Lord is?

In your imagination, picture a man with dark hair and eyes, of Mediterranean descent. Not the one I was talking about before. This man, too, is nearly naked, and He is covered in blood. He has been beaten beyond recognition. He is the one from whom men hide their faces. The crowd cheers, thirsty for violence. In His pain and agony He cries out for His beloved Jerusalem, "Father, forgive them, for they know not what they do." He's dying. Do you see Him? Look at Him. He is the Lord God Almighty, and He's going to hell for you, His Bride.

Look at Him. And listen for the theme song.

FOURTEEN

THE OMEN

(Revelation 7)

O NE SUNDAY A FRIEND OF MINE came up to me after the service and said, "Thanks, Peter, for preaching on the Revelation. To tell you the truth, I read it years ago, and it scared me so badly I haven't read it since."

"That's just the way I felt," I said.

For the longest time, I had trouble with this book. Part of my problem was watching *The Omen* when I was a young believer in high school. In the movie, this poor kid named Damien shaves his head and finds out he has the number 666 tattooed on the top of his head, which is a major bummer because now that means he's the antichrist.

That movie really stressed me out. I used to ask myself, "Am I *really* saved?" I thought about shaving my head to check for a number. I even prayed a few times, "Jesus, please don't let me be the antichrist."

I'm not, which is good news for my congregation. (Wouldn't that be embarrassing to go to the church with the antichrist for a pastor?)

Just reading the Revelation can scare the whatever right out of you. Try being a shepherd and feeling doubly accountable to get all the sheep to conquer. No wonder so many preachers are scared and grumpy. They have to preach this stuff and feel a millstone around their neck.

In chapter 6 the Lamb begins to unwrap the scroll. The four horsemen ride across the face of the earth, as in Zechariah 6:5, where the horsemen are referred to as the four winds. After the horsemen, we see the witnesses under the altar. They have been slain like slaughtered lambs, given white robes, and told to wait until the full number of their brethren come in, who will all be killed as they were.

When the sixth seal is opened, the stars fall, the sky rolls up, everybody runs for cover, and the people cry out, "Who can stand?" That is a great question, especially if you read ahead to the seventh seal in chapter 8: hail, fire, blood, death; darkness in the heavens; demon locusts from the pit of hell; horses that breathe fire and sulfur.

Who can stand? Who will conquer?

That is the burning question in the minds of these in the seven churches in Asia Minor who are recipients of the Revelation. Each of the messages to the angels of the seven churches ends with a phrase like this: [to him who conquers] " . . . they will be clad with white garments" (Sardis); or " . . . I will write on him the name of my God and my own new name (like a seal) on their foreheads" (Philadelphia). But at the end of chapter 6 all these terrified people are crying out for the mountains and rocks to fall on them and hide them from the wrath of God. "And who can stand before it?"—end of chapter. Then chapter 7 opens:

REVELATION 7:1–17: *After this I saw four angels standing at the four corners of the earth, holding back the four winds of the earth, that no wind might blow on earth or sea or against any tree. Then I saw another angel ascend from the rising of the sun, with the seal of the living God, and he called with a loud voice to the four angels who had been given power to harm earth and sea, saying, "Do not harm the earth or the sea or the trees, till we have sealed the servants of our God upon their foreheads." And I heard the number of the sealed, a hundred and forty-four thousand sealed, out of every tribe of the sons of Israel, twelve thousand sealed out of the tribe of Judah, twelve thousand of the tribe of Reuben, twelve thousand of the tribe of Gad, twelve thousand of the tribe of Asher, twelve thousand of the tribe of Naphtali, twelve thousand of the tribe of Manasseh, twelve thousand of the tribe of Simeon, twelve thousand of the tribe of Levi, twelve thousand of the tribe of Issachar, twelve thousand of the tribe of Zebulun, twelve thousand of the tribe of Joseph, twelve thousand sealed out of the tribe of Benjamin.*

After this I looked, and behold, a great multitude which no man could number, from every nation, from all tribes and peoples and tongues, standing before the throne and before the Lamb, clothed in white robes, with palm branches in their hands, and crying out with a loud voice, "Salvation belongs to our God who sits upon the throne, and to the Lamb!" And all the angels stood round the throne and round the elders and the four living creatures, and they fell on their faces before the throne and worshiped God, saying, "Amen! Blessing and glory and wisdom and thanksgiving and honor and power and might be to our God for ever and ever! Amen."

Then one of the elders addressed me, saying, "Who are these, clothed in white robes, and whence have they come?" I said to him, "Sir, you know." And he said

*to me, "These are they who have come out of the great tribulation; they have
washed their robes and made them white in the blood of the Lamb.*

> *Therefore are they before the throne of God,*
> > *and serve him day and night within his temple;*
> > *and he who sits upon the throne will shelter them*
> > *with his presence.*
> *They shall hunger no more, neither thirst any more;*
> > *the sun shall not strike them, nor any scorching heat.*
> *For the Lamb in the midst of the throne will be their shepherd,*
> > *and he will guide them to springs of living water;*
> *and God will wipe away every tear from their eyes."*

WHO CAN STAND? *These* guys can stand. But who *are* they? Jehovah's
Witnesses? Seventh Day Adventists? Branch Davidians? One hundred forty-
four thousand crackerjack, celibate, commando, end-times Jewish warriors?
Just who are these guys? There are a whole slew of opinions about who they
are and how to make sense of this chapter. So I'd like to point out some of
the basic interpretive principles I've been using all along for understanding the
Revelation:

1. *The Revelation should be relevant to the seven churches in Asia Minor,*
   because it's addressed to them, and "the time is at hand."

2. *The Revelation should be relevant to us,* because "blessed are those who
   hear and read."

3. *The context of the Revelation is all of Scripture*—this book is absolutely
   loaded with Old Testament references and allusions, such as Hebrew
   word pictures, poetic forms, and manners of speaking.

4. *John's other writings and Paul's writings give us our theological vocabulary.*
   John's Gospel and his epistles should help us understand how John talks
   in the Revelation. We also know that John is writing to, and is part of,
   churches that were evangelized and discipled by Paul. We know from
   Acts that Paul taught for two years in Ephesus, and "all" of Asia came to
   hear him. By this time, they probably would have viewed Ephesians and
   Colossians as Scripture (see 2 Peter 3:16).

5. *The Revelation is a kairology, not a chronology.* Don't get stuck on
   counting. Take meaning more seriously than space and time. Through
   macrophysics and microphysics we have come to realize that space and

time are relative to meaning and to light. Long before that, and more importantly, Scripture itself revealed the same thing. With God, our math (space and time) doesn't work.

$$1 = 3$$
$$3 = 1$$
1 = 7 spirits before the throne
7 spirits before the throne = 1
1 day is as a thousand years
A thousand years is as a day

NUMBERS ARE FLUID AROUND ETERNITY, but meaning *(logos)* is light—Jesus. And all things are relative to Him. So pay attention to meanings before you get caught up in your own mathematics.

Many commentators refer to chapter 7 as an interlude, because it breaks a series of seven. We love to count things. But who's to say that the counting isn't an interlude in eternity? Which comes first?

John sees four angels holding back the four winds, which probably allude to the four horsemen. They have not yet harmed earth, sea, or tree. Then John sees another angel with the seal of the living God. The 144,000 are sealed *before* the wind begins to blow.

What does the number 144,000 mean?

- It equals 12 x 12 x 1000.

- The New Jerusalem is built with the 12 names of the 12 tribes of Israel and the 12 names of the 12 apostles of the Lamb.

- The dimensions of the New Jerusalem are 12,000 x 12,000 x 12,000 *stadios.*

- The 144,000 is Israel, because the text says so. But for Paul and John we are Israel, grafted in as the true sons of Abraham. A lot of weird stuff is going around churches these days because we have forgotten that God broke down the dividing wall of hostility and made us one (Ephesians 2:15). Twice already in the Revelation (2:9; 3:9) John has referred to people who say they are Jews but are not. They are of the synagogue of Satan.

  Christians should *hate* anti-Semitism, not because we love Jews but because we *are* Jews. We love our brothers and sisters who haven't yet come to the Messiah. A person is a Jew who is one inwardly, not outwardly, writes Paul in Romans 2:28–29. We are "the Israel of God" (Galatians 6:16).

BUT WHY IS ISRAEL NUMBERED LIKE THIS? Bible scholar Gordon Fee explains that every numbering of Israelites in the Old Testament was for one purpose—going to war. This is an army of twelve tribes, each with twelve divisions of one thousand adult men. They show up again later in the Revelation (14:1–5) with the name of God inscribed on their foreheads like a seal, singing a new song. They've kept themselves pure from women, which was an Israelite practice for soldiers going into war. This is an army, and they are called "firstfruits" of the great harvest of the redeemed. Firstfruits were a type of sacrifice in the temple. According to James, "Of his own will he brought us forth by the word of truth that we should be a kind of first fruits of his creatures" (1:18).

Notice that John only *hears* the numbering of the troops (7:4). A few verses later (7:9), he sees a multitude of people from all nations and languages, wearing white robes like those who were slain under the altar under the fifth seal. They sing a song, which is basically the new song.

John hears the 144,000. John sees a multitude. Hold onto that thought.

Modern poets rhyme *sounds*. But Hebrew poets rhymed *meanings*. They would say the same thing a second time, with a similar but slightly different meaning.

The group that John *hears* and the group that John *sees* form a rhyme of meaning. I think that basically they are the same—and in some way refer to *all* believers. This bears out if you trace the clues of the signature seals on their foreheads, the new song, and the servants of God throughout the book. But most importantly, when John said the angel had the seal of the Living God, all the believers in and around Ephesus would have thought one thing, and John would have *known* they would think of one thing: Ephesians 1:13–14. "In him you also, who have heard the word of truth, the gospel of your salvation, and have believed in him, were sealed with the promised Holy Spirit, which is the guarantee of our inheritance until we acquire possession of it, to the praise of his glory."

Paul taught that every believer is sealed with the very presence of the Spirit of the living God. Jesus sends His Spirit to teach us, guide us, and guard us for the day of redemption: "My sheep hear my voice, and I know them, and they follow me; and I give them eternal life, and they shall never perish, and no one shall snatch them out of my hand. . . . and no one is able to snatch them out of the Father's hand" (John 10:27–29). The Spirit emanates from the Son and the Father.

Paul also writes, "In all these things we are *hypernikcomen* [more than conquerors] through him who loved us. For I am sure that neither death, nor life, nor angels, nor principalities, nor things present, nor things to come, nor powers, nor height, nor depth, nor anything else in all creation, will be able to separate us from the love of God in Christ Jesus our Lord" (Romans 8:37–39). If you have given yourself to Him . . . believed in Him, then you are *stuck* with Him—and He is stuck with you! That's why Paul told the Ephesians, "Do not grieve the Holy Spirit of God, in whom you were sealed for the day of redemption" (4:30). Make it easy for Him—don't grieve Him!

The 144,000 are *at least* sealed with the Spirit of the living God. I also believe they are us—or at least represent us. That's based on my sixth principle of interpreting and preaching the Revelation.

6. *We should* at least *preach and believe what Scripture says clearly in other places.* Then, who really cares if there's some bizarre tribal army of celibate, ethnic Jews with nifty little cross tattoos on their foreheads somewhere in the distant future after we've been raptured off the face of the earth? My friend, that might be nice, but we are sealed with the presence of the living God.

Who cares if we get a little tattoo? We're sealed with the Spirit from before the throne—the Spirit of Jesus Himself. Did you notice we're sealed even before the winds begin to blow? Before the horsemen ride and the trumpets sound? And when the wrath of God does come, as in the fifth trumpet, and the demon locusts fly out of the pit of hell, they will be commanded not to harm anyone with the seal of God upon their forehead.

Yeah, we suffer tribulation in this world. But none of our suffering is wrath, because Jesus the Lamb has taken all wrath for us. For us, all tribulation is now a tool for *love.* Parents call it "discipline." But you who are in Christ were sealed *before* the wind began to blow, *before* the horsemen began to ride. You were sealed, according to Paul and John, *before you were born,* before you did one good thing. That means you were . . . *chosen.* Elected, predestined, and saved by nothing but 100 percent grace (Ephesians 2:8). Therefore you were sealed even before you confessed Jesus with your lips. He said to his disciples, "You did not choose me, but I chose you" (John 15:16). His Spirit chose you to choose Him even when you were dead. Even then He was guarding your heart and watching your spirit.

What if you actually believed that, not just with your head but with your heart?

What if you actually believed that you have been *saved,* and every moment you are being sanctified—because you are sealed with the very presence of the living God and the blood of the Lamb? What if you were truly convinced that even now you are seated in the heavenlies with Him, and *nothing in all creation* can separate you from the love of God in Christ Jesus?

Preachers are afraid to preach this stuff, and I know why. It's because they feel that millstone around their neck, and they trust in their own strength.

A friend told me about struggling for years with his preacher father. His father had told him once upon a time, "I won't preach grace, because people use it as an excuse for sin." And people *do* use it as an excuse for sin. If you use grace as an excuse for sin, saying to yourself, "I'm saved by grace. Why not let sin abound?" you don't understand. And you may need to ask yourself, "Did I ever really believe? Did I really ever give myself to Him?"

But if we don't preach grace, we preach the law. We preach . . . flesh, pride, fear—and fear can't conquer. Jesus said in Matthew 7:12, "This is the whole law and the prophets"—love. And John writes, "There is no fear in love, but perfect love casts out fear. For fear has to do with punishment, and he who fears is not perfected in love. We love, because he first loved us" (1 John 4:18–19), before the wind began to blow.

And Paul reminds us that Satan, your opponent, was disarmed at the cross. So what does he fight with now? Fear . . . inspired by lies . . . propaganda.

So you may be saved, you may be sealed, and you may be filled with an immeasurable greatness of power beyond all comparison, yet you may be absolutely impotent for the kingdom of God, because you're cowering in the corner in fear. God says to you, "Fear not!" Why? Because it's a wonderful gift, but also because He wants you, child of God, to step on the head of that serpent and conquer.

Did you notice that it's the army that gets sealed with the guarantee of salvation? God desires fearless, graceful, powerful, sacrificial, joyful warriors.

> Stand therefore, having girded your loins with truth, and having put on the breastplate of righteousness, and having shod your feet with the equipment of the gospel of peace; besides all these, taking the shield of faith with which you can quench all the flaming darts of the evil one. And take the helmet of salvation, and the sword of the Spirit, which is the word of God. (Ephesians 6:14–16)

In short, put on Christ. Believe the seal—salvation. The armor of God is believing the seal of God. And in believing that, you conquer.

If you've given your life to Christ, you are on a mission from God. Paul reminded us not to be frightened in anything by your opponents. Fear not. You might be thinking to yourself . . . *Fear not? Wait a minute. If I live like that, I could get hurt!* Yup.

I could get killed! Yup.

Maybe even tortured—like being crucified! Yup—hallelujah; praise Jesus! For you would be sealed like Him: "For on him has God the Father set his seal"

(John 6:27). Dying with Jesus, you conquer with Jesus . . . dying in faith.

All those in the multitude in the second half of Revelation 7 have the white robes of those sacrificed under the altar. They are cleansed by the blood of the Lamb, and they share in the sufferings of the Lamb. They stand before the throne *now* (present tense), serving in His temple *now* (present tense), singing "Salvation belongs to our God" (present tense), but they shall hunger and thirst no more (future tense). And God will wipe away every tear (future tense). That implies that they're hungry and thirsty now, and have tears now, yet they stand before the throne in the temple now.

Yet *we* are the temple, and the writer to the Hebrews says we should enter the throne room of grace with boldness (4:16).

So who are these hungry, thirsty, tear-stained people who stand before the throne of grace and sing, "Salvation belongs to our God"? Where have we ever seen something like that?

The elder turns to John and says, "These are they who *are* coming out of great tribulation" (not "who *have come*"; in the Greek it's actually a present participle, translated out by the translators trying to make sense of what's going on; but the elder doesn't actually say that). This is still God's army, and they are fearlessly singing in tribulation, for Jesus told them, "In this world you will have tribulation." You *will.* "But be of good cheer [imperative tense; a commandment], for I have overcome the world" (John 16:33).

Paul writes, "[Do not be] frightened in anything by your opponents [it's a commandment again . . . principalities and powers, world rulers of this present darkness]. This is a clear omen to them of their destruction, but of your salvation, and that from God" (Philippians 1:27–28).

When Paul and Silas sing in the Philippian jail . . . when Peter and John rejoice on the steps of the temple, their backs still dripping with blood from being flogged . . . when Richard Wurmbrand dances in his Romanian prison cell with joy . . . when Sudanese Christians meet under the banyan trees in Africa for worship . . . when my abused friend sings songs of joy to Jesus in His temple, which is us . . . when Jesus recites the first line of Psalm 22 as He bears our hell, suffering on the cross. Oh yeah! The kingdom conquers.

Who *are* these guys in Revelation 7, suffering yet singing with joy, "Salvation belongs to our God, who sits upon the throne, and to the Lamb"?

Us! Haven't you sung that in church? It's us, wherever believers gather in Jesus' name and sing to His glory. So fear not: You are not the antichrist, but you *are* the omen. So stand up, go to war, and make that ancient serpent tremble. *Worship.*

FIFTEEN

PRAYER FROM THE OTHER SIDE OF SILENCE

(Revelation 8:1–5)

REVELATION 5:8: *And when he had taken the scroll, the four living creatures and the twenty-four elders fell down before the Lamb, each holding a harp, and with golden bowls full of incense* [thumiama], *which are the prayers of the saints."*

IN THE REVELATION, God is absolutely sovereign over mountains, sky, and stars; the kings of the earth; and the great dragon and his demons from the pit. Not one of those things changes history or moves God. They are all pawns in His hand. Yet right before He opens the scroll, the Lamb upon the throne smells something—your prayers.

In John 14:13 Jesus says, "Whatever you ask in my name, I will do it, that the Father may be glorified in the Son." In Matthew 21:21–22, when Jesus is going into Jerusalem, up Mount Zion, He says, "If you have faith and never doubt . . . even if you say to this mountain, 'Be taken up and cast into the sea,' it will be done. And whatever you ask in prayer, you will receive, if you have faith."

In Revelation 1:6 John writes that Christ has made us kings and priests. We reign on earth through prayer. I've seen it in places like Romania, where the dictator was toppled by the prayers of the saints, in silence and in prison cells. Our prayers are far more powerful than any of us know.

But if you're like me, you may be saying, "Okay, that's great. But I have tried it, and it doesn't work. I pray, and it's like heaven is silent. *Nothing.*"

Some would say, "Just pray *more*. Think what we could do with more prayers and more people praying!" Do you get many Internet prayer requests? You may have seen the kind that end with " . . . if you love God and you believe in prayer, pass this on to six other prayer warriors and do not delete this message."

More people praying, *more* words. If God is leading you to pray for somebody on the Internet, by all means do so. But will we be heard for our many words? Jesus said that the Gentiles "think that they will be heard for their many words" (Matthew 6:7).

Others might say, "It's not about *many words;* it's about the *"right words"*—like reciting the prayer of Jabez, or saying "in Jesus' name" at the end of every prayer. But if it's simply a matter of saying the *right words,* I think the Bible calls that witchcraft, divination, magic. Not *prayers* but *incantations.* Then people silently reject Jesus when such incantations don't work. Worse yet, if they *think* they work, they begin playing the harlot with God or whoever listens to those prayers.

Does prayer *work?* That's a little like asking, "Peter, did your date with Susan work?" Or one of my children asking a sibling, "Hey—did your talk with Dad *work?*" Usually, when my children are trying to get something with many words—"Please . . . please . . . *please,* Dad!"—or with the right words—*"Mom* said. She got me a pop. In the name of Mom, get me a pop!"—odds are it won't work. Yet I long to hear my children speak my name and share their hearts.

In Matthew 6 Jesus teaches, "In praying, do not heap up empty phrases as the Gentiles do; for they think that they will be heard for their many words. Do not be like them, for your Father knows what you need before you ask him" (vv. 7–8). When my kids were little, I knew what they wanted. I could read their brains in the candy aisle. But I still wanted to hear them call my name, "Daddy."

Jesus continues: "Pray then like this: Our Father [Abba, Daddy] . . . in heaven" (v. 9). He says to pray *like* this, not pray *exactly* this. The key is not magic words or even *many* words. The key lies in something Jesus said to His disciples during His last night with them, the night He was betrayed, before He was crucified. He repeats His promise with a twist, now speaking about God the Father: "If you ask anything of the Father, he will give it to you in my name. Hitherto [heretofore; up till now] you have asked nothing in my name; ask . . . that your joy may be full" (John 16:23–24).

For three years they have hung out with Jesus, the man Himself. He had taught them the Lord's Prayer. But then He says, "So far you have not asked *one thing* in my name." Maybe "in the name of Jesus" is more than five little magic words. Perhaps it requires a journey *with* Jesus all the way to Mount Calvary.

Perhaps you are feeling frustrated with prayer. You pray—and it's not that you don't get a classy new car or genuine pearls, it's that God doesn't seem to be responding *at all.* You start wondering not only whether prayer really works, but if you even matter to God. Is He your Father, or are you an orphan? Heaven is silent.

BACK TO THE REVELATION . . . . The slaughtered Lamb on the throne smells those prayers and begins opening the seals. He opens the first six seals, and we see conquest, warfare, famine, and death. We see martyrs, and we see the sky roll up and the stars fall. Finally, in chapter 8, the Lamb on the throne opens the seventh and final seal. "When the Lamb opened the seventh seal, there was silence in heaven for about half an hour" (v. 1).

Silence after *all that noise*—the heavenly worship, the four living creatures, the twenty-four elders who never stop singing?

Silence frustrates us and makes us anxious. Other people pray and hear voices, but when *you* pray there is silence. You try many words; you try better words. *Silence.*

Then people come along and say things like, "If God seems distant, guess who moved?" Or "God is talking all the time. All you have to do is tune in." Is God an almighty chatterbox, and you just can't find His call numbers?

Remember, John is the beloved disciple. He is *in* the Spirit *on* the Lord's Day, and all of heaven is silent! Yet John also wrote, "Those around the throne never stop singing, 'Holy, holy, holy is the Lord God Almighty.'"

Silence, yet all reality is upheld by the word of His power. Heaven is silent, but maybe God is still speaking somehow. Maybe the silence is part of the heavenly song.

For those of you who are frustrated by the silence in your ears and the voices in other people's ears, I want to remind you that there are different ways of hearing. Some have gifts that others don't have, and that's by design. But if you come to Jesus and proclaim Jesus as your Lord, Jesus Himself says you have heard his voice: "My sheep hear my voice" (John 10:27).

So stop stressing about "if you hear." Love, trust, and obey Jesus, and you *do* hear.

Yes, sometimes sin gets in the way and blocks us from hearing. If you know of sin, confess it and get it out of the way. But *sometimes* heaven *is* silent. And sometimes silence *says* more than words and *does* more than words. Silence cleanses us of . . . *us.* It prepares us to hear.

Moses spoke to God face-to-face, like a man talking with a friend, the

Scripture says. But before that he was exiled forty years in the backside of the wilderness! God was preparing him in the silence for the day he would hear this: "Moses, Moses, I AM."

Jesus was without sin. Yet immediately after He was baptized in the Jordan in the Spirit, the Holy Spirit led Him into the desert for forty days and forty nights. After that, He came preaching the kingdom.

David, the man after God's own heart, wrote, "For God alone my soul waits in silence" (Psalm 62:1).

Sometimes heaven is silent, yet silence is part of the song. Revelation is like a great anthem. It builds and builds, one theme on top of another theme, through the seals, until the seventh seal is opened. Then all at once! . . . *silence.* Our hearts anticipate the crescendo. Good music is structured that way. Silence makes us long for God's crescendo. All of heaven is silent with anticipation.

Or maybe . . . *God* is silent with anticipation?

When you are silent in a conversation, you are anticipating and inviting the other person to speak. For seven chapters God has been speaking to John, and for thousands of years God has been speaking through creation and futility, and now silence.

Perhaps *He* is inviting, anticipating, longing for someone else to speak. As a father anticipates the day his baby, out of the silence and babbling, finally says a word—a *logoi:* "Dada." When that happens, the daddy screams to everyone else around, "Quiet! Listen! Jonathan just said, 'Dada'!" He holds his breath, and everyone quiets down to listen for the word "Dada." In Aramaic, "Abba."

Jesus said, "Hitherto you have asked nothing in my name." A lot of babbling that doesn't make much sense, but no word, no *"logos."* Then comes the cross, and they do ask "in His name."

Paul writes, "When we cry, 'Abba! Father!' it is the Spirit himself bearing witness with our spirit that we are children of God, and if children, then heirs, heirs of God and fellow heirs with Christ, provided we suffer with him in order that we may also be glorified with him" (Romans 8:15–17).

When my children first spoke "Dada" out of the silence, out of the babble, I communed with them. My flesh and blood was speaking to me. And I would move mountains to hear it.

"Pray this way," says Jesus: *"Abba,* who art in heaven . . ."

In C. S. Lewis's *The Horse and His Boy,* when Aslan shows up in the dark silence to the runaway Shasta, the boy whispers, "Who are you?" The Great Lion replies, "One who has waited long for you to speak."[1]

Perhaps the Lion of Judah, the Lamb on the throne, has been speaking to you all your life. Now He has unwrapped your scroll, and with silence—deep calling to deep—He beckons you: "Speak to me."

"Abba Father"; "God save me." "God save" in Hebrew is "Yeshua." In Greek, "Jesus." Silence is an invitation to speak. And the word spoken out of the silence is the best.

REVELATION 8:1–2: *When the Lamb opened the seventh seal, there was silence in heaven for about half an hour. Then I saw the seven angels who stand before God, and seven trumpets were given to them.*

After the silence, John sees the seven angels who stand before God and are given seven trumpets (8:2). I think these seven angels are the seven eyes of the Lamb, who are the seven lamps on the seven lampstands, the seven spirits who are the Holy Spirit sent out into all the world speaking in the seven churches and our hearts, speaking even through the seven trumpet blasts. Trumpets proclaim things, like the Day of Atonement—Yom Kippur.

REVELATION 8:3–6: *And another angel came and stood at the altar with a golden censer; and he was given much incense to mingle with the prayers of all the saints upon the golden altar before the throne; and the smoke of the incense rose with the prayers of the saints from the hand of the angel before God. Then the angel took the censer and filled it with fire from the altar and threw it on the earth; and there were peals of thunder, voices, flashes of lightning, and an earthquake.*
Now the seven angels who had the seven trumpets made ready to blow them.

THIS OTHER ANGEL breaks the series of seven trumpets, which is part of the series of seven seals, as if we have another glimpse into the eternity that produces the series of sevens or is the *goal* of the series of sevens. Everything in this picture is connected by the words "and also"—*kai* in Greek—as if it is all-contiguous or eternal. An eternal picture of God on the throne, the Spirit before the throne, and this "angel."

People argue about the identity of this angel, but it's clear what he's doing: he's a priest offering incense on the altar in the temple. That's what Hebrew priests did each day, after anointing themselves with an oil of myrrh and other spices. They used an incense made of frankincense and other spices at the morning and evening slaughter of the sacrificial lamb.

In Leviticus 16, however, God commanded Aaron to offer incense *in* the Holy of Holies. *Within* it, before the ark—the Mercy Seat—the throne of God, he was commanded to take a censer full of coals from the altar and two handfuls of incense and go *behind* the curtain and put the incense on the fire of the golden altar, which was right before the Lord. And the smoke from that incense was said to protect Aaron lest he die, as he threw the blood of sacrifice upon the Mercy Seat—the throne of God—the ark of the covenant.

And somewhere along the line, the trumpets sounded, proclaiming Yom Kippur, the Day of Atonement.

Only the High Priest was to go behind the curtain and make this offering of incense and sacrifice before the throne. And scholars think that it was probably the custom that this incense offering was made in silence. I read somewhere that it probably took about . . . half an hour.

This angel is the high priest. The angel mediates the covenant; the angel mixes our prayers with incense he is given, and they ascend before God. Then the angel takes the golden censer and casts it upon the earth.

Who is this *angel* messing with our prayers?!

Angel means "messenger." Recognize that not all angels are like our pictures in popular culture. In the Old Testament, for example, the angel of Yahweh is clearly not like other angels. He is addressed as God Himself. He appears as a man. He wrestles with Jacob and calls him "Israel." He stops the hand of Abraham about to sacrifice his son on Mount Carmel. He speaks to Moses from the burning bush on Mount Sinai. He shows up all over the Old Testament. If you saw him, I believe you'd call him "Jesus." So who is this angel mediating our prayers?

Paul tells us that "There is one God, and there is one mediator between God and men, the man Christ Jesus, who gave himself as a ransom for all, the testimony to which was borne at the proper time" (1 Timothy 2:5–6). *One mediator.*

Hebrews 7–8 spells it out: Jesus is our high priest—He Himself is the sacrifice whose own blood is spread on the altar. The most natural way to translate the prepositional phrase in Revelation 8:3 is not "stood at the altar," but "stood on the altar." Jesus is the bleeding Lamb on the throne, and made sacrifice once for all. Yet the author of Hebrews writes, "He always lives to make intercession for them" that draw near to God through Him (7:25). That's *us.* Jesus takes your prayers and mixes them with His incense, *thumiama,* meaning "fragrant odors," like myrrh the priests used in the anointing and frankincense that was put in the censers as incense.

Where does Jesus get this fragrance? It is given to Him. As an infant king, He received frankincense and myrrh from Eastern kings. Mary anointed Him with costly aromatic oil on His way to Jerusalem to die. Jesus said, "It was intended that she should save this . . . for the day of my burial" (John 12:7). On the cross, Jesus smelled of that fragrance. They took His dead body and covered it in fragrances, as was the Jews' custom. Jesus mediates our prayers through His sacrificial death on the cross.

Even as He hung there in space and time, people prayed. A thief prayed. I think a Roman centurion may have prayed, "Oh God, who *is* this man?" People in the crowd must have prayed, "God, where *are* you?" And though they crucified Him, Jesus prayed, "Father, forgive them, for they know not what they do."

His prayer fragranced and purified their prayers. Then the censer was cast upon the earth, and the centurion dropped to his knees saying, "Surely this was the Son of God." The thief said, "Remember me when you enter into your kingdom."

And the earth shook,
and the rocks split,
and the tombs were opened,
and He lives to make intercession for you.

Paul says that we don't know how to pray as we should. Perhaps that means that if you pray, "God, I *really* want a classy new car and some genuine pearls," then Jesus mixes your prayers with His sacrificial incense and maybe He prays something like this: "Oh Father, forgive her for her small, little heart. What she really means by asking for that classy car is that she craves security. She wants to know that she's more valuable to you than all the pearls in the world."

He intercedes *for* us, and through His Spirit He causes us to intercede. He uses His silence to purify our hearts and entices us to speak. And with His Spirit He enters our silence and enables us to call out, "Word"—"Abba Father." Even when we are dead. Even when we shout, "Crucify." Even when we cover the dead silence in our hearts with noise. Even when we're dead in our own sins, He causes us to make a true confession.

As Jesus hung on the cross from the sixth hour to the ninth hour, the sky grew dark. Then at the ninth hour Jesus lifted His head and cried with a loud voice, "My God, my God, why have you forsaken me?"—the first line of Psalm 22. You see, *that's our line!* It's *our* prayer to be prayed from the depths of hell in silence and death. In a cursed world He speaks our curse to God. He prays *our* prayer to God.

Psalm 22 is a cry for salvation. Then Jesus says, "Into your hands I commit my spirit. It is finished." And the curtain in the temple rips from the top to the bottom, the earth shakes, the rocks are split, and the tombs are opened. He enters our silence, our deadness, and He speaks where we cannot even speak—out of the silence, a right confession.

We see here more than we can begin to comprehend. But at least, I hope you get this: When you pray, be silent before Him, before His cross, before His body broken and blood shed. *Be silent;* then speak.

But how do we get silent? We are addicted to words! We use them out of fear as weapons. So how can we surrender to God's silence? Take time to get rid of your words. Don't worry about them; confess them. *Then* be silent before Him. If words come to your heart out of that silence, speak them, because they are probably not your words.

"We need prayers of words, yes," writes Madeleine L'Engle, "the words are the path to contemplation; but the deepest communion with God is beyond words, on the other side of silence."[2] But how can I be silent enough to ever speak or pray God's words? I've covered my terrified heart with noise.

I want to leave you with a picture. It's the only time I ever saw a little boy named Jarek sit still in perfect silence. He was four years old, and I was performing the marriage ceremony of his mother, Janielle, to a man named Andy. Both Janielle and Andy had recently come to Christ.

Jarek was Janielle's son from a former relationship, and he really didn't know who his father was. He didn't really have a daddy. Jarek's skin was much darker than Andy's, so people could tell he was not Andy's boy. I think Jarek *knew* it. Out of his fear and anxiety he was always restless and running about, never sitting still. During the ceremony he did the ring bearer thing, and then he was all over the place and wouldn't sit still. By the time we got to the vows he was quarantined in the front row with relatives on either side holding him down.

As I began to lead bride and bridegroom in the ring ceremony, with Jarek squirming and making noises, all at once Andy stopped me. "Peter, I have to say something."

He turned around with everybody watching. Jarek was still squirming in his seat. Andy said, "Jarek." The boy froze. "Jarek, I love you with all my heart," Andy said. "And I will always be your daddy, and you will always be my son." And Jarek did not move the rest of the service.

I don't know the next word Jarek spoke, because he was silent for the rest of the service, but I pray that it was this when he saw Andy: "Daddy."

Be stunned to silence by the relentless love of your Abba revealed in Jesus . . . then speak. The Father is silent, waiting for you to speak. The Son died so that you could speak. The Spirit enters the deadness of your heart, giving the word to speak.

God waits in hushed anticipation, just to hear you say His name. Pray, "Abba . . . Jesus."

REMEMBER, PRAYER CAN MOVE MOUNTAINS. But big deal. Your prayer moved God from Mount Zion, the temple mount, and Mount Sinai all the way to Mount Calvary, the Hill of the Skull. He goes there to hear His children speak, "Abba . . . Jesus."
"Daddy . . . save."

SIXTEEN

WARNINGS ON A GOD–CURSED WORLD

(Revelation 8:6–9:21)

I ONCE READ about a pastor who tried for years to get some brothers to consider God and their prayer life, but to no avail. One day, one of the brothers was bitten by a rattlesnake. At that, the family finally called the pastor to come pray. When he arrived, he prayed, "Oh wise and righteous Father, we thank Thee that Thou didst send this snake to bite Sam. . . . And now, Oh Father, wilt thou send another rattlesnake to bite Jim, and another to bite John, and another really big one to bite their old man?"

REVELATION 8:6–9:19: *Now the seven angels who had the seven trumpets made ready to blow them.*

The first angel blew his trumpet, and there followed hail and fire, mixed with blood, which fell on the earth; and a third of the earth was burnt up, and a third of the trees were burnt up, and all green grass was burnt up.

The second angel blew his trumpet, and something like a great mountain, burning with fire, was thrown into the sea; and a third of the sea became blood, a third of the living creatures in the sea died, and a third of the ships were destroyed.

The third angel blew his trumpet, and a great star fell from heaven, blazing like a torch, and it fell on a third of the rivers and on the fountains of water. The name of the star is Wormwood. A third of the waters became wormwood, and many men died of the water, because it was made bitter.

The fourth angel blew his trumpet, and a third of the sun was struck, and a third of the moon, and a third of the stars, so that a third of their light was darkened; a third of the day was kept from shining, and likewise a third of the night.

Then I looked, and I heard an eagle crying with a loud voice, as it flew in midheaven, "Woe, woe, woe to those who dwell on the earth, at the blasts of the other trumpets which the three angels are about to blow!"

And the fifth angel blew his trumpet, and I saw a star fallen from heaven to earth, and he was given the key of the shaft of the bottomless pit; he opened the shaft of the bottomless pit, and from the shaft rose smoke like the smoke of a great furnace, and the sun and the air were darkened with the smoke from the shaft. Then from the smoke came locusts on the earth, and they were given power like the power of scorpions of the earth; they were told not to harm the grass of the earth or any green growth or any tree, but only those of mankind who have not the seal of God upon their foreheads; they were allowed to torture them for five months, but not to kill them, and their torture was like the torture of a scorpion, when it stings a man. And in those days men will seek death and will not find it; they will long to die, and death will fly from them.

In appearance the locusts were like horses arrayed for battle; on their heads were what looked like crowns of gold; their faces were like human faces, their hair like women's hair, and their teeth like lions' teeth; they had scales like iron breastplates, and the noise of their wings was like the noise of many chariots with horses rushing into battle. They have tails like scorpions, and stings, and their power of hurting men for five months lies in their tails. They have as king over them the angel of the bottomless pit; his name in Hebrew is Abaddon, and in Greek he is called Apollyon.

The first woe has passed; behold, two woes are still to come.

Then the sixth angel blew his trumpet, and I heard a voice from the four horns of the golden altar before God, saying to the sixth angel who had the trumpet, "Release the four angels who are bound at the great river Euphrates." So the four angels were released, who had been held ready for the hour, the day, the month, and the year, to kill a third of mankind. The number of the troops of cavalry was twice ten thousand times ten thousand; I heard their number. And this was how I saw the horses in my vision: the riders wore breastplates the color of fire and of sapphire and of sulphur, and the heads of the horses were like lions' heads, and fire and smoke and sulphur issued from their mouths. By these three plagues a third of mankind was killed, by the fire and smoke and sulphur issuing from their mouths. For the power of the horses is in their mouths and in their tails; their tails are like serpents, with heads, and by means of them they wound.

AND NOW, "May God bless you and keep you and make His face to shine upon you and give you peace." Wait a *minute!* What the heck was going on there? I've been studying this section for a long time, and I'm *still* not sure what all this is.

There are things going on that we *do* see, like people dying. And there are things going on we *don't* see, like the golden altar—just as we see conquest, warfare, famine, and death without seeing the four horsemen in space and time.

I'm not sure what we see or when it happens objectively in space and time. Did the hail, fire, and blood fall three thousand years ago in the plagues upon Egypt, or do these events happen again in the future? Has it been falling now for thousands of years as hail, lightning, and bloodshed worldwide? Or all of the above? And what does it mean?

The first trumpet—"hail, fire, and blood"—is like the first and seventh plagues on Egypt, as God was about to take Israel to the Promised Land. So a person could wonder, "Gosh, are we supposed to be leaving this place . . . going somewhere?" That's a good question. The first, seventh, eighth, and ninth plagues on Egypt are here in these trumpets.

At the second trumpet, a great, burning mountain is cast into the sea, and one-third of the sea turns to blood. Some people think the mountain is Babylon, and there is support for that view in the book of Jeremiah (51:25, 42). Some think the mountain is Mount Zion, because in A.D. 70, probably not long before the Revelation was written, Rome obliterated Zion and ruled the sea.

Many informed people think the Revelation is all about the destruction of Jerusalem, and they have strong reasons for that view. In the Gospels, it's difficult to tell when Jesus is referring to the destruction of Jerusalem and when He is speaking about the end of the world. In the Olivet discourse He speaks about *both together.*

Many people think this burning mountain is a volcano—Mount Vesuvius in Italy, which in 79 A.D. actually *was* a great, burning mountain cast into the sea, killing nearly fifteen thousand people along the way.

At the third trumpet, a great star falls to earth. At any time astronomers could look up in the sky and see a comet hurling towards earth, and Bruce Willis with all his rocket jocks couldn't stop it. When this star hits the water, it turns a third of the water bitter. It is the opposite of the story of Marah: When the Israelites came to the bitter water, Moses cast a tree into it, and it turned sweet. In Revelation 8–9 it's as if God's hand is being removed from His people, undoing His blessing: He will give disobedient Israel wormwood to eat and poisoned water to drink (Jeremiah 9:15).

At the fourth trumpet, a third of the light from the heavenly bodies is kept from shining, like an ash cloud from Mount Vesuvius, or the plague of darkness on the Egyptians, or the locust cloud in the prophecies of Joel, or what Peter quotes on the Day of Pentecost to explain what was happening that day two thousand years ago:

"This is what was spoken by the prophet Joel: 'And in the last days . . . I will pour out my Spirit upon all flesh, . . . And I will show wonders in the heaven above and signs on the earth beneath, blood, and fire, and vapor of smoke; the sun shall be turned into darkness and the moon into blood, before the day of the Lord comes.'" (Acts 2:16–20)

These are the last days, says Peter. So tonight you might see a blood-red moon.

The fourth of the seven trumpets undoes what God did on the fourth of the seven days of Creation. Maybe God is uncreating, or re-creating: seven days in Genesis—seven seals, trumpets, and bowls in the Revelation.

At the fifth trumpet, the locusts are released from the abyss. A locust's life span is five months. But these locusts don't act like other locusts. They don't afflict and eat plants; they afflict *people*. They have crowns, and men's faces with women's hair and lion's teeth. They are clearly demonic, under the control and authority of the ancient serpent.

The ancient historian Josephus recorded that during the horrific, six-month siege of Jerusalem, roving bands of possessed, Jewish transvestites raped and murdered their fellow Jews in the condemned city. They had women's hair, men's faces, and lions' teeth. (You didn't see that one coming, did you?)

Hal Lindsey suggests the locusts may be black Cobra helicopters spraying nerve gas from their tails. Some Catholics have argued the demon locusts are Lutherans. Whatever they are, it's *really bad*.

I believe I've actually talked to some of the locusts. I think they're demons. They hide behind crowns and human faces and gorgeous women's hair, but they long to inflict you with pain. If you're a believer, you battle them. They can harass you and keep you in fear, but they themselves cannot truly harm you. For you are sealed with the seal of God, the Holy Spirit, and they have been disarmed. However, even though *they* can't kill you, they can possess the godless people of this world, kings and soldiers and armies, who *can* kill you.

At the sixth trumpet, a great army is released from over the Euphrates, killing a third of mankind. I suspect this pictures people and armies under the control of demons. Rwanda, Bosnia, Serbia, the Sudan, Cambodia, the Third Reich . . . those were far more than just angry people.

Just this cavalry is 200 million strong. There is no single army this big on earth. Maybe this is all the evil armies that have ever marched over the face of our earth. Or maybe this is the Battle of Armageddon. Perhaps it's a poetic description of the Parthian cavalry north and east of the Euphrates. Others say it's obviously a poetic description of the siege of Jerusalem . . . just like the fall of Jericho, which was preceded by seven trumpets blown by seven priests as the people marched around the city seven times.

If you were in Jericho on the walls, I'm sure about the sixth time around you would have thought, "What the heck is going on?" And after six trumpet blasts, we wonder the same thing.

After six trumpet blasts, it appears that all *hell* is going on; all hell is breaking loose. Actually, only one-third of hell is breaking loose, as if it's a warning for the other two-thirds. So for those who die, maybe these *are* the bowls of wrath (they parallel the trumpets). But for the two-thirds, they are a warning.

The trumpets are part of the seals. Broken seals reveal mysteries. Blaring trumpets announce news. I suppose that whether the news is good or bad depends almost entirely upon which side of the wall you are standing . . . just like the plagues were good news to the Israelites but pretty bad news to the Egyptians.

> Good news if you're planning to leave,
> bad news if you call Egypt home.
> Good news if you're inheriting the Promised Land,
> bad news if you're highly invested in Jericho.

These trumpets proclaim news—a message. We don't know the details, and maybe we're not *supposed* to know all the details. That way . . .

. . . whether we look back in time and see Mount Vesuvius, the fall of Jericho, the plagues, and the fall of Jerusalem;

. . . whether we look in the paper today and see earthquakes, disasters, and demonic activity;

. . . whether we look into the future and see predicted seismic activity in California, global warming, and Armageddon . . .

No matter which direction we look, the message comes across loud and clear: You are living in a "God-damned" world. And I choose my words carefully, theologically, and biblically.

If you're offended at my words, I understand. You may have some cultural moralisms to sort through. But you should somehow inform your children that God cursed the earth. It's a damned world. You may say, "That's cursing!" No, it's not. God already did the cursing. You're living in a God-cursed world that *will* be consumed with fire.

Maybe you find this offensive not because of swear words, but because you're on the wrong side of the wall. Maybe you're highly invested in Jericho and Egypt, and I just *really* insulted your investment portfolio.

This *is* a God-condemned, cursed, damned world, and you don't need black Cobra helicopters to tell you so. As you read this, millions die in wars, famines, and natural disasters. Afflicted by demons, men rape little girls and murder people for sport. The creation literally devours itself. One organism lives off the death of another. The world calls it "the survival of the fittest," and we think it's *normal.*

The truth is, you may take your last breath this evening, and all those things are just warnings, symptoms of disease. For long ago and not far away, God said to the man, "The day you eat of the fruit of the tree you shall surely die"—the law.

In rebellion the man and woman ate, and I believe on that day they *did* die. They became the walking dead, their hearts shut off to God, unable to see, incapable of real love. But on that very day God came to them, and in the deepest love, He cursed the world. In Genesis 3:17 God says to Adam, "Cursed is the ground for thy sake" (KJV). And on that day God cursed the dragon and cast it to earth as a snake.

God subjected the world to futility in hope—hope of *what?!* Our repentance.

Demons, wars, famines, black helicopters . . . they *may* be our enemies, but they are not the real problem. The disease is our *own, dead,* unrepentant hearts. We don't love; we don't trust; we don't depend on God. We depend on ourselves, the works of our hands, and the things of this world.

The trumpets sound, and what do we do? Get better insurance policies, take vitamins, hire more police. Maybe even get religion to impress God and help make this world a better place. But God *cursed* this world. *Wake up.*

It's like we're dead on a ship bound for hell, and we don't know it. God fires a torpedo, and now it's a condemned, sinking ship. Satan's the captain and doesn't want to lose his cargo, so he runs up and down the hallways of the ship yelling, "You can have all the steaks you want! All the drinks are free! Hey, no rules—you can play soccer in the grand ballroom! Live the good life!"

If that doesn't work, and we wise up and begin to look around and say, "Hey, the ship is sinking!" he says, "Well, then don't play soccer in the grand ballroom—get to work! Grab a hammer and some tools, and we'll fix this ship ourselves. Go to church every Sunday and do good deeds . . ."

What does God want the whole time? *Abandon ship.* Stop trusting the works of your own hands and repent. Cry out for salvation! God doesn't really have to launch torpedoes; all He has to do is remove His hand, and creation begins to devour itself. The demons rage, the armies march, the serpent strikes, and we taste hell—the wrath of God.

Maybe a war, famine, or plague would do America some good, and we'd have a revival.

REVELATION 9:19–21: *The rest of mankind, who were not killed by these plagues, did not repent of the works of their hands nor give up worshiping demons and idols of gold and silver and bronze and stone and wood, which cannot either see or hear or walk; nor did they repent of their murders or their sorceries or their immorality or their thefts.*

DID YOU GET THAT? Six trumpets, a lot of hell breaking loose, and *nobody . . . nobody . . .* repents. Nobody! They just trust in the works of their own hands and get more religion—that is, idolatry. Snakes, by themselves, do not produce repentance.

Some folks think that Christians are all about chasing snakes into their homes and then prophesying doom. But I don't think we're called to prophesy doom like Joel and Elijah. When people say, "Man, this world bites," your job is to say, "Amen!" In fact, more than that, say, "Did you know this is a God-cursed world?" But we're not to be messengers of doom—bad things—but rather messengers of Jesus—good news . . . in the midst of doom.

Next John sees another mighty angel (10:1). John receives a scroll, and he's told to prophesy about many nations, tongues, peoples, and tribes. And "the testimony of Jesus is the spirit of prophecy" (Revelation 19:10). Then we see two witnesses who prophesy the testimony of Jesus. And when they *do,* people give glory to God. They repent. And then the last trumpet sounds.

What *is* the testimony of Jesus, the spirit of prophecy? It's right in front of us. The slaughtered Lamb is sitting on God's throne, and *He* opens the seal; *He* opens the scroll.

The seventh, and last, trumpet anticipates the last plague. Remember the final plague—slaughter of the firstborn? John 3:16 says, "For God so loved the world that he gave his only Son, that whoever believes in him should not perish but have eternal life." He is the Passover Lamb for us, the new Israel.

The good news in the midst of the God-cursed world is that God so loved this God-cursed world that—dare I say it?—God cursed God. "Christ redeemed us from the curse of the law, having become a curse for us—for it is written, 'Cursed be every one who hangs on a tree'" (Galatians 3:13). In Christ, God offered His only son, the sacrificial Lamb, in our place. Trumpets always sounded in proclaiming sacrifice on the Day of Atonement.

In Christ, God bore our hell, suffered our cross, and died in our place. Not only to atone, not only to save, but also to bear our pain:

- He boards the sinking ship.

- He is born in a manger.
- He feels the pain of every soldier in battle.
- He weeps over Jerusalem.
- He whimpers with every beaten and abused child hiding in a closet.
- He communes with us in all our sufferings.

In that communion He allows us to taste the hell that *He* bore for us, exposing His heart and calling to us, "Would you lose yourself now? Would you stop trusting the works of your hand? Would you surrender to my love?"

"And I when I am lifted up," said Jesus, "I will draw all men to myself." "Cursed is every man that hangs on a tree," said God in the Old Testament. Jesus came to be bitten by the snake, but He crushed the snake's head, and God raised Him from the dead—the testimony of Jesus.

I'll never forget the testimony of one of my dad's friends. John Rankin and my dad both fought in World War II. John was a tank driver in Europe. His job was to ride the iron horse spewing fire, smoke, and sulfur, right into hell.

John's partner in driving in the tank was a believer. He told John that Christ loved Him so much He took John's curse for him in a cursed world, and then rose victorious after His death on the cross. John *could* believe that the world was cursed—he was tasting it. But he did not repent.

One day they were riding "unbuttoned"—heads exposed at the neck. The engine was so loud they had to speak to each other through a tube. The partner yelled through the tube, "John, what are you going to do about Jesus?"

John, trying to put him off, said, "What do you mean?" He didn't hear anything, so he repeated, *"What do you mean?"* He still didn't hear anything, so he turned and looked. His friend's head had been completely blown off by enemy fire.

The trumpet had sounded. That night John surrendered his heart to the love of God in Christ Jesus our Lord. It was the power of a testimony of Love in the midst of a cursed world.

Trumpets are sounding all over. A Lamb has been sacrificed for you. Repent.

SEVENTEEN

THE BITTERSWEET GOSPEL

(Revelation 10)

W HEN I WAS A YOUTH PASTOR, I tried just about everything to get the kids in the back row of the youth room to be quiet and listen to the Word of God.

I stripped to my underwear and put on the armor of God . . .

I shaved my head and ate goldfish . . .

I refereed a live chicken-wrapping contest . . .

I employed wonderful exegetical tools of systematic theology and principles I had learned in seminary . . .

And *still* the kids in the back row would not quit yakking and listen to the Word of God.

God has done all kinds of things to get *us* to listen. He sent the prophets, the law, burning mountains, global catastrophes, promises of lands flowing with milk and honey, principles to live by . . . and still we harden our hearts and refuse to listen.

Finally, one Monday night the kids in the back row *did* listen. But *I* wasn't speaking. It was one of our volunteers. If you saw Kyle you'd think, "Well, there's a model citizen. I hope my kids grow up to be like him." But this night he stood in front of the youth group and told a story that until just a few days earlier he had never told anyone—not even his wife. It was about a time when he lay on the floor of his apartment for three days without moving, surrounded by knives, pills, and instruments of death, because he wanted to die.

Although he had professed Christ as a high schooler, in college Kyle was enticed into selling cocaine. Before long he was living a double life, flying back and forth between San Diego and San Francisco with cocaine strapped to his body, enthralled with the money and the adventure. Eight months into it, he was sitting in the back of a limousine, talking to a supplier in the front seat behind smoked glass about how he was having trouble collecting on one of his accounts. The supplier began to lecture Kyle on the need to enforce discipline. "If you'd like me to have him killed, I will."

All at once it hit Kyle like a ton of bricks. He wasn't a *success;* he was a *drug dealer* talking about having someone snuffed for money. All his life, all his history, all his chronology had led to this. He went home and sank into the abyss.

For three days he lay on the floor of his apartment absolutely horrified at himself. Then he prayed, and at *that* point he knew he had a choice: death or Jesus. He would either kill himself—suicide—or he would die with Jesus—salvation.

On the third day, the phone rang. It was his high school youth pastor, who had no clue what was going on. But for Kyle it was the sweet sound of grace, and it was then that he chose Jesus—or that Jesus raised him. As Kyle wept bitter tears in front of all those kids that Monday night, the gospel was entirely sweet. The kids in the back row did not move a muscle.

Revelation 10 is about halfway through the book. Except for the first three chapters recording the letters to the seven churches, the book has centered around this incredible scroll from the right hand of God, containing the Word of God—the meaning and *Logos* of God . By the end of chapter 9, all the seals are broken and all but the last trumpet has sounded. We've seen warfare, famine, plague, death, earthquakes, burning mountains, hideous demons from hell, horrific armies marching across the face of the earth. Yet as chapter 9 concludes, "The rest of mankind, who were not killed by these plagues, did not repent" (v. 20). The kids in the back row *still* would not shut up and listen.

REVELATION 10:1–3: *Then I saw another mighty angel coming down from heaven, wrapped in a cloud, with a rainbow over his head, and his face was like the sun, and his legs like pillars of fire. He had a little scroll open in his hand. And he set his right foot on the sea, and his left foot on the land, and called out with a loud voice, like a lion roaring; when he called out, the seven thunders sounded.*

Chapter 10 opens as John sees a mighty angel—*angelos;* messenger— coming on the clouds of heaven. In the first chapter, John writes of Jesus, "Behold, he is coming with the clouds"—not "he *will* come," but *"is"* (1:7). This *angelos* has a rainbow around his head. The rainbow is a symbol of God's covenant of grace, remember? It was given to Noah.

The face of this *angelos* shines like the sun, just as Jesus' face shone in chapter 1. He stands on sea and land, a symbol of his sovereignty over all things. His voice is like a lion roaring (there is only one Lion in the Book of Revelation). When he speaks, the seven thunders sound. Seven thunders! Like the voice of God in Psalm 29. This *angelos* acts just like the manifest glory of God (see Ezekiel 1-3) and the Son of Man (Daniel 7, 12).

Jesus *is* the Son of Man, the manifest glory of God. I believe Jesus *is* the angel of the Lord—the angel of Yahweh. The Book of Revelation is entitled, "The Revelation of Jesus." Not every angel is Jesus. But I think this one is. He *brings* the Word of God. He *reveals the* Word of God. He *is* the Word of God.

In His hand is a *bibliaridion,* which is a small *biblion,* a small scroll. The scroll may be the same as, or a smaller version of, the scroll in the right hand of God, but the two are clearly linked. All seven seals are now broken on that big scroll, and the scroll in the hand of the angel—the messenger—is open. The *angelos* roars, and the seven thunders sound.

REVELATION 10:4: *And when the seven thunders had sounded, I was about to write, but I heard a voice from heaven saying, "Seal up what the seven thunders have said, and do not write it down."*

THAT'S WEIRD. Seven is the number of creation. There are seven seals, seven trumpets, seven thunders, and seven bowls. We've talked about how I think they are theodicies; that is, explanations of the sufferings and pains of this world. Broken seals reveal the glory of God; Jesus is revealed in the midst of tribulation. Trumpets proclaim news; Jesus is *heard* in the midst of tribulation. Now there are seven thunders, and John is commanded not to write them down. I think that means there are more purposes in our sufferings and tribulations than we could even begin to comprehend. And there is more to Jesus our Lord than we are able to know.

In 2 Corinthians 12:2 Paul said he ascended into the third heaven, and heard things there that he could not utter, that it was unlawful for any man to speak. The thunders are the third series of sevens. Perhaps the sevens are all levels of heaven, meaning, reality, or dimensions within creation. Whatever the case, Jesus is more than we know.

REVELATION 10:5–7: *And the angel whom I saw standing on sea and land lifted up his right hand to heaven and swore by him who lives for ever and ever, who created heaven and what is in it, the earth and what is in it, and the sea and what is in it, that there should be no more delay, but that in the days of the trumpet call to be sounded by the seventh angel, the mystery of God, as he announced to his servants the prophets, should be fulfilled.*

THE TRUMPET CALL TO BE SOUNDED is the last trumpet. In 1 Corinthians 15:52 and 1 Thessalonians 4:16, Paul teaches that at the last trumpet we will be raised—raptured—caught up in the air—with Christ. The trumpet sounds in the next chapter. But here in 10:7 John wrote something strange: "In the days of the trumpet call to be sounded"—as if that trumpet call lasts for days, or occurs in many days. In those days of the trumpet call, the mystery of God, as He announced *(evangellizo,* or "evangelized") to His prophets will be fulfilled—finished—accomplished.

What *is* this mystery of God? Colossians 2:2: *Jesus.* The work of Jesus. The gospel of Jesus the Christ. Romans 16: the gospel of Christ. Ephesians 3:4: the gospel of Christ. Ephesians 1:9–10: The mystery of God's will is to unite all things in Christ. According to Paul, this was accomplished when God raised Christ from the dead and made Him sit down in the heavenly places at His right hand.

The mystery of God is the life, death, and resurrection of *Jesus.*

Now this *angelos standing* on sea and land declares that there will be no more delay in revealing this mystery. What he actually says in the Greek is, "There will be no more *chronos.*" The King James Version translates it, "There will be no more time."

We read at the start of the Revelation, and we'll read it again at the end: the *kairos* is at hand: *God's* time—eternity—kingdom time. The *kairos* is at hand and there will be no more *chronos.* Eternity has invaded temporality. It gets weirder than this, for there will be no more *chronos* in the days of the seventh trumpet call when the mystery is fulfilled . . .

. . . as if in the *last* days eternity will be continually invading temporality.

. . . as if in the *last* days the eternal kingdom of God will be overpowering the kingdoms of this world and our own little kingdoms.

. . . as if in the *last* days the gospel of Jesus the Christ will be preached, and people will listen.

According to Peter in Acts 2, these *are* the last days. And eternity *is* invading temporality. And that means a whole lot. It's fun to speculate about it. I've wondered if it means that when believers die, they hear the seventh trumpet, and Jesus comes for them, just like He said He would in John 14 ("I will come to you" [v.18]). They see Him coming on the clouds of heaven. ("He is coming with the clouds," says John, "and every eye will see him" [1:7].) Jesus said to the thief on the cross, "This day you will be with me in paradise." I think that means the thief saw Him coming, and He came *soon*. And He came in that thief's generation, so that that thief did not "pass away" or "sleep" like his ancestors the Jews waiting for the Messiah. He saw Jesus coming on the clouds of heaven at the very same moment that *I* will see Jesus coming on the clouds of heaven: the boundary between all of our chronologies and God's eternity.

It's just speculation, and I don't know. But I *do* know this: When you surrender to Christ, you surrender your *chronos*—your chronology or history—to His eternity. You pass from death to life, from old to new. In Christ, *you* are no longer your chronology. You are no longer the things that you have done in the past, and you are no longer the things you may do in the future. You are defined entirely and utterly by the eternal grace of God in Christ Jesus *right now*. And His grace transforms all your time.

REVELATION 10:8–11: *Then the voice which I had heard from heaven spoke to me again, saying, "Go, take the scroll which is open in the hand of the angel who is standing on the sea and on the land." So I went to the angel and told him to give me the little scroll; and he said to me, "Take it and eat; it will be bitter to your stomach, but sweet as honey in your mouth." And I took the little scroll from the hand of the angel and ate it; it was sweet as honey in my mouth, but when I had eaten it my stomach was made bitter. And I was told, "You must again prophesy about many peoples and nations and tongues and kings."*

IN THE FINAL VERSE OF THIS CHAPTER, John is told to prophesy *again*. How has he already prophesied? It's not the first nine chapters of Revelation, because he just heard them. He hasn't told anybody yet. How has he already prophesied? Most of his life he has born testimony to Jesus. And now this prophesying is the content of the little scroll proclaiming Jesus. This scroll contains the Word of God. Maybe the big scroll is the Word of God, Jesus in all of His fullness, and the little scroll is the Word of God, Jesus through John—John's testimony, John's Gospel, 1, 2, and 3 John, or all of the above. Whatever it is, it is the Word of God—the good news of God—coming through John.

It's clear that although all heaven waits with eager anticipation for the opening of the scroll, and all the earth shakes and the dragon rages, and kingdoms rise and fall, and armies march across the face of the earth, the Word of God—the content of the scroll—*will not* be revealed through any of these incredible things. The Word of God will be revealed through something better: a little old man exiled on the Isle of Patmos, seven little struggling churches in Asia Minor, and you.

Paul says that the mystery of God, hidden for ages, is now revealed through the church to the principalities and powers in the heavenly places (Ephesians 3:9–10). You reveal God's glory in Christ to angels and demons, and to peoples, nations, tongues, and tribes. And although they did not repent in all the cataclysms of history, they *listen* to you. They repent, and eternity invades chronology. The kingdom comes when you ingest the Word and speak it.

John is told to *eat* the scroll. It is sweet to the taste but bitter in his stomach. In his mouth, the gospel is sweet. God saves sinners because He loves them. But the gospel is bitter, hard to digest, in John's stomach. Maybe it's because it's so huge—the seven thunders, eternity invading temporality, the mysteries of the ages.

Every week I preach I get a bitter stomach. I think, "God, who am *I* to talk about this?!" But sometimes I get a bitter stomach for a different reason. It's so sweet to think God loves you, until you realize that God loves *you* . . . unabridged, naked *you*. Only by the grace of God do we ever have the courage to truly see ourselves. "Amazing grace, how sweet the sound that saved a wretch like me." Saved . . . that's sweet! A wretch . . . that's bitter.

I prayed with a friend once who by God's grace had remembered a very dark period in her life. She was horrified at herself. She wept and wept and wept. I had my arm around her, praying with her as she was weeping, and finally she cried out, "Jesus, I want to die. I just want to *die!*" And she heard these words: "You *are* dying." At that, I felt peace enter her body. She was dying and rising.

Several years ago I had my own miraculous encounter with God in prayer. He showed me I had gone to seminary and worked in a church and compiled an impressive chronology of good deeds because in my heart I hated His Bride, the Church, for what I had seen her do to my pastor father. All my good deeds were infected with hell because I wanted to *show* her—I wanted to *beat* her.

In that moment I saw myself, and I lay on the floor for hours, weeping. Then there came a great peace. God was crucifying Peter Hiett's proud chronology so I could no longer love Peter Hiett for all his good deeds, but only by grace. That's a bitter meal, realizing self needs to die. I couldn't excuse that self, I couldn't pay for that self, and if I killed that self there would just be more self.

After Peter denied Jesus, Scripture records that Jesus looked at Peter, and Peter looked at Jesus. Then he ran out and wept bitterly. He took the bitter meal, repented of himself, and surrendered himself to Jesus for death, and he was born again. And on Pentecost Peter preached, and it was sweet.

If the gospel has never seemed bitter to you, you need to spend less time talking about Jesus and more time looking at Jesus. For in seeing Jesus, you see yourself. And that can be hard on the stomach. The undigested gospel is not gospel, it's religion . . . and law . . . works . . . condemnation . . . and death. Instead of being the salt of the earth and the light of the world, we become a political position, preaching "I'm right and you're wrong!" Is that the gospel? It may feel sweet to my stomach, but to the world it's bitter on my lips. It should be the other way around: the gospel bitter in my stomach but sweet on my lips for the world. God saves sinners, "of whom I am chief"—that's digested gospel on Paul's lips (1 Timothy 1:15 NKJV).

So eat the scroll and preach the Word. You *are* a new creation in Christ. We have all sinned and fallen short of the glory of God, but you are no longer your chronology. You are *His eternity.* And the words that come to your lips after you have seen yourself at the foot of the cross will be the sweetness of the gospel for a dying world.

Does it now make sense to you that Kyle spoke, and the kids in the back row shut up and listened?

EIGHTEEN

END-TIMES SUPERHEROES

(Revelation 11:1–19)

REVELATION 11:1–19: *Then I was given a measuring rod like a staff, and I was told: "Rise and measure the temple of God and the altar and those who worship there, but do not measure the court outside the temple; leave that out, for it is given over to the nations, and they will trample over the holy city for forty-two months. And I will grant my two witnesses power to prophesy for one thousand two hundred and sixty days, clothed in sackcloth."*

These are the two olive trees and the two lampstands which stand before the Lord of the earth. And if any one would harm them, fire pours out from their mouth and consumes their foes; if any one would harm them, thus he is doomed to be killed. They have power to shut the sky, that no rain may fall during the days of their prophesying, and they have power over the waters to turn them into blood, and to smite the earth with every plague, as often as they desire. And when they have finished their testimony, the beast that ascends from the bottomless pit will make war upon them and conquer them and kill them, and their dead bodies will lie in the street of the great city which is allegorically called Sodom and Egypt, where their Lord was crucified. For three days and a half men from the peoples and tribes and tongues and nations gaze at their dead bodies and refuse to let them be placed in a tomb, and those who dwell on the earth will rejoice over them and make merry and exchange presents, because these two prophets had been a torment to those who dwell on the earth. But after the three and a half days a breath of life from God entered them, and they stood up on their feet, and great fear fell on those who saw them. Then they heard a loud voice from heaven saying to them, "Come up hither!" And in the sight of their foes they went up to heaven in a cloud. And at that hour there was a great earthquake, and a tenth of the city fell; seven thousand people were killed in the earthquake, and the rest were terrified and gave glory to the God of heaven.

The second woe has passed; behold, the third woe is soon to come.

Then the seventh angel blew his trumpet, and there were loud voices in heaven, saying, "The kingdom of the world has become the kingdom of our Lord and of his Christ, and he shall reign for ever and ever." And the twenty-four elders who sit on their thrones before God fell on their faces and worshiped God, saying,

> *"We give thanks to thee, Lord God Almighty, who art and who wast,*
> *that thou hast taken thy great power and begun to reign*
> *The nations raged, but thy wrath came,*
> *and the time for the dead to be judged,*
> *for rewarding thy servants, the prophets and saints,*
> *and those who fear thy name, both small and great,*
> *and for destroying the destroyers of the earth."*

Then God's temple in heaven was opened, and the ark of his covenant was seen within his temple; and there were flashes of lightning, voices, peals of thunder, an earthquake, and heavy hail.

AND THAT'S THE END . . . not of the book, but the end. For the last trumpet is blown and the temple is opened. But right before the end there is a great showdown between good and evil. In 11:7, for the first time in the Revelation, we meet the beast that ascends from the bottomless pit. It's probably the antichrist. "Children, it is the last hour; and as you have heard that antichrist is coming, so now many antichrists have come; therefore we know that it is the last hour" (1 John 2:18). That was written around A.D. 75. If *that* was the last hour, this is *really* the last hour! And many antichrists *have* come. But wouldn't you like to know the name of the big one still to come—the one whom Jesus will slay "with the breath of his mouth" at His return (2 Thessalonians 2:8)?

Over the last two thousand years, there have been many candidates for antichrist. In the twentieth century, the most likely candidate would have been Adolf Hitler, who murdered six million Jews.

After Hitler, probably the biggest candidate was Anwar Sadat. As a young Egyptian, Anwar Sadat admired Hitler because Hitler hated the British (who occupied Egypt) and the Jews. In the 1970s, after he became president of Egypt, Sadat attacked Israel in the Sinai. Several years later, he did an about-face and signed a peace treaty with Israel. U.S. Christians likened this new Egyptian "pharaoh" to the one who had seemed like an enemy and then signed a covenant with Israel as in Daniel 9:27. But Sadat was assassinated and didn't come back to life.

Many Christians suspected Jimmy Carter next—after all, he facilitated the Egypt-Israel treaty. In his 1980 book *Countdown to Armageddon,* Hal Lindsey observed that Jimmy Carter was groomed by the "trilateral commission," which clearly smacked of one-world, end-times government.

We can laugh now, but what do we do about the antichrist that is to come? Don't you want to know who it is to come? Don't you want to know how to read . . .

> the times and the seasons,
>> the plagues and the famines,
>>> the wars and geopolitical events of our day,
>>>> what happens with the nation of Israel, and
>>>>> the meaning of the United Nations . . .

so you can make a difference?

In the *Left Behind* series, the name of the antichrist is Nicolae Carpathia, and the tribulation saints live in a bunker reading the times and the seasons so they can battle well and make a difference. But the real superheroes of the tribulation are two freaky witnesses who show up on the new temple mount: Elijah and Moses. They have the power to consume their enemies with fire from their mouths. And Nicolae Carpathia can't touch them until the time of their testimony is complete (which is about book 7).

In the Revelation, John doesn't really tell us who these two superhero witnesses are. However, clearly, in the Revelation and in all of Scripture, every believer is called to be a witness *(martys in Greek, from which we get our word martyr)*.

In the *Left Behind* series, the tribulation saints live in a bunker reading the times and the seasons. In Acts 1, the last time we see Jesus' earthly body, His disciples gather with Him and ask:

> "Lord, will you at this time restore the kingdom to Israel?" He said to them, "It is not for you to know times or seasons which the Father has fixed by his own authority. But you shall receive power when the Holy Spirit has come upon you; and you shall be my witnesses in Jerusalem and in all Judea and Samaria and to the end of the earth."
>
> And when he had said this, as they were looking on, he was lifted up, and a cloud took him out of their sight. And while they were gazing into heaven as he went, behold, two men stood by them in white robes, and said, "Men of Galilee, why do you stand looking into heaven? This Jesus, who was taken up from you into heaven, will come in the same way as you saw him go into heaven." (Acts 1:6–11)

That's kind of weird. Jesus says, "It's not for you to know times and seasons . . . but you shall be my witnesses."

How are you doing at being a witness? Why don't you do it *more?* Maybe you're like me, and . . .

- you don't know what to say, and you don't want to sound canned, like you're reading a tract.
- you don't have all the answers to all the questions.
- you secretly worry, "What if some of *their* questions damage my faith?"
- you say, "I can't witness like *other* people can."
- you think you're weak.
- you're convinced it won't make a difference.

The Revelation was written to seven little churches in Asia Minor—but chapter 11 must not be bankrupt of meaning for us. So if there are two freaky, fire-breathing prophets in a reconstituted Israelite temple in the distant future for a three-and-a-half-year period, that's just *fine.* But it must mean *more* than that, to have meaning for the Church throughout history. Otherwise, the Revelation becomes voyeuristic Bible trivia. And it's *not.*

It is about *you* being a witness *now.*

So if you say, "I can't witness; I don't know what to say!" eat the scroll like John did, because it's not so much *what* you say as who you *are.* You are called to *be* a witness. Digest the Word of God and live it out.

A shepherd feeds his sheep not so they'll regurgitate the meal on his feet but so the sheep will digest it and turn it into wool. God saves you by grace in Christ Jesus. Digest the fact that you are a sinner, and you will be a witness: compassionate, humble (they are dressed in sackcloth), and genuine. It won't be canned; it will be *life* in you.

"But I don't have all the answers!" If this is your cry, let me give you a three-word phrase that will help you immensely and bring great glory to our Father where there has been a great deal of pain: *I don't know.*

You're not called to testify to the meaning of hominid fossils as they relate to Hebrew verbs in Genesis 1. And you're not called to bear witness to the meaning of everyone's sufferings. The seven thunders are sealed up; you can't know. But you *are* called to bear witness to Jesus, whom you *do* know.

"But I might get into a debate, and what if I lose *my* faith?" As soon as John is told to testify, he is given a rod and told to measure the sanctuary or temple. Lots of people think this proves that the temple will be rebuilt in Jerusalem. But with what will it be rebuilt? In chapter 3 Jesus says, "To him who conquers I will make him a pillar in the temple of my God." We *are* the temple.

Because of John's witness, the true church is built, set aside, and sealed even while the nations trample the outer courts . . . the *visible church,* perhaps. But you belong to Jesus; He will not let you go. You are His sanctuary. The true Church.

"But I can't preach the gospel eloquently or give prophetic messages from God." *Fine.* But let's look at these witnesses. They are given 1,260 days to prophesy, which is forty-two months, which is the amount of time nations are given to trample the Holy City, which is three-and-a-half years—or "time and times and half a time," the amount of time the woman is protected in the wilderness, the amount of time allotted to the beast to blaspheme, the amount of time stated in Luke 4:25 and James 5:17 that Elijah stopped the rain from falling. It is also the amount of time Antiochus Epiphany defiled the temple (before Jesus came), the amount of time the Romans seized Jerusalem, the amount of time Nero persecuted the Church, and the duration of Jesus' ministry on earth in His body.

Three-and-a-half is also a broken seven. Seven is God's perfection. Three-and-a-half is the time of trouble and rebellion. And at the end of Daniel, Daniel asks this man in linen, who appears to be the Son of Man hovering above the waters between two witnesses, "How long till the end of these wonders when Israel is delivered and dead people receive eternal life and stuff like that?" This man raises his hand like the messenger in Revelation 10, and instead of saying, "There will be no more time," in Daniel the man says, "It will be for a time, times and half a time." Then he tells Daniel, "Go your way, . . . because the words are closed up and sealed until the time of the end" (Daniel 12:5–13 NIV). And Daniel is told to seal the scroll. In the Revelation *John* is told to leave the scroll open, "for the time is at hand" (22:10 KJV).

I don't know what it all means, but it at least means that this is the time of the end. I think this is time, times, and half a time. It's the time of the Church bearing testimony in the last days. And this is the time of the two witnesses. They *are* the two olive trees (ref. Zechariah 4:11).

The two witnesses are technically, in the Greek, one body—singular. In 11:8-9a, it's "body"—singular. In verse 9b it's "bodies"—plural. Although they are many, they are one body. And they have powers like Moses and Elijah: stopping rain like Elijah and sending plagues like Moses.

Moses and Elijah appeared with Jesus on the Mount of Transfiguration as witnesses. These two represent the law and the prophets. "The law and the prophets bear witness to . . . the righteousness of God" (Romans 3:21–22). That is, they bear witness to . . . Jesus. The fact that there are two witnesses is important. The Old Testament law stipulated time and time again, "Nothing shall be established without the testimony of two witnesses."

So it is not enough for you to hear the testimony of Moses. You must also hear the testimony of Elijah, and vice versa. The gospel of Jesus involves a reasoned, systematic witness and a visionary, poetic, ecstatic witness. They are both prophetic, and both the testimony of Jesus.

law and prophet
Moses and Elijah
logos and *rhema*
principle and passion
mind and motion
reason and feeling
left-brained and right-brained
Baptists and Pentecostals
maybe even . . .
male and female
female and male
. . . but at least two witnesses.
Two witnesses; one Jesus.

Satan will try very hard to get the witnesses fighting with each other. It used to bother me that Christian witness was so diverse, but now I see that Jesus is *way* too big and *way* too colorful and *way* too personal for any one witness.

Your witness, child of God, is unique, priceless, and irreplaceable. Do not be somebody else. Eat the scroll, digest the Word, and then speak the same truth: Jesus.

Two different witnesses, but the same fire proceeds from each of their mouths. After Jesus told His disciples that they would be His witnesses, He told them to go to Jerusalem and wait for the promised Holy Spirit. On the Day of Pentecost the Holy Spirit showed up, "And there appeared to them tongues as of fire, distributed and resting on each one of them" (Acts 2:3).

In the Gospel of John, Jesus breathed on His disciples before He left and said, "Receive the Holy Spirit. If you forgive the sins of any, they are forgiven. If you retain the sins of any, they are retained" (20:22–23). And He told them the Spirit would be His witness, and "convince the world concerning sin and righteousness and judgment" (John 16:8).

The Holy Spirit is the Word of testimony and judgment on *your lips* when you testify of Jesus. So if you say, "I'm weak," the Word—Spirit of God—isn't. You speak fire when you speak Jesus.

If you say, "I tried it and it didn't work," biblically I'm forced to say to you, "You're wrong!" The Word of God will not return void but will accomplish the work He has for it (Isaiah 55:11).

As you testify, the world is judged not by you but by the Word. Grace received or grace denied. More than that, I have found (and I believe Scripture bears me out) that we are just *terrible, terrible* judges of when something "works."

In the witnesses' lifetime, they see only persecution and rejection. In fact, the beast and his people are allowed to *kill* them. And nobody repents. When Jesus was killed, everybody scattered, just like He said they would. If we had been there, I think we would have said, "Obviously those three-and-a-half years of *His* life did not work." The witnesses are raised after three-and-a-half days, and then an earthquake hits, and *then,* after they have ascended in a cloud, the people in the Revelation for the first time repent and give glory to God. It "worked" when nothing else in the entire Revelation had "worked" so far! It "worked," but they were no longer around (at least on earth) to see it.

Do you realize you are sowing seeds that may not germinate for forty or fifty—or two thousand—years? Paul writes that you have already been raised. John writes that you already have eternal life. And they both argue that your faith in the midst of suffering and tribulation is the witness God desires. It's the seed that bears fruit.

The seed of the Church is the "blood of the martyrs"—witnesses—who praise God with resurrection life even as they die. Yet these two witnesses seem to be more than that. They die, stay dead, and then ascend in a cloud. These two witnesses sound an awful lot like Jesus, almost like they're His *body* or something.

They are.

You testify to a Jesus who is a living presence within you. I think that's why Jesus desires *people* as witnesses, not just textbooks, computers, or tracts. We are witnesses to a living person who inhabits our bodies. We are *His* body and He lives *His* life in us.

In the end, even though these two witnesses die at the hands of the antichrist these saints end up conquering the antichrist and the dragon "by the blood of the lamb and the word of their testimony." Jesus *is* the Word of our testimony.

Finally the last trumpet sounds. The curtain in the temple rips from top to bottom. "Then God's temple in heaven was opened" (Revelation 10:19). Peace with God. And we are raised with Jesus. The end.

We digest the Word, but in the end we find the Word has digested us. We are the body of the Word of God. We are the body of Christ in this world.

So whether or not there are two freaky, weird witnesses in the reconstituted temple in Jerusalem in the year 2059 . . . I don't really care. Because they're *boring* compared to you. You are the end-times superheroes.

HITLER IS DEAD, Anwar Sadat won the Nobel Peace Prize, and Jimmy Carter failed so miserably at being the antichrist that he won the Nobel Peace Prize too. Who knows? Maybe Jimmy even told Anwar about Jesus. If He did, that's how you battle an antichrist—with fire, Holy Spirit fire, love. You may be battling an antichrist right now (many antichrists have come—1 John 2:18). We don't conquer with well-laid military plans, secret hideouts, and legislation regarding the modern nation of Israel. We conquer with the blood of the Lamb and the word of our testimony, even if we die—especially if we die— which is to live.

Nineteen

The Location of the Lost Ark

(Revelation 11:15–19)

In the movie *Raiders of the Lost Ark,* Indiana Jones and museum curator Marcus Brody explain to Egyptian officials the ark of the covenant and why the Nazis want it. "The Bible speaks of the ark leveling mountains and laying waste to entire regions," says Brody. "An army which carries the ark before it is invincible." That's cool.

Wouldn't you like to get your hands on the ark and take it with you to your in-laws' house or the office? "Hey, boss . . . about that raise . . . I want to show you something here behind my desk. It's the *ark of God!*"

The word *ark* simply means "container." But this, the ark of the covenant, was special. God gave Moses very detailed instructions for how it was to be built. Inside, it carried the stone tablets inscribed with the Ten Commandments—the Word of God to Israel. On top of the ark were two golden cherubim with wings outstretched over what was called the Mercy Seat, which was like God's throne on earth, where God told Moses He would meet with him. God also gave very elaborate instructions for the tabernacle (or "tent"), where they were to keep the ark of the covenant, and elaborate instructions for the veil that was to separate the ark of the covenant from the people.

At the end of the Book of Exodus, the cloud that led the Israelites (the glory and presence of God, the angel-messenger of the Lord, and the fire that spoke from the bush) . . . well, He descends and fills the tabernacle.

When they carried the ark across the River Jordan and the priest's feet touched the water, the Jordan parted like the Red Sea. When they carried it into battle against Jericho, on the seventh day, the seventh time around, when the priests had blown the seventh trumpet, the walls came tumbling down, and the Israelites began to occupy the Promised Land. (Throne, covenant Word, cherubim, sevens, trumpets . . . sounds familiar.)

An army that carries the ark is invincible. The only problem is, what army *can* carry the ark? In the movie, when the Nazis finally get hold of it and open it, a blast of lightning, wind, and Spirit is released, killing everyone except Indiana Jones and Marian, who both averted their gaze from the swirling images. Through the deafening noise, one archaeologist exclaims, "It's beautiful!" before he meets his doom. Then the visible power returns to the ark, and the lid slams shut.

I love that reaction. It *was* beautiful. The problem was, *he* wasn't.

In Leviticus 15, when the ark was brand-new, two sons of Aaron went behind the veil in front of the ark, and they died. God informed Moses, "Oh yeah, Moses, one important thing: Tell Aaron that before he goes behind the veil before the ark of My presence, he must make these blood sacrifices and cleanse himself for the atonement of sins, or else he'll die."

The ark is an incredible power, but it's not a magic power. Lots of people refuse to believe in the power of God because it's not magic—that is, scientific: It doesn't simply respond to their conditions. My wife is a power, but she's not a magic power . . . I've found that out. She's a *personal* power. The ark was a personal power. It mattered who used it and how. People didn't really *use* the ark; the ark used *them*. They didn't really *judge* the ark; the ark judged them. What happened to you in the presence of the ark was your judgment.

As the Israelites carried the ark into battle, it would judge by rewarding the people of God with victory and destroying the destroyers of Israel with the wrath of God. With the ark, the kingdoms of Palestine became the kingdom of Israel. But it wasn't a magic power. And it wasn't an automatic power. The Israelites still had to march and fight. And it required faith.

In fact, it seemed that God liked to put the Israelites in ridiculous circumstances that required a whole lot of faith. Then He revealed His power.

Oh, you bunch of tired wandering slaves; this is what I want you to do. Take my box and march around the mightiest city in all of Palestine, blow some trumpets, make some noise, and all the walls will fall down." And if they don't? Well, then I guess the Israelites get slaughtered or starve to death in the desert. God has a way of putting us in such situations.

Not a magic power; not an automatic power; but an absolutely awesome, horrific power.

Powers like that can be very hard to live with. Once the Philistines captured the ark from sinful Israel, but it destroyed the idol in their temple and brought only misery. In terror they sent it back to Israel on a cart.

Some Israelites looked inside it and died. Years later, King David went to get the ark. But one of his friends, Uzzah, reached out his hand to steady the ark, and the Lord "broke forth on Uzzah" (2 Samuel 6:7), killing him on the spot.

An army that carries the ark is invincible. But what army can carry it?

When David finally brought it properly into the city of Jerusalem, he danced with joy. Yet in the next chapter he thought, "Hey, I should build a temple for it." I think I understand his reasoning: "We need more than just a tent to contain this thing—we need a big, stone temple." You put uranium and plutonium in a cement vault, not a pup tent. Jesus is wonderful as long as you keep Him in one of those big, stone churches.

That very night, God spoke to David through the prophet Nathan: "Tell . . . David, Would you build me a house to dwell in?" Then he explained that He moves with His people. "Say to my servant David, 'The LORD declares to you that the LORD will make you a house. . . . I will raise up your offspring [seed] after you, and I will establish his kingdom. He shall build a house for my name, and I will establish the throne of his kingdom for ever. I will be his father and he shall be my son'" (2 Samuel 7:5, 11–14).

This son of David must be more than simply Solomon, who built the stone temple in Jerusalem. Do you remember what Jesus said about the stone temple? "Destroy this temple, and in three days I will raise it up." He *did* build a temple. And it *does* contain the presence of Almighty God.

Whatever happened to the ark? After King Josiah in the seventh century B.C., the ark drops out of history. In Jesus' day they didn't know where it was, but there were hopes and rumors that it would reappear in the temple in the messianic age. The veil would open, and there it would be. In A.D. 70, the Romans came along and utterly obliterated the temple.

No temple, no ark, no manifest presence of God, no power . . .and how they longed to find that ark!

In Scripture, after King Josiah the ark is not seen again until a short time after A.D. 70 when it is seen by a little, old, political prisoner exiled on the island of Patmos by Rome (the new Babylon). He hears a trumpet—the seventh trumpet—and he sees the ark in the temple.

By Revelation 11:15, six of the seven trumpets have sounded. John has been told to measure the temple, and that's when we see the two witnesses, who I believe are a picture of us looking like Jesus. They ascend into heaven.

The seven trumpets comprise the seventh seal. At the seventh trumpet that great scroll from the throne of God is now entirely open.

REVELATION 11:15–19: *Then the seventh angel blew his trumpet, and there were loud voices in heaven, saying, "The kingdom of the world has become the kingdom of our Lord and of his Christ, and he shall reign for ever and ever." And the twenty-four elders who sit on their thrones before God fell on their faces and worshiped God, saying,*

> *"We give thanks to thee, Lord God Almighty, who art and who wast,*
>> *that thou hast taken thy great power and begun to reign*
> *The nations raged, but thy wrath came,*
>> *and the time for the dead to be judged,*
> *for rewarding thy servants, the prophets and saints,*
>> *and those who fear thy name, both small and great,*
> *and for destroying the destroyers of the earth."*

Then God's temple in heaven was opened, and the ark of his covenant was seen within his temple; and there were flashes of lightning, voices, peals of thunder, an earthquake, and heavy hail.

THE TEMPLE IN HEAVEN IS OPENED; the veil is ripped from the top to the bottom; the great scroll is unwrapped. And behold, in chapter 12, verse 1, what do we see? A pregnant woman about to give birth. She gives birth to a baby that we know.

He is the Word of God;

He is the Word of our testimony.

He is the testator and mediator of the new and eternal covenant.

He is the presence of God;

He is the Angel of the Lord;

He is the King of glory, and they wrapped Him in swaddling clothes and placed Him in a manger (those Hebrews might have even used the word *ark*.)

I believe that great scroll is the new, eternal covenant, the Word of God, which includes all things. The earthly body of Jesus is like the ark. And now the ark is in His temple.

In Revelation 11:15 the seventh and last trumpet is sounded. The apostle Paul said, "At the last trumpet . . . the dead will be raised imperishable" (1 Corinthians 15:52). For *me*, that's in the future. Yet Paul and John talked in several places as if it were in the *past*.

In Colossians and Ephesians (Paul's letters to these seven churches in Asia Minor to whom the Revelation is *also* addressed) Paul writes as if they've already been raised. In Colossians 3:1 he writes, "If then you have been raised with Christ." He tells them in Ephesians, that they are seated "with him in the heavenly places" (2:6), like it's a done deal! You *are* the temple of the Lord, seated in the heavenlies.

At the seventh trumpet, voices cry out, "The kingdom of the world has become the kingdom of our Lord and of his Christ" (11:15). We don't see that yet, but Jesus said in Revelation 1 that He is the "ruler of the kings of the earth."

In Matthew, after Jesus arose He said, "All authority in heaven and on earth has been given to me. Go therefore and make disciples of all nations" (Matthew 28:18–19).

Paul writes in Ephesians 1:22, "[God] has put all things under [Christ] and has made him the head over all things for the church." It's as if Jesus has already won, and now He's just unwrapping and unfolding His victory in space and time through *us*. He has taken His great power and begun to reign.

The kingdom came with Jesus; it's growing in space and time, coming through us—the Church. And through us—the Church. The destroyers of the earth—Satan and all his evil works—are destroyed.

In Ephesians Paul writes, "[This] is the plan of the mystery hidden for ages [the Gospel]; that through the church [us] the manifold wisdom of God might now be made known to the principalities and powers" (Ephesians 3:9). Our job is to deliver a message to Satan: *You lost!*

The Church reveals the new covenant—

the Word—

the gospel—

in the days of the seventh trumpet call.

At the seventh trumpet is judgment. We know that the judgment day is in our future. Yet John records Jesus saying, "'Now is the judgment of this world, now shall the ruler of this world be cast out; and I, when I am lifted up from the earth, will draw all men to myself.' He said this to show by what death he was to die" (John 12:31–33).

Judgment is *now*, as if we're standing before the ark of the covenant now. How can that be?

When the Son of Man comes in all his glory . . . he will sit on his glorious throne and divide the nations. . . . And the king will say to those on his right, "Enter into the kingdom prepared for you. For I was hungry and you gave me food. I was naked, and you clothed me. I was sick and in prison, and you came and visited me." And those on his right will say to him, "But Lord, when did we see you hungry, sick . . . ?" And he will say, "Whatever you did to even the least of these, my brethren, you did to me" (see Matthew 25:31–40).

Jesus said "even the least of these, *my brethren*." Who are His brethren? *Us, the Church.* "What you do to my people you do to me." Why? Because He is present in His people and known in His people. They are His temple. And this is the judgment: He is saying, "Do you love Me? Do you want Me? The lowly, weak people in this room are My tabernacle, My moving temple. My glory is hidden in their weakness. And what will you do in My presence?" *Judgment.* There *is* a judgment day to come. Yet *now* is this world judged. There *will* be a consummated kingdom, but all kingdoms belong to Jesus the Christ *now,* and He uses them for His purposes. Through the Church He unfolds His victory in space and time.

When Jesus the Christ hung upon that Roman cross, He cried, *"It is finished!"* It *is.* And at that moment the veil in the temple ripped from the top to the bottom. And behold!—the ark wasn't there.

Now John looks and sees the temple. I think that's the temple he measured at the beginning of chapter 11. (Suddenly we saw the witnesses martyred, and then they ascended into heaven.) So now the temple is in heaven, and he looks, and it's open. Behold, within it—within *them*—is the lost ark of the testimony! The Church carried the testimony.

The ark of the covenant is in the temple. If Indiana Jones had paid attention in Sunday school, he would have known: the ark is in the temple. The Word of God, "the mystery hidden for ages and generations but now made manifest to his saints. To them God chose to make known how great among the Gentiles are the riches of the glory of this mystery, which is Christ in you" (Colossians 1:26–27).

When my son Coleman was little and learned that Jesus was inside him, he used to put his fingers in his ears and yell, "Jesus, I can't hear You! Are You in there?" I don't know if he ever heard an audible voice or not, but he *did* hear Jesus. Because Coleman will tell you—Jesus is in there. That's the gospel. The ark is in the temple. Jesus is in his heart.

This isn't just a sentiment or a manner of speaking; it is a basic doctrine of our orthodox faith. So how can it be that little Coleman Hiett is not utterly destroyed by the presence of God, like those Nazis in the movie and David's friend Uzzah? What army *can carry* the ark of the covenant? Coleman. The Church.

How can this be? Because of the "blood of Jesus, by the new and living way which he opened for us through the curtain, that is, through his flesh"—His sacrifice (Hebrews 10:19). Jesus, the very presence, glory, and love of God, the messenger of the Lord, died that we may enter and that He may enter us and live in us—His temple, His people. The ark *is* in His temple—His Church, and the army that carries the ark *is invincible!*

In fact, it's already finished in all eternity. Do you hear what the Lord is saying to the little churches in Asia Minor up against the Roman Empire in the height of its glory? "I am in your midst. I walk among the lampstands. And

I am in My temple, which is My people. My seven little churches, we will topple the Roman Empire and the great dragon and the beast and the whore of Babylon. For the gates of hell cannot stand against My Church." The greatest power unleashed in the sons of Adam on the face of earth was contained in those seven little churches in Asia Minor. History bears that out.

Do you hear what the Lord is saying to us in His Church today? "My ark is in My temple. And My temple is a tabernacle, and it moves—don't you *dare* think that you can leave Me in some stone building somewhere. I move with My people."

There is an "immeasurable greatness of his power in us who believe" (Ephesians 1:19). But it's not magic. And it's not automatic. It's the person of Jesus. He wants us to have faith, for He does not take us by force. Satan will, if he gets the opportunity, but not Jesus. He romances our hearts. He suffered and died for us that we would surrender in love. That is the greatest power of all: The slaughtered Lamb is on the throne. He is the power of God unto salvation. That power dwells in you; Christ lives His life in you when you walk by faith in Him.

The seven churches toppled the Roman Empire. I met some of the believers who toppled the Romanian government. Richard Wurmbrand was a prisoner in a Romanian cell, and he tells about the years when he was tortured and beaten and left to starve. A young atheist was thrown into his prison cell one day, screaming, "I *hate* God, and leave me alone!" Wurmbrand shared his faith with him anyway, but still young Joseph would not believe.

During that time Wurmbrand loved the other prisoners in the cell. He would give his food when they were hungry and he was hungry. In winter he risked freezing to death by tearing out the lining of his jacket and giving it to Joseph.

One day Joseph said to him, "We've read nearly everything that Jesus *said,* but still I wonder what He was like. I mean, what was He like to know as a man?"

Wurmbrand thought for a moment and then replied, "Years ago when I was in room four there was a pastor there who lived like Jesus. He gave himself away, and he loved everyone there. One day a committed communist asked him, 'What was Jesus like?' In a moment of great courage and great humility, this pastor said, 'Jesus was like me.' The communist said, 'If he was like you, then I love him.'"

Joseph looked at Wurmbrand and said, "If Jesus is like *you,* then I love Him too."[1]

The ark is in the temple, and the army that carries the ark is *invincible.*

TWENTY

BORN-AGAIN BIRTH PAINS

(Revelation 12:1–6, 13–17)

ONE SUNDAY I walked up to the microphone at church and said, "I had a really hard week, so I'm not going to preach. I'll just close the service in a short prayer and we'll go home early. And if you're thinking I ought to preach anyway . . .

"Well, none of you knows what it's like to be a pastor of a large church with crises and confidences you have to keep, and also be a boss to a bunch of people in this Christian fishbowl, holding them accountable while making sure they still like you at the same time.

"You don't know what it is to preach week after week, year after year, to feel as if you get up and *bleed* on people . . . spill your heart, and then they criticize you and step on it. Then next week you have to go right back, sit in your office, and wonder what God wants to say to everybody . . . because you need to bring them a 'fresh word' from the Lord. You stare at some text that is utterly confusing, and even if you kind of understand it, then you have to serve it up simple to everybody. Sometimes I sit there in my office in absolute *anguish*."

Then I said, "I know what some of you are thinking: 'We *all* have hard weeks.' But you don't know. *You don't understand. You're not me.*"

Well, you may be thinking what folks in church were thinking: *Oh, right. Peter, you don't have a clue what I'm going through. You don't know what it's like to be diagnosed with cancer, and have no health insurance. You're not stuck in a bad marriage. You don't know the anguish I live with from my past, but I'm still here! You don't know the daily struggle of chronic fatigue and pain! You couldn't possibly understand. Nobody understands . . . not even God! God could never know what it's like to be me: poor and oppressed, born into poverty, rejected by friends and family and church, abandoned by my father, feeling the weight of the*

152

world on my shoulders, sin and shame heaped on my back, godforsaken, like I've been stripped and beaten and nailed to the wall naked—crucified!

Wait a minute. Sydney Carter wrote a poem about that . . .

> But God is up in heaven
> And he doesn't do a thing,
> With a million angels watching,
> And they never move a wing. . . .
> It's God they ought to crucify
> Instead of you and me,
> I said to this Carpenter
> A-hanging on the tree.[1]

SO FAR IN THE REVELATION, we have seen incredible anguish. For the last eight chapters—anguish. It's all been a part of opening this incredible scroll in order to deliver its Word. Now the scroll is open.

REVELATION 12:1–6, 17: *And a great portent appeared in heaven, a woman clothed with the sun, with the moon under her feet, and on her head a crown of twelve stars; she was with child and she cried out in her pangs of birth, in anguish for delivery. And another portent appeared in heaven; behold, a great red dragon, with seven heads and ten horns, and seven diadems upon his heads. His tail swept down a third of the stars of heaven, and cast them to the earth. And the dragon stood before the woman who was about to bear a child, that he might devour her child when she brought it forth; she brought forth a male child, one who is to rule all the nations with a rod of iron, but her child was caught up to God and to his throne, and the woman fled into the wilderness, where she has a place prepared by God, in which to be nourished for one thousand two hundred and sixty days. . . .*

[In verses 7–16 there is a great war in the heavenlies, and Satan is cast down. He pursues the woman and is thwarted.]

Then the dragon was angry with the woman, and went off to make war on the rest of her offspring, on those who keep the commandments of God and bear testimony to Jesus. And he stood on the sand of the sea.

SO THE SCROLL IS OPENED, with all heaven and creation wondering what's in it, and a woman delivers a baby. Almost all Bible teachers are unanimous on the identity of that baby: it's the Word of God, Jesus. But who is the *woman?* That's the confusing part.

Catholic theologians have argued that she's Mary. But she's kind of *large* for Mary. Some argue that she's Eve, and that makes some sense. Long ago, Eve had a run-in with the dragon in the Garden. He tempted her and she fell, along with Adam. God cursed the dragon, casting it to earth: "Upon your belly you shall go, and dust you shall eat all the days of your life. I will put enmity between you and the woman, and between your seed and her seed; he [her seed] shall bruise your head, and you shall bruise his heel." Then God said to Eve, "I will greatly multiply your pain in childbearing; in pain you shall bring forth children" (Genesis 3:14–16). Anguish.

Clearly Jesus is that promised seed. But technically, Eve didn't give birth to Jesus, except through a long genealogy—a lineage—of other mothers. So some people have argued that that woman in Revelation 12 is that genealogy, or that the woman is Israel. The woman is clothed with the "sun, moon, and stars." Joseph had a dream of his family in which they were "sun, moon, and stars." So it seems the woman must *at least* be Israel, and *at least* Eve, and *at least* Mary, and somehow that genealogy from Eve to Mary.

By the way, that genealogy makes for some rather sordid ancestors in Jesus' past. Eve was the mother of all sinners, the original sinner. Abraham pimped his wife. David, Jesus' great-great-great-grandfather, murdered the husband of Jesus' great-great-great-grandmother Bathsheba so he could have sex with her. Gentile blood was infused through a harlot, Rahab. Jesus was of the house of Judah, but that was only because his great-great-great-great-grandmother Tamar disguised herself as a prostitute and got her father-in-law, Judah, to have sex with her. Quite a lineage. And just like the stable where Jesus was born, Jesus doesn't seem all that concerned about hiding the mess.

Think of it: The promised seed from God Himself implanted in poor, teenaged, peasant flesh from that lineage; then born in desperation and confusion in a stinking barn in an occupied and oppressed country. Talk about *anguish.*

So maybe He *does* know what it's like. Maybe He really did empty Himself and take the form of a slave. Maybe He really is born of the woman in anguish. Maybe he really did wrap Himself in flesh like mine and . . . had gas and heartburn . . . and smelled like gym socks after a long hike. And maybe when He was tired, He was tempted to get drunk . . . have sex . . . go to bed and stay in bed and never preach! Maybe He was tempted like that, or do you not believe that He was tempted in every respect, "as we are, yet without sin" (Hebrews 4:15)?

Jesus was born in space and time, in Bethlehem of Judea, to Mary the virgin. Yet Revelation 12 seems to refer to more than simply Jesus' birth to

Mary in Bethlehem . . . and to more than His life in Palestine (in 12:5 he is caught up to the throne, and it doesn't even mention the cross).

Yet after the child is taken up into heaven, this woman has more offspring. These children bear testimony to Jesus, and that hardly sounds like Israel, at least the Israel we normally think of. Yet Paul and John taught that we—the Church— *are* Israel. And we are Jesus' brothers and sisters, right? But wait—Jesus said, "Whoever does the will of my Father in heaven is my brother and sister and mother" (Matthew 12:50). We *are* Christ's brothers and sisters, and that means we have the same father as Jesus. But that also means we have the same *mother* as Jesus, and we *are* that mother! So then the woman must be God's people throughout time . . . whoever does the will of the Father throughout time.

How could Jesus be born and live and ascend more than once in Bethlehem and Palestine? How could Hebrews state that Jesus was tempted in every way as I am and you are? He was never a woman who was raped! He never had to moderate a session meeting during a budget crisis! And how is it that *I* could be His mother? How could I be that woman in Revelation 12?

In Galatians Paul writes, "It is no longer I who live but Christ in me" (2:20). How did He *get* there? Paul goes on to tell the Galatians that he— Paul—is in travail—birth pangs—*with* them "until Christ be formed" in them (4:19). Like Jesus said, His followers are His mother . . . which seems to mean Jesus is born of the Church somehow, impregnated with the seed [*sperma* in Greek] of God the Father, the Word of God.

Jesus born of you as mother, and born in you, formed in you—that seems weird, but it's what we sing at Christmastime. "Oh holy child of Bethlehem, descend to us we pray; cast out our sin and enter in, be born in us today." It's not just a song.

In 1 John 3, John writes that God's seed is in us who belong to Him. In the Gospel of John, Jesus says to Nicodemus, "You must be born again" (3:3). We throw that phrase around so much, I think we've come to believe that being "born again" is an easy, instantaneous process. Well, after four kids I suspect it's not such an easy, instantaneous process. The fertilization, on the other hand, is rather instantaneous and easy. Maybe fertilization, receiving the seed—the Word—is the instantaneous part, but pregnancy and delivery can really hurt and last awhile! Maybe we should expect some born-again birth pains—*anguish*.

The woman is in anguish to deliver. In fact, the anguish is so great, we really can't do it. "We're born of the spirit," Jesus says, the Spirit of Jesus. The Word is the seed implanted in us, and we're born together with Him. The *me* that is born again is *Him* in me. "No longer I who live but Christ in me" (Galatians 2:20). Christ in me is to live. He's born of me in me—the *new me*.

In Matthew 24, when Jesus sits His disciples down and talks of wars, earthquakes, and famines, He is describing all the broken seals and sounding trumpets we've been looking at in the Revelation. Then He calls them *birth pangs*. Who's being born?

Paul writes, "We know that the whole creation has been groaning in travail together until now; and not only the creation, but we ourselves, who have the first fruits of the Spirit" (Romans 8:22-23). Who's being born? According to Paul, the sons of glory . . . us . . . the Church . . . the body of Christ. Christ in us is being born.

In Revelation 12 the woman—we who believe—is clothed with "sun, moon, and stars": creation. The creation is like our delivery room. Jesus is born *of you* and *in you* . . . in anguish. His life is born in my filthy, anguished stable of a heart.

So He knows. He understands. He feels what His body feels. I am His body; you are His body. He was born into His earthly flesh in Bethlehem of Judea, but He's also born into my body here and now. That means that I'm known, and I am not alone. That is wonderful news!

But it's also challenging news, because I can never say to Him, "You're not me!" because He *is;* or, "You don't understand!" because He *does*. When He tells me to do something like get up off my lazy tail and endure, I can't use those old lines and excuses on Him. We all long to be known, yet we all hang on to *not* being known, because we use our secret anguish as an excuse and justification for sin. Yet when we do that, it traps us deeper and deeper into defeat, sin, loneliness, and more anguish. The father of lies knows that.

We close our own ears because we tell ourselves, "No one can speak into my anguish." That's a lie. Jesus can. He has authority to speak into your anguish because He is born in your anguish. *Of course* He writes, "My seven churches, I know your works, and I know your tribulations, and I know where you dwell." It is where He dwells. When Christ addresses the "Spirit" or "Angel" in each of the seven churches, I suspect it is His own Spirit born in them, into their mess and anguish, in order to deliver them.

Babies are born in anguish ever since that day in the garden long ago when God prescribed anguish in delivery. The woman in Revelation 12 is in *anguish* to be delivered.

When we deny the anguish in our hearts and don't face it;

when we deny our own shame and failure and sin;

when we hang on to that anguish as a weapon against God;

when we use those places of secret anguish as a trump card for the day of judgment; ("Oh, yeah, God, *You* don't know what it's like! *You're* not me!")

when we refuse to surrender our places of anguish to Jesus . . .
we refuse the birth of His life in our lives.

For the Christ is born into those places of anguish. "You will find him wrapped in swaddling clothes and lying in your manger."

So many people want to see the King of Glory, but they won't be caught dead in a stable, especially their own stable. It's too humiliating.

I have some amazing stories of Christ born in people's anguish—when they've surrendered memories of sin and shame. But since you've read this far and hopefully encountered the Word through me, I think I should tell you that almost every week I sit in my office, and I struggle and scratch, and my honest prayer is, "God, what the heck are You doing?!?" I want to run from the anguish. Yet now, after all these years, I have to admit, although it scares me: the word is born in my anguish. When I am weak, He is strong. I come to see the Savior in the very place where I need to be saved. I surrender my anguish, and then it's His anguish. And He conquers it. That's who He is: the Savior.

He knows all my anguish because it's *His* anguish. But if it's His, then it's His eternally and always, which means it was His anguish before I was even born. Here's the deeper truth: Not that He's come to know my anguish, but that He allows me to taste His—the anguish of loving a fallen world . . . and the joy of redeeming it.

Listen to Jesus in John 16:20–22: "You will be sorrowful, but your sorrow will turn into joy. When a woman is in travail she has sorrow, because her hour has come; but when she is delivered of the child, she no longer remembers the anguish, for joy that a child is born into the world. So you have sorrow now, but I will see you again and your hearts will rejoice, and no one will take your joy from you."

When my oldest son, Jonathan, was born, he was nearly six weeks early. My wife had twenty-four hours of intense labor and a ruptured placenta, and we didn't even know where the hospital was. We didn't know if Jonathan would live, and I wasn't sure my wife would either.

I've never seen a person in such anguish. There was blood everywhere, and she was passing out on the table from pain and exhaustion. I remember thinking, *You'd better enjoy this baby, if he lives, because you'll never have another one.*

As the doctor pulled Jonathan out and held him up in front of my wife, bloody and screaming, the very first words out of her mouth were, "Oh . . . ! I want another one!"

Joy.

Your anguish, sorrow, suffering, and guilt can be your own private hell, or it can be the birthplace of the King of Glory.

The woman is in anguish to deliver . . . the Word in you, Christ in you. Surrender your anguish, and soon you will see Him. And no one will *ever* be able to take your joy away from you.

TWENTY-ONE

THE DRAGON

(Revelation 12:7–17)

J. R. R. TOLKIEN wrote, "It does not do to leave a live dragon out of your calculations, if you live near him."[1]

> **REVELATION 12:7–14:** *Now war arose in heaven, Michael and his angels fighting against the dragon; and the dragon and his angels fought, but they were defeated and there was no longer any place for them in heaven. And the great dragon was thrown down, that ancient serpent, who is called the Devil and Satan, the deceiver of the whole world—he was thrown down to the earth, and his angels were thrown down with him. And I heard a loud voice in heaven, saying, "Now the salvation and the power and the kingdom of our God and the authority of his Christ have come, for the accuser of our brethren has been thrown down, who accuses them day and night before our God. And they have conquered him by the blood of the Lamb and by the word of their testimony, for they loved not their lives even unto death. Rejoice then, O heaven and you that dwell therein! But woe to you, O earth and sea, for the devil has come down to you in great wrath, because he knows that his time is short!"*
> *And when the dragon saw that he had been thrown down to the earth, he pursued the woman who had borne the male child. But the woman was given the two wings of the great eagle that she might fly from the serpent into the wilderness, to the place where she is to be nourished for a time, and times, and half a time.*

"Time, times, and half a time" (v. 14) is three and a half years, 1,260 days. It's the length of Jesus' earthly ministry. It's also Daniel's time of the end. I believe it's the time we are in *now.* "Now . . . the accuser of our brethren has been thrown down" (v. 10).

REVELATION 12:15–17: *The serpent poured water like a river out of his mouth after the woman, to sweep her away with the flood. But the earth came to the help of the woman, and the earth opened its mouth and swallowed the river which the dragon had poured from his mouth. Then the dragon was angry with the woman, and went off to make war on the rest of her offspring, on those who keep the commandments of God and bear testimony to Jesus. And he stood on the sand of the sea.*

That's us! And we're at war.

I love to hear World War II stories from my dad, who trained infantry troops stateside before he was shipped out to the Philippines, especially when he sits down with another old guy and shares memories. They do it in great cheer. Old *dragon slayers.*

The story goes that one evening after a day of training, a soldier came into my father's barracks and said:

I've had it! I'm sick of this place, and I'm sick of you and your demanding ways. Yesterday morning you had us marching at 8:00, 9:30, and 11:00— you don't appreciate *me,* and you don't appreciate my *needs!* The restroom facilities are entirely inadequate. What's more, you have some serious boundary issues. You violate my boundaries. I signed up for this war because I heard that Bob Hope entertains the troops. I haven't heard Bob Hope once! And I don't like the songs we sing—in fact, I don't like *any* of the music. Frankly, I don't like *you!* You probably have some kind of border-line passive-aggressive personality disorder. If something doesn't change, I'm out of here!

Of course that didn't happen in World War II. It happened in church. My father trained troops in our nation's army, and my father trained troops in the kingdom's army, the Church. I grew up in the Church, and stuff like that was commonplace. To an objective observer it might just have appeared that the Church had not included the dragon in their calculations.

Sometimes I worry that we have not included the dragon in *our* calculations. When we sing worship songs, we're going to war! When we pray, we're going to war! When we give, we're going to war! When we serve dinner at the shelter, we're going to war! When we marry, have kids, and invite our neighbors to church, we're going to war!

And that changes things.

You pray more,

and give more,

and sing louder,

and complain less.

In 12:9 we learn that the dragon is "the old serpent who is called the devil" who tempted Adam and Eve and would one day be crushed by the seed of the woman. Devil means "slanderer" or "accuser." He is also called *Satan,* which means "adversary" or "enemy." Satan is in thorough rebellion against God, and "there is no truth in him" (John 8:44)

But in John 1:9 we read, there is a "light that enlightens every man." All men have some truth shining in them. Satan has *no truth* in Him . . . he is thorough in his darkness and rebellion. He deceives the whole world. Jesus said that Satan is a murderer and the father of lies, that he lies "according to his own nature" (John 8:44). I read somewhere that the chief punishment of the liar is not so much that he is not believed, but that he *cannot* believe.

Satan does not believe. In the words of John, "The light shines in the darkness, and the darkness has not [understood, comprehended, or] overcome it" (John 1:5). For, in the words of Tolkien, "He weighs all things to a nicety in the scales of his malice . . . the only measure he knows is desire, desire for power; and so he judges all hearts."[2] He does not see truth, and he does not comprehend love. He is the liar entirely trapped in his own lies.

And Satan *is not* the equal opposite of God. He is not the "dark side of the force." Evil does not have an independent existence. It is always corrupted good. You can never tell a lie unless there's a truth to tell the lie about. I believe Satan is a negation or a corruption. We really battle him, but I can't truly say he's a live dragon, for Jesus is the Life.

In the Old Testament, Satan appears in the throne room of God and accuses the children of Adam. Satan knows the *law* . . . but not love. He calls God to God's own justice, but not for the same reason. God is just because He is love. Satan is a legalist because he is malice.

Satan's great strength used to lie in his power of death. If God's law declared death, somehow Satan could satiate his lust for destruction. He was free to destroy. But Jesus took our flesh and blood and died that He might *destroy* the one who had the power of death (Hebrews 2:14–15). Destroy the destroyer.

Now Satan is thrown down in an absolute rage. Why? Because God has done what is inconceivable, incomprehensible to Satan. He has acted in absolute and perfect sacrificial love by dying for us.

What Satan thought to be his greatest victory—destroying that Messiah, the prophet Jesus—turned out to be his greatest defeat, his own destruction. For God was in Christ that day, reconciling the world to Himself, that their sins would not be counted against them.

So Satan goes to the throne room to accuse the sons of Adam. He looks at the throne and what does he see?—*that man* he destroyed on the cross. He sees the second Adam, the very Lamb he slaughtered . . . on the throne. Verse 7 says that Michael fought the dragon, as prophesied in Daniel 12. In verse 11 it says we (or they) conquer, but it's all by the victory of the Lamb.

Never forget that all this revelation of victory is the scroll unwrapped by a bleeding Lamb on the throne. Satan looks and sees not only that Lamb resurrected on the throne, but everyone throughout time who has trusted Him. Jesus bore their destruction on His cross, so all those who were with Him in His death now are with Him forever in His resurrection—an eternal communion of life. Jesus is with them in every moment of their lives, *kairos* invading *chronos,* eternity invading temporality. Eternal life *now.*

This is an "eternal gospel" (Revelation 14:6); the lamb was slain from "the foundation of the world" (13:8). This happened beyond time. Yet I believe that Satan is a creature of time, as we are, and therefore he didn't see it coming. He did not and *would* not.

When Jesus reached Jerusalem in the last week of His life and proclaimed, "Now is the judgment of this world, now shall the ruler of this world be cast out" (John 12:31), Satan didn't have a *clue.* As he destroyed Jesus on the cross, he destroyed *himself* and all his works for all time. This was the plan for the fullness of time, to unite all things in Christ. And Satan flipped the switch that shone the light: Jesus always wins.

The love of God in Christ Jesus our Lord *always conquers,* everywhere and every when. Even when He dies—*especially* when He dies—He conquers.

The loud voice cries, "Rejoice then, O heaven . . . ! But woe to you, O earth and sea, for the devil has come down to you in great wrath, because he knows that his time is short!" (12:12). Satan doesn't know the truth, for the truth is Jesus. He will not commune with truth. But he knows his time is short, and now he is sentenced to watch the victory of Jesus unwrapped in all space and time, even through us, especially through us.

Jesus always wins. He knows that now.

I used to wonder, "Then why does Satan still fight? What's his plan?" Satan has no plan (like God does), because he has no meaning at heart. Oh, he has *plans,* and he has *schemes,* and he has *wiles,* but they all serve and feed his childish rage. So he rages in complete and "hole-hearted" childish, evil fury. And if he could, right now, he would destroy us all on the spot. But he can't, for he has been disarmed.

Paul wrote in Colossians that when Christ died on the cross, He disarmed the principalities and powers (2:15). They cannot accuse anyone before God, so they have no grounds for destruction. Satan can only operate within the bounds of God's redemptive purposes in Jesus Christ our Lord. Yet verse 17 says he still makes war. How does he?

In Revelation 12:14, the dragon continues to pursue the woman, the people of God. The woman is given the two wings of the great eagle, but the serpent pours a river of water from his mouth after the woman. *What* comes out of the serpent's mouth?

Lies,

slander,

accusations,

propaganda.

We live in a *river* of lies. The river threatens to sweep the woman and the Church away, but the earth opens its mouth and swallows the river. Have you ever been weighed down by all the lies? Wondering if God even exists, and if God even cares about you? Then you go for a walk in he woods or stand on the top of a fourteen-thousand-foot peak. And the wounded earth itself begins to swallow the river. Creation, even subjected to futility, proclaims the glory of God.

You see, the dragon can no longer accuse you in the heavens, so he will accuse you on earth, to divide the people of God and make you cower in fear: *You are so wicked and sinful, God couldn't possibly love you. Surely He couldn't forgive that—and neither will your so-called friends. You'd better protect yourself. . . sew some fig leaves together and hide out of fear.*

Cover the anguish. Don't look into the stable, and don't go near the Hill of the Skull. Don't confess your sins. Play it safe. If the facilities aren't good enough, turn back. If it's taking a lot of effort, give up. Quit fighting.

He makes war with the river from his mouth. The river is a propaganda campaign to get us, the Church militant, to surrender to an unarmed man. Never surrender to him.

Do not give Satan any ground to feast on your fear, guilt, or shame. Confess it all to Christ and confess one to another, so your brother or sister can pronounce that you're forgiven. Then Satan is thwarted. Christ calls you to war in order to proclaim and exhibit His eternal victory in every moment of space and time. Your confession to another is His victory of grace. But He wasn't joking—it *is* a war.

It is a fight. Jesus said, "In the world you have tribulation; but be of good cheer, I have overcome the world" (John 16:33). *Good cheer? In war?* Yes.

In *Perelandra* by C. S. Lewis, Ransom the hero battles the "un-man"—Satan. And Lewis writes:

> Then an experience that perhaps no good man can ever have in our world, came over him—a torrent of perfectly unmixed and lawful hatred. . . . It is perhaps difficult to understand why this filled Ransom not with horror but with a kind of joy. The joy came from finding at last what hatred was made for. As a boy with an axe rejoices on finding a tree . . . so he rejoiced in the perfect congruity between his emotion and its object.[3]

Never hate human beings, for they are the prize to be captured with sacrificial love. But *Satan is your enemy!* He longs to drink the blood and eat the flesh of the children of Adam. He craves the terror of your children. He delights in death, genocide, rape, and torture.

He *is* evil, and I abhor him. It's a privilege to stick the knife of the Word of God in his bloodless gut.

Christian, you were born to be a warrior, and this *is* your war. At last you know who your enemy truly is, so slay the dragon in the joy of the Lord, and *do not fear!* In Christ you have already won.

Watch out for arrogance and the lust for power—those things are of the dragon. Christ has conquered, and this is the joy: *He is in you. His victory is in you. Heaven is upon you.*

When the seventy disciples rejoiced that demons were subject to them in Christ's name, Jesus said, "I saw Satan fall like lightning from heaven. Behold, I have given you authority . . . over all the power of the enemy. . . .Nevertheless, do not rejoice in this, that the spirits are subject to you; but rejoice that your names are written in heaven" (Luke 10:18–20).

In Revelation 12:14, the woman is given the two wings of the great eagle. At one point while I was studying this passage I prayed, "God, who is this great eagle?" The very next morning I got a call from someone in our congregation. "Peter, you wouldn't believe what I saw last week in church!" she said. "During worship I looked out the windows and suddenly I saw this *immense eagle!* Its wings were stretched out over the mountains, and it was looking at us screeching. At first I thought it was angry screeching, but it was His intense holiness. It was the Lord. Its beak was open, and I heard it shriek these words: 'Church of the living God, I give you all power and dominion to accomplish my will on earth as it is in heaven. Take hold of what I give you. Let Christ be your banner and song.' Then it quoted the Song of Solomon: 'His banner over you is love.'"

In Exodus, God tells the Israelites that he bore them up on eagles' wings (19:4). *We are given* those eagles' wings—authority. The loud voice in heaven cried, "They have conquered him by the blood of the Lamb and the word of their testimony, for they loved not their lives even unto death. Rejoice then, O heaven . . . !" We conquer when we claim and believe the blood of the Lamb in our own lives and share it with others . . . even, and especially, unto death. That blood is . . .

> grace,
>> mercy,
>>> the love of God to us.

To us it's sweet, but to the dragon it's the knife twisted in his bloodless gut . . . poison. It's the blood of the Lamb on the throne, declaring that the dragon has *no* grounds for destruction, and he himself is defeated. His time is short. At the cross, the dragon tried to ingest the body and blood of the second Adam, the uttermost Adam, Jesus. It destroyed Satan. Take our Lord—body and blood—and you become His body and blood. And Jesus, the Word of the testimony, is in you. Your testimony is a knife in the dragon's gut and communion wine is fire.

We overcome by the blood of the Lamb and the word of our testimony, living not our lives even unto death. To die is to life forever. Satan's old weapon (death) is now your moment of greatest victory. What seem to be Satan's greatest victories are his greatest defeats. In defeating Satan, Jesus exhibits His conquest of sacrificial love.

If you haven't surrendered to Christ, you're living in darkness and lies. Satan is the father of lies. You yourself have no power over him, but are subject to bondage by him. Surrender to the Way, the Truth, and the Life: call on Jesus. Confess your sins, believe Christ's grace, and claim Him as your Lord. Ingest His body and blood (communion). You become His body and bleed His blood. The body and blood of the Dragon-Slayer.

TWENTY-TWO

POLITICS AND RELIGION: DOUBLE-TROUBLE

(Revelation 13)

REVELATION 13:1–10: *And he stood on the sand of the sea.*

And I saw a beast rising out of the sea, with ten horns and seven heads, with ten diadems upon its horns and a blasphemous name upon its heads. And the beast that I saw was like a leopard, its feet were like a bear's, and its mouth was like a lion's mouth. And to it the dragon gave his power and his throne and great authority. One of its heads seemed to have a mortal wound, but its mortal wound was healed, and the whole earth followed the beast with wonder. Men worshiped the dragon, for he had given his authority to the beast, and they worshiped the beast, saying, "Who is like the beast, and who can fight against it?"

And the beast was given a mouth uttering haughty and blasphemous words, and it was allowed to exercise authority for forty-two months; it opened its mouth to utter blasphemies against God, blaspheming his name and his dwelling, that is, those who dwell in heaven.

IN REVELATION 17 an angel appears to tell John, "The waters that you saw . . . are peoples and multitudes and nations and tongues" (v. 15). He also tells John that the ten horns are ten kings that have not yet received royal power (v.12), and that the seven heads are seven mountains upon which the harlot of Babylon sits (v. 9). Remember: Rome is the "city on seven hills."

The angel also tells John that the seven heads are seven kings, five of whom have already fallen, one is, and the other yet to come (v. 10). This means the beast is alive and kicking at the time of the Revelation.

The angel also reveals that "the beast that was and is not" is actually an eighth head, yet it shall ascend out of the bottomless pit. It seems this beast won't die and stay dead. It can't be killed by normal means.

At the time of the Revelation, the Roman emperor Nero, the fifth emperor of the empire, had recently died of a self-inflicted head wound. A myth circulated among the empire that he would be back. Nero's death in A.D. 68 resulted in mass confusion, civil unrest, and three suitors for the throne. It appeared the empire was doomed . . . until it almost miraculously revived in A.D. 69 through Emperor Vespasian. The world was in awe at Rome's resilience. In wonder they exclaimed, "Who can fight against it?" (see Revelation 13:4).

People often argue about the exact identity of the heads and the horns, but if you study Scripture, obviously this beast *at least* refers to governments such as Babylon, Persia, and Greece . . . the lion, the bear, and the leopard . . . that rise out of the sea in Daniel 7. A fourth beast in Daniel 7 has ten horns . . . which appears to be Rome. At the end of chapter 7 these four beasts are defeated by one like the "son of man" coming on the clouds, the Ancient of Days (v. 13). Yet the saints will suffer for a time, times, and half a time (v. 25)—forty-two months.

The four beasts also take the form of a large statue in Nebuchadnezzar's dream in Daniel 2. Babylon is the head, and it seems that Persia is the chest, Greece is the loins, and Rome is the legs and ten toes. In the dream a rock "cut out by no human hand" (v. 34) crashes into the toes of the statue. The statue crumbles, and the rock grows into a great mountain, eventually filling the entire world—an *eternal kingdom.* We know who that rock is—the Ancient of Days, the son of man, our Lord Jesus.

It would seem that the beast is *at least* the spirit or energy behind governments that war upon the people of God and blasphemously exalt themselves above God and His Christ. Such governments in the past were those that persecuted Israel; at the time of the Revelation, it was Rome persecuting the Church. At this time of John's vision, there were ten kings and a head still to come. Behind them all is the seven-headed dragon.

Paul reminded us that we "are not contending against flesh and blood, but against the principalities, against the powers, against the world rulers of this present darkness, against the spiritual hosts of wickedness in the heavenly places" (Ephesians 6:12). John tells us that we battle against the beast from the sea.

In 1950 the great Dutch theologian Hendrik Berkhof wrote a seminal book entitled *Christ and the Powers,* in which he argued that Paul saw the principalities and powers as structures of earthly, human existence, "social facts," "ideologies," and "nations."[1] These principalities and powers were created by God, but like humanity, had fallen.

Clearly, evil is organized. It works through governments, institutions, and peoples, what John calls "the world," as opposed to "the earth," which swallows the lies of the dragon. "We are of God, [but] the whole world is in the power of the evil one" (1 John 5:19). The *whole world.* Yet Revelation 1:5 says Jesus is "the ruler of kings on earth." Everything the beast does is allowed or granted to him. The beast is allowed to blaspheme the name of God and His dwelling—those who dwell in heaven, *us,* the Church.

Rome was the beast that blasphemed the seven churches in Asia Minor. Rome was the beast that crucified Jesus. A Roman soldier thrust a spear in His side. The whole world was amazed at the power of Rome. Studying history, *I've* been amazed at the power of Rome! How on earth did they rule such a vast empire? Answer: According to John, by the beast and the dragon.

What about today? Where's the seven-headed beast now? Obviously we still battle against the world rulers of this present darkness. John wrote, "Children, it is the last hour; and as you have heard that antichrist is coming, so now many antichrists have come" (1 John 2:18). Well, where *is* he now?

In his book *Marx and Satan,*[2] Richard Wurmbrand makes some fascinating connections between satanism and people such as Joseph Stalin, Friedrich Engles, and Karl Marx. Historians will argue Marx's involvement with satanism, but it's hard to argue with the hundreds of millions of dead strewn across the twentieth century. Marx was *not* an atheist. He was a God-hater.

Hitler was a God-hater, a mass murderer of the Jews and a violent persecutor of the Church—the Israel of God. It's well-known that Hitler was involved in the occult.

In 1973 historian and occultist Trevor Ravenscroft wrote a book entitled *The Spear of Destiny.* This spear purportedly was the lance the Roman soldier stuck in Christ's side as He hung dead on the cross. This spear has an amazing history, and legend had it that whoever possessed the spear could conquer the world. In 1938 Hitler annexed Austria and obtained all the relics in the Hoffburg Museum, including the spear. In 1944 he placed it in an underground vault.

On April 30, 1945, at 2:10 P.M., American forces took possession of the vault, including the spear. Eighty minutes later Hitler killed himself in a bunker in Berlin. (Suicide, like Nero.)

Hitler once spoke of the day he first saw the spear:

> I stood there quietly gazing upon it for several minutes quite oblivious to the scene around me. It seemed to carry some hidden inner meaning which evaded me. . . . I felt as though I myself had held it before in some earlier century of history. That I myself had once claimed it as my talisman of power and held the destiny of the world in my hands.[3]

What a freaky, weird story. But maybe Hitler was like a horn on that horrific beast. Historians will argue about Hitler's involvement with satanism, but it's hard to argue with six million systematically murdered and tortured corpses.

Nazism is mostly dead. Communism is greatly weakened. But the dragon and the beast are still at work. Where? Think about the more than thirty million babies (that's what we call them if we want them; fetuses if we don't want them) aborted in our nation since *Roe v. Wade.* If you've been party to that, remember Jesus is always there to forgive and He makes all things new.

Maybe abortion is too subtle. In the Sudan, Muslims have crucified Christian fathers, raped and forced circumcision on Christian mothers, then sold their children into slavery. Thousands upon thousands . . . and it's barely reported in the Western press. This past week, a friend came to my office to talk to me about the Sudan, to make sure I knew what was happening. We asked ourselves, "What can we do about it?"

The U.S. military could obliterate the Sudan. But we don't. My friend and I discussed the confusing politics and the role of government. We wondered, "How can we conquer? What can we do?" And I thought of an answer . . . but I was afraid to say it.

How do we conquer the beast?

REVELATION 13:7-10: *[The beast] was allowed to make war on the saints and to conquer them. And authority was given it over every tribe and people and tongue and nation, and all who dwell on earth will worship it, every one whose name has not been written before the foundation of the world in the book of life of the Lamb that was slain. If anyone has an ear, let him hear:*
> *If any one is to be taken captive,*
> *to captivity he goes;*
> *if any one slays with the sword,*
> *with the sword must he be slain.*
> *Here is a call for the endurance and faith of the saints.*

"If any one is to be taken captive, to captivity he goes" (Jeremiah 15:2). That's destiny.

"All who take the sword will perish by the sword" (Matthew 26:52). That's Jesus.

Then there's a call for "endurance and faith." Beware of what this beast can do to you. Beware when fighting the dragon lest you become the dragon.

REVELATION 13:11: *Then I saw another beast which rose out of the earth; it had two horns like a lamb and it spoke like a dragon.*

This second beast comes from the earth or land, a word often used to refer to Israel. In Genesis 1:1 God forms the land from the chaotic sea. The dragon is emulating the One on the throne. The first beast fakes death and resurrection; the dragon and the two beasts in chapter 13 form a mock trinity. *Antichrist* doesn't simply mean "opposite Christ," but "imitation Christ"—"mock Christ."

This beast from the land looks like a sacrificial lamb but it talks like a dragon.

REVELATION 13:12–18: *It exercises all the authority of the first beast in its presence, and makes the earth and its inhabitants worship the first beast, whose mortal wound was healed. It works great signs, even making fire come down from heaven to earth in the sight of men; and by the signs which it is allowed to work in the presence of the beast, it deceives those who dwell on earth, bidding them make an image for the beast which was wounded by the sword and yet lived; and it was allowed to give breath to the image of the beast so that the image of the beast should even speak, and to cause those who would not worship the image of the beast to be slain. Also it causes all, both small and great, both rich and poor, both free and slave, to be marked on the right hand or the forehead, so that no one can buy or sell unless he has the mark, that is, the name of the beast or the number of its name. This calls for wisdom: let him who has understanding reckon the number of the beast, for it is a human number, its number is six hundred and sixty-six.*

A "HUMAN NUMBER" would imply that the other numbers in Revelation—such as forty-two, seven, and three and a half are *not* merely human. But *this* number we are invited to calculate. It was common in that day to do so. On a wall in Pompeii you can find this graffiti: "I love her whose number is 545." In that day every letter in the alphabet was assigned a numeric value and then added together to get the number of the name.

The number of the beast is 666, but some ancient manuscripts record 616. Emperor Nero's name is spelled two ways: in Hebrew, one way adds up to 666; the other way adds up to 616.

Emperor Nero captured Christians and then rolled them in pitch, tied them to poles, and set them on fire as human torches in the coliseum at night. Then he drank and watched as other Christians, sown into animal skins, were torn apart by wild dogs. After Nero killed himself with a fatal wound to the head, the empire later revived and under Emperor Domitian continued the persecution of Christians, only much worse. Persecutions were inflicted on those who wouldn't bow down to worship before statues or images of Caesar.

The Jews were officially exempt from this decree, but they would often betray Christians, handing them over to the Roman *Concilia,* who enforced the cult of the emperor. This practice was especially strong in Asia Minor. Those who wouldn't worship the emperor were often excluded from buying and selling, and often faced death. However, their names were written in a book. They were sealed and marked by God for resurrection, just as the others who bowed down to Caesar were marked with the beast for destruction.

Now, if you are worried about my interpretation, let me say, I don't know the future. I don't *know* what will happen. Prophecies can have many fulfillments. So if someone comes up to you one day and asks, "Hey, dude, can I tattoo the number 666 on your hand or forehead?" just *walk away.* Just say no! I really hope the mark is that obvious, but I'm afraid the dragon is probably more subtle than that.

I believe the first beast is evil politics throughout history, and the second beast is evil religion. Don't compromise; don't receive their mark. The 666 really is a human number. It is *six,* the number of fallen, incomplete humanity, three times over.

So how do we know this beast? It's marked with fallen humanity. It looks like religion; it looks like a lamb . . . but listen closely. Beast talk is all about self-improvement, psychology, sociology, and business. It's all about human striving: shame, fear, power, and pride. Human politics and human religion together are *lethal.*

In Germany they worshiped Hitler. And communism is more than politics; it's a religion. Historically, one of the more popular candidates for beast and antichrist was the visible Church and the pope. In the Middle Ages, the pope was politics and religion, seated in Rome of the seven hills. Many popes were entirely immoral and corrupt, enforcing religion with power. During the Inquisition, thousands were systematically tortured and burned at the stake. And the popes ordered the Crusades against the Muslims in Palestine and even in the Sudan.

Beware when fighting the dragon lest you become the dragon. Well . . . what about the Muslims in the Sudan and Afghanistan today? How *do* we conquer the beast?

In Revelation 13:7 the beast is allowed to make war on the saints and conquer them. It reminds me of something else John recorded. When our Lord Jesus was drenched in blood, crowned with thorns, and standing before the Roman governor Pilate, He said, "You would have no power over me if it were not given to you from above" (John 19:11). He had already said, "My kingdom is not of this world. If it were, my servants would fight" (John 18:36).

This so unnerved Pilate that he sought to release Jesus. He said to the mob, "Behold, your king."

But the chief priests who presided over the sacrificial lambs each day
in the temple,
the chief priests of the land of Israel,
who had so ardently fought against the Roman beast,
cried out before the mob,
"We have no king but Caesar!"
Caesar—the beast from the sea.

Beware when fighting the dragon lest you become the dragon.

And so the religious leaders of Israel delivered Jesus to the Roman beast, just as the synagogues in Asia delivered Christians to the Roman *Concilia*. Satan, who had so earnestly desired this, delighted as the beast strung up Christ on that cross, and it was a Roman soldier who thrust a spear in His side.

REVELATION 14:1: *Then I looked, and lo, on Mount Zion stood the Lamb, and with him a hundred and forty-four thousand who had his name and his Father's name written on their foreheads.*

Jesus conquered by being conquered. He conquered with sacrificial love. We conquer with the blood of the lamb and the word of our testimony, loving not our lives even unto death.

So my friend and I sat in my office discussing the persecution in the Sudan.

Having just read Revelation 13 and wondering how we could conquer, I finally said something like this:

> Well, I guess maybe we could pray that God (and it would have to be *God* calling people to this) would raise up two or three thousand white, upper-middle-class American folks who would leave here and to the Sudan . . . sneak across the border . . . that is, leave Laodicea and just go sit with their brothers and sisters in Smyrna . . . leave America and just go sit with their brothers and sisters in the Sudan. And if the Arabs came down on them in a fury and crucified two or three thousand Americans in the desert, things would change! The U.S. military would be put on alert. I bet the slave trade would stop. But even more powerful than that, the gospel would be proclaimed. And satanic lies placed in the hearts of Muslims dating back to the Crusades—when the Church became the beast—those lies might be broken. The rider on the white horse would come and we would conquer not just governments but human hearts.

I know, it's just a wild thought, but that is how our God "disarmed the principalities and powers and made a public example of them, triumphing over them in [Christ]" (Colossians 2:15).

I've come to believe that John 12:31 is the key to understanding the Revelation: *"Now* is the judgment of this world; *now* shall the ruler of this world be cast out; and I when I am lifted up from the land will draw all men to myself."* He was speaking of His crucifixion. The word *draw* is probably best translated "romance," as in *I will romance all men to myself.* You romance a lover because that's the only way you can get her heart to surrender in the freedom of love. There is no greater power.

The beast and the dragon thought they held Christ to that cross with the power of iron nails, but they were only the *means* purposed before the foundation of the world. Nails, beast, and dragon cannot pin the Son of God to wood because they are not *powerful* enough. Only His own relentless love could ever do a thing like that.

One day very soon, when this world of illusions and lies is finally burned away, we will see beyond a shadow of a doubt that nothing is more real or powerful than love. "God *is* love," said John (1 John 4:8).

I'm not suggesting that politics and organized religion have no place, but that they have no power . . . no *real* power . . . no power to conquer the world.

When the dragon inspired the beast from the land and the beast from the sea, when the high priest in the land delivered Jesus to the Roman governor, when God allowed the two beasts to conquer Christ by nailing Him to the cross (and Christ humbled Himself even unto death) . . . it was precisely then that our Lord conquered the world.

It was also then that a Roman soldier stood in front of the cross and looked at the glory of God shining in the face of Christ. I like to think that *he* was the one holding that spear of destiny and that he was the first to say, "Surely this was the Son of God."

At that moment an incredible rock "cut out by no human hand" crashed into the Roman Empire, and it began to fall! And the kingdoms of this world began to crumble. And that rock in Nebuchadnezzar's dream began to grow into a great mountain. It is growing still, here and now. It is an *eternal kingdom* that cannot be stopped!

Tragically, Hitler did not really know it *was* a spear of destiny. But all destinies are God's destiny. This was the plan for the fullness of time, to unite all things in Christ, and through Him to reconcile all things to Himself, making peace by the blood of His cross.

So we conquer by *being* conquered with and in love. As that Roman soldier held the lance, he was conquered by Jesus as Jesus conquered the world. The beast's supreme weapon is killing. Our supreme weapon is dying . . . with Christ.

Twenty-Three

The Revelation on TV

(Revelation 14:1–13)

ONE TUESDAY MORNING in September as I was getting dressed, I began
to wonder about the sermon I had preached that Sunday. I had just taught on
Revelation 13, the beast, and its connections to totalitarian governments and
religion. We had even mentioned Afghanistan and Islam. I had begun to
wonder if all that was just too far away and unreal. I decided: *This* week I'll
just bring it home . . . talk about how we're to die to ourselves not just in
places like Rome and Afghanistan and the Sudan, but in our marriages . . . and
our budgets . . . and what videos we do and don't bring home from
Blockbuster. Because every time we're obedient in faith to Jesus, we die to sin
and we die to this world. The Revelation can seem so unreal, apocalyptic,
irrelevant. I wanted to bring it home.

Then a call from my sister interrupted my thoughts. "Peter and Susan,"
she said, "turn on your TV right now."

When I turned it on, I saw one of the World Trade Center towers
billowing with smoke, a huge, gaping wound in its side. Then another
airplane; then another tower on fire; then a report that one of the towers had
fallen. Then, all at once, before my eyes on live TV, I saw the other tower
crumble all the way to the ground. Then the picture I will never forget:

There seated on the water was Lady Liberty, holding her torch, facing the
east, as if beckoning, "Give me your tired, your poor, your huddled masses
longing to breathe free"—and behind her the great city, the United Nations,
Wall Street . . . billowing with fire and smoke, the World Trade Center fallen
to the ground.

At that point the Revelation seemed so relevant it took my breath away.
God was telling His story—telling *history.*

175

REVELATION 14:1–5: *Then I looked, and lo, on Mount Zion stood the Lamb, and with him a hundred and forty-four thousand who had his name and his Father's name written on their foreheads. And I heard a voice from heaven like the sound of many waters and like the sound of loud thunder; the voice I heard was like the sound of harpers playing on their harps, and they sing a new song before the throne and before the four living creatures and before the elders. No one could learn that song except the hundred and forty-four thousand who had been redeemed from the earth. It is these who have not defiled themselves with women, for they are chaste; it is these who follow the Lamb wherever he goes; these have been redeemed from mankind as first fruits for God and the Lamb, and in their mouth no lie was found, for they are spotless.*

They conquer *by being conquered in love.*

They conquer the ancient dragon while being conquered by his beast.

"They conquer by the blood of the lamb and the word of their testimony, loving not their lives even unto death" (Revelation 12:11).

They conquer by following the Lamb wherever He goes . . . He goes to a cross.

They conquer, and they are *us*. We are like "first fruits redeemed from the earth" (James 1:18). We are the Church militant: 144,000 sealed servants of God, the Israel of God, 12 tribes x 12 divisions, each soldier devoted to war, and therefore figuratively celibate like the ancient Israelites. We are to be undefiled by idolatry—in Scripture, idolatry is whoredom.

We are those in Hebrews who "have come to Mount Zion and to the city of the living God, the heavenly Jerusalem, and to innumerable angels in festal gathering, and to the assembly of the first-born who are enrolled in heaven, and to a judge who is God of all, and to the spirits of just men made perfect, and to Jesus, the mediator of a new covenant, and to the sprinkled blood that speaks more graciously than the blood of Abel" (12:22–24).

We conquer by the blood of the Lamb. We conquer with the power of the cross, the romance of God—even by dying for our very enemies.

Jesus said, "Love your enemies and pray for those who persecute you" (Matthew 5:44). But in light of 9-11, you might prefer another scripture. How about this one: "When you find the unfaithful, strike off their head till you have made a great slaughter among them." That one's from the Koran, Sura 47.

The dragon is trying to get you to convert. But Jesus is *also* trying to get you to convert. Today, Muslims are in an identity crisis, asking, "Is this what Islam leads to?" They are also asking, "What does Christianity lead to?" If we retaliate in kind, I doubt they'll ever read the Bible. Instead they'll read us, and say, "Well, it's just the same old song."

So what then should our president do? Honestly, I don't know. I suppose he should "bear the sword" as a "servant of God." That's the role of government in Romans 13:4. Presidents can do that, a bit. But a guy named George who loves Jesus . . . he can do *so much more*. He can go on national TV and weep for New Yorkers, children in Afghanistan, and soldiers in Iraq. He can weep like Jesus wept over the city of Jerusalem (before He let her kill Him). He can sing a different song.

I love our government. I just can't kid myself that it can preach the gospel with guns, as if the kingdom were a kingdom of *this world*. In Revelation 14, the 144,000 unharmed, slaughtered saints of God—the army of God—sing a different song on Mount Zion.

REVELATION 14:6–13: *Then I saw another angel flying in midheaven, with an eternal gospel to proclaim to those who dwell on earth, to every nation and tribe and tongue and people; and he said with a loud voice, "Fear God and give him glory, for the hour of his judgment has come; and worship him who made heaven and earth, the sea and the fountains of water."*

Another angel, a second, followed, saying, "Fallen, fallen is Babylon the great, she who made all nations drink the wine of her impure passion."

And another angel, a third, followed them, saying with a loud voice, "If any one worships the beast and its image, and receives a mark on his forehead or on his hand, he also shall drink the wine of God's wrath, poured unmixed into the cup of his anger, and he shall be tormented with fire and sulphur in the presence of the holy angels and in the presence of the Lamb. And the smoke of their torment goes up for ever and ever; and they have no rest, day or night, these worshipers of the beast and its image, and whoever receives the mark of its name."

Here is a call for the endurance of the saints, those who keep the commandments of God and the faith of Jesus.

And I heard a voice from heaven saying, "Write this: Blessed are the dead who die in the Lord henceforth."

"HAPPY," "BLESSED" . . . they are the conquering, conquered saints singing with Jesus on Mount Zion. This isn't just pie in the sky by and by; heaven invades *now* in Christ by faith. We have come to Mount Zion. These are suffering saints dying with Christ even now. So how can they sing like this when the world lies in ruin?

In 14:8 an angel flies through declaring, "Fallen, fallen is Babylon the great. She made all nations drink the wine of her impure passion." Babylon's actual fall isn't described until chapter 18, but maybe she's already fallen in the hearts of these singing saints, so she no longer has any more power over them.

Strangely, we obsess over the beast and the antichrist, yet we hardly ever mention the great harlot. But she takes up more space in the book. She's another one of the principalities and powers, like the beast. In chapter 17 we learn that she sits on the beast, or political power. All the kings of the earth have fornicated with her, and all the peoples of the world are drunk with the wine of that fornication (17:2).

The angel tells John that the whore is the great city that has dominion over the kings of the earth. It is clear that she is the economy and culture of Rome, but she is also Babylon and Egypt and Sodom. She is the global economy that thrives under an empire due to free trade. The kings of the earth *hate* her because of her power over them, but they're in bed with her because they want her pleasures.

Economy isn't necessarily corrupt. There is another economy in the Revelation as well, that of the New Jerusalem—the people of God, the Bride of Christ.

Husbands are to give their lives (their seed) to their brides in order to bear fruit (life). But Satan tempts them to give their seed (their life) to harlots in order to bear death. In Revelation the kings of the earth are playing the harlot rather than loving the Bride.

Men lust after harlots, sleep with them, and then hate them and hate themselves.

Men lust after idols, worship them, and then destroy them and destroy themselves.

Men turn the economy into an idol, go to bed with it, become enslaved to it, and then they hate it and it kills them. The beast and the kings fornicate with the whore, and then in Revelation 17:16 they hate the whore, desolate her, and burn her with fire. Satan's kingdom devours itself.

So the whore of Babylon appears to be an idolatrous world economy. In Revelation she's pictured as the goddess Roma or Cybelle, seated on the waters and the seven hills. Not the Great Mother goddess, but the "mother of harlots and of earth's abominations" (17:5), and the merchants (traders) of the earth have grown rich with the wealth of her wantonness.

If she were around today, where would she be?

I bet she'd try to be seated in the world's richest economy and most influential city. I bet the nations would be united around her, addicted to her intoxications—dependent on her while resenting her. I bet she'd sell her goods with blasphemies, promising cars could save your soul and blue jeans could give you an identity. I bet she'd be the leading producer and distributor of pornography worldwide. I bet she'd consume the vast majority of the world's resources, growing rich and fat while the world starves.

I bet she'd be defended by people who preach free trade (which is good) but then abuse their freedom as license for evil. And even though freedom would be the song, it would be idolatrous freedom, placed above God, who is love. So human life would no longer be sacred, and it wouldn't surprise me if much of her wealth had been built on the backs of slaves (Revelation 18:13).

Sometimes I think we Americans are pretty stupid to worry about the beast. The odds, even now, of your being killed in a terrorist attack are remarkably slim. But maybe we ought to be a bit on guard against the harlot and what she's up to. She's seductive, and the people of God are seduced by her (18:4).

If I had been a Palestinian Arab Christian kid (yes, there are many of them; isn't it ironic?) living in the West Bank that September Tuesday and reading the Revelation, I think I'd see Osama bin Laden as the beast in bed with the harlot, dependent on her for his $300 million, yet hating her.

Then I would notice that the beast flew his planes right into the World Trade Center next to Wall Street and the United Nations. I'd watch them fall and burn behind a statue of a woman holding a torch, a gift to America from France, reminiscent of the Goddess of Reason from the French Revolution and Republic, and also patterned after the Mother Goddess by its sculptor Augustus Bartholdi (the seven horns on her crown are the seven seas, and the torch symbolizes enlightenment).

I must confess that as a poor, oppressed, Palestinian kid, I'd be tempted to *dance*, not because American children, mothers, and fathers lay dying—they would be abstractions to me at that point—but because the whore had fallen. I'd be tempted to dance, the way we might have been tempted to dance at the end of a war with Iraq or Afghanistan, not because children, moms, and dads were burning in the desert—at that point they would be abstractions to us—but because the beast had been mortally wounded.

Pay attention here: I *did not* say that the Statue of Liberty is the whore of Babylon. Idols have power only if you idolize them. But understand this: Our statue of liberty is not a woman holding a torch of enlightenment beckoning "give me your tired, your poor, your huddled masses." That is an idol. No government, no religious system, no economy can give you liberty. *Our* statue of liberty is the *cross*. And the Spirit cries, "Come to me all you who are weary and heavy laden and I will give you rest" (Matthew 11:28).

How can the saints sing
    when the world is in ruins?
        They're free from this world
           and belong to another.
That's liberty, and only God can give it to you.

I also *did not say* that the World Trade Center or Wall Street or the people *in* the Towers were the whore of Babylon. *Every one* of them is a priceless treasure for whom our Lord died on a cross. Nor did I say that the U.S. is the whore of Babylon. But I *will* say this: She *is* seduced by her and infected with her demons (Revelation 18:2).

An expert on terrorism commented that these attacks struck the heart of America—her military and her economy. If our *military* is our heart, say hello to the beast! And if our *economy* is our heart, we have the heart of a harlot. And if we turn our country into a whore, we will *hate* her. Don't pledge allegiance to the flag before you pledge allegiance to the cross! Love America as never before. And what is America? To God, she's dearly beloved people. And what is her heart? God wants to give her a new heart. And how will He give her that heart? Not through government, not through some religious program, not through the economy, but through *you*—the saints—singing the new song on Mount Zion. No one else in heaven and on earth can sing it but you.

So romance the Bride: Sing the song to her and tell her who she is. She is hidden in the people, the New Jerusalem coming down. But you cannot romance the Bride if you're in bed with the harlot.

At the fall of Babylon in chapter 18, a voice cries from heaven, "Come out of her, my people" (v. 4). Do you get the picture? In Scripture when a man goes into a woman, she gets pregnant. The voice is crying, "Stop giving your heart and your life to the harlot."

Give your heart to the Bride and bear the fruit of the kingdom. Stop spending your life, your heart, your passions, your treasure on consumer idolatries. Stop consuming! Stop calling yourselves "consumers" and start calling yourselves "creators." Love the Bride in America, in the Sudan, in Palestine, Israel, and Iraq.

In the middle of the rubble of the World Trade Center, the relief workers found a cross, five stories high. A cross can turn a harlot into a bride. We've all been harlots . . . yet we are the Bride in a new world.

How, then, do the saints on Mount Zion sing while the world lies in ruin? They belong to another world already, and it is invading this one. No longer intoxicated by the harlot, they begin to see the beauty of the Bride. They begin to believe the furious love of the Bridegroom. Dead to this world and alive to another, they are the ones who *change* this world.

"Consider yourself dead to sin [this world] and alive to God," writes Paul in Romans 6:11. We are constantly being given up to death. Now listen one more time to this line from the Revelation: "Blessed [happy] are the dead who die in the Lord" (Revelation 14:13).

On that Tuesday afternoon, I was racked with a million emotions but surprised by one. For in the midst of sorrow and grief, compassion and mourning, I must admit something in me felt like singing. I think I was hearing a voice from another world . . . "Come out, Peter. Come out of her."

I ached for victims; I mourned for my own investments in Babylon—my way of life. But the Revelation was so *entirely relevant*. It was so relevant it felt like this world was losing its grip on me and I was ready to go . . . *home*.

That Tuesday evening, like hundreds of thousands of people in other churches in America, we gathered together. We had communion: body broken, blood shed, slain Lamb. The Lamb and the saints gathered on the mountain, and we *sang well*.

TWENTY-FOUR

THE NOT-SO-GRIM REAPER

(Revelation 14:13–20)

THE REVELATION IS ONE HUGE SYMPHONY, and they never stop singing to the glory of the Lamb on the throne. Heaven is music!

That's interesting, because at certain times in certain places,—Afghanistan and Iran, for instance,—music is, or was, illegal. The world feels such a need right now to point out that Christianity and Islam are basically the same thing. At least on the surface, however, there is a striking difference between the two: Christians sing a lot, and many Muslims do not. In fact, many Orthodox Muslims do not sing at all, because it's forbidden. Currently, a debate continues in the Islamic community about whether or not it's a sin to sing (anything more than chanting the Koran).

Last year on my sabbatical, I did some reading in the Koran. I was amazed that it has no music—no songs, no poetry. At one point Muhammad writes that those who err follow poets. Yet the Bible is *packed* with poetry—more than most people realize, because we read it in English. And it is filled with admonitions to sing and "Rejoice always."

My son Coleman would be in big trouble in some Muslim countries because he will *not stop singing.* He sings about *everything* . . . putting on his underwear . . . walking up the stairs . . . it drives us old people nuts! He can't help it. Coleman has so much *life* in him it flows out in a song all the time.

In Revelation 14, the 144,000 are singing on Mount Zion with the Lamb. And we're singing with them right here, because we have come to Mount Zion (see Hebrews 12).

REVELATION 14:13: *And I heard a voice from heaven saying, "Write this: Blessed are the dead who die in the Lord henceforth." "Blessed indeed," says the Spirit, "that they may rest from their labors, for their deeds follow them!"*

Their "deeds" follow them. . . . I wonder if that's why a lot of people think world religions are the same—they assume that all of them are just a matter of doing good deeds on earth followed by reward in heaven. Maybe we should ask, what makes a good deed *good?*

REVELATION 14:14–15: *Then I looked, and lo, a white cloud, and seated on the cloud one like a son of man, with a golden crown on his head, and a sharp sickle in his hand. And another angel came out of the temple, calling with a loud voice to him who sat upon the cloud, "Put in your sickle, and reap, for the hour to reap has come, for the harvest of the earth is fully ripe."*

The one on the cloud must be Jesus. But then another angel comes out of the temple (we *are* the temple) and appears to boss Jesus around (Jesus is the Son of man and the Lord of the harvest, v. 14), telling Him to swing His sickle. Who could this be? I think maybe it's the Holy Spirit calling from our hearts, "Come and get it, Jesus. They're ripe."

REVELATION 14:16: *So he who sat upon the cloud swung his sickle on the earth, and the earth was reaped.*

Jesus said:

- "Henceforth you will see the Son of man coming on the clouds of heaven" (Matthew 24–30). What's He doing?—Reaping.
- "Lift your eyes; the fields are white, ripe for harvest" (John 4:35). They are ripe *right now.*
- "When the grain is ripe, at once the reaper puts in the sickle" (Mark 4:26). Ever since the cross, Jesus has been harvesting this earth, His kingdom of good deeds.

Get the picture? The saints broken and bloodied sing on Mount Zion, and suddenly there is *fruit.* Fruit happens.

The Israelites put the choir in front of the army to sing, and they conquer. Broken, humbled slaves walk through the desert, sing, and the walls of Jericho come falling down. And they possess the Promised Land.

Paul and Silas, broken and bloodied, sing in the Philippian jail. The earth shakes, walls come tumbling down, and they evangelize Europe. *That's fruit.*

Jesus, broken and bloodied, sings from a cross the first line of Psalm 22: "My God, my God, why have you forsaken me?" He dies before he can finish the song, yet in dying He gives birth to a new creation, like a seed dropped into broken, fertile soil.

In Isaiah 54:1 we read: "Sing, O barren one, who did not bear . . . ! For the children of the desolate one will be more than the children of her that is married." *Sing . . . sing* and bear fruit!

In Scripture folks *sing* in hard times, and stuff grows.

Jesus tells His disciples about a fig tree that has been barren for three years. The master wants to cut it down, but the gardener says, "No, wait . . . I'll go around the base of the tree, break up the soil, and throw some *koprion* on it ['I'll dung it,' KJV]. Maybe it will bear fruit then" (Luke 13:6–9).

The fig tree is Israel. God *loves* Israel and we are Israel. God loves us more than we can begin to comprehend. Yet it is amazing how broken ground and manure make stuff grow . . . help a seed to grow.

In Scripture, good deeds are fruit. We don't make fruit; all we do is prepare the soil and make sure it's fertile, broken, and humble in order to receive the implanted seed. "Blessed [happy] are the dead who die in the Lord . . . that they may rest from their labors" (Revelation 14:13). *Rested*—the Greek tense here (aorist middle subjunctive) indicates that it could be something that has already happened here on earth. We are to strive to enter God's rest, according to Hebrews 4, and good deeds then follow. Jesus says that the harvest grows while the farmer sleeps and "he knows not how" (Mark 4:26–27)—he works to break the soil and plant the seed, but it grows while he rests from his labor. Fruit doesn't happen by your own effort. It's something *God* does: like wheat, like grapes, like children.

There is imitation fruit, but the real deal is made by God. Imitation fruit is made by humans. Last year when I read the Koran, I was struck by how *human* it is. No stories, no songs, no poems. Just advice, law. But the Bible spans thousands of years with many different authors through whom God spoke . . . poems, stories, songs. It's one tremendous story from front to back. And when there is law, it's law to help you understand a person. Law within a story. In the

Koran, law is small and good deeds are small (Sura 47: "Allah wants some but not all of your money"). So, in the Koran, evil is so small that some people are good enough. In the Koran, because good is small and evil is small, *grace* is small. Allah is merciful for only those who deserve it. (Sura 4:108: "Allah is forgiving, merciful . . . but loves not those that deceive themselves.")

In the Bible, *everybody* deceives himself! In the Bible, *everybody* is dead in his trespasses and sins! In the Bible, *no* one is good but God alone! So in the Bible, *grace is everything.* For we are all saved by one hundred percent grace "through faith, and this not of ourselves, lest any should boast" (Ephesians 2:5).

The Koran struck me as so human—it's about human energy and human kingdoms, so it participates in human violence while motivating men with other-worldly rewards, such as big-eyed virgins feeding them fruit on couches in the Garden of Eden.

I can see the attraction there, but it teaches that *I* can do it. *I* can pay. I can *buy some* of those heavenly virgins. That is, pay for love—that's harlotry. If I act like I've earned my bride, I make her out to be a harlot. Do you think if you're good enough you'll get into heaven? In Christianity, heaven isn't just a place; it's a person. And thinking you can pay for that person is the depth of depravity.

Islam is entirely different from Christianity, but it is almost exactly the same as most run-of-the-mill American civic religion: "Just do good deeds, and God will let you in." "It's not Jesus (the person of God)." "Just be good, and you can get God's stuff." Those good deeds are imitation fruit—man-made, and worse than no fruit—products of hell.

Jesus says His kingdom is like good seed sown in a field, but the enemy has also sown tares—weeds that look like wheat (Matthew 13:24–30). Jesus says, *Don't try to remove the tares because you'll wreck the wheat. At the harvest they'll be separated.* The harvester knows; Jesus knows . . . but it's very hard for us to tell.

People want me to tell them whether or not we should go to war, if the president is right or wrong, and what exactly is the good deed to do. I usually reply, "I don't know."

A book like the Koran *does* know. It will tell you exactly what to do. The Bible, especially the New Testament, doesn't really tell you. So Christians have argued for two thousand years about whether it's a sin or a duty for a Christian to serve in the military and fight in a war. I wish we had time to discuss all the views, but in the end, maybe God doesn't want us to get all our answers from a book. Jesus said, "You search the scriptures because you think that in them you have eternal life. And it is they that bear witness to me; yet you refuse to come to me that you may have life" (John 5:39–40).

Maybe good deeds are *good* because of the song you sing in your heart when you do them. Externally it may look the same, but the Father knows love songs. To whom are you singing?

My closet is full of videos of musicals, which is strange because I *hate* musicals. But *these* musicals I love, because my kids are in them. They are from church and school, and you wouldn't understand them very well because the videos show only the parts where my kids sing, and only my kids in those parts. What I love is not the words that my kids sing out loud (they're the same words that all the others sing, and besides, they're usually off-key), it's that I know my five-year-old is singing them out of a heart that is thoroughly in love with me. They're singing *to me.* For a daddy, that's the measure of a good deed . . . a good song.

Did you know that the words to the song of the Lamb—the new song that no one else can learn—appear to be printed in Revelation 15? Perhaps it's not the words themselves that matter most but the heart with which we sing them, as children of God.

My favorite song is:

> I love you a bushel and a peck,
> A bushel and a peck and a hug around the neck.

Only one person in the world can sing it truly: the one who loves me more than any other guy in the whole world. For a bridegroom, that's the measure of a good deed—a good song. She used to sing it to me in high school; now she's my wife, and that song has borne great fruit: Jonathan, Elizabeth, Rebecca, and Coleman.

God is a Daddy, and Jesus is the Bridegroom. And they both are one farmer growing fruit . . . love, joy, peace, patience, kindness, goodness, gentleness, faithfulness, self-control. . . . This fruit cannot be grown simply by human effort. We can only prepare the broken and fertile soil in surrender to the Father and the Bridegroom.

You can practice notes and rehearse the score, but if you really want to play the song, at some point you have to surrender to it and *lose* yourself in the music. Interestingly, *Islam* means "surrender." But I suspect most Muslims attempt to surrender to the law—the score—to play the notes without hearing the song. A song can sweep you away. You can lose your *self* in a song.

Christians also have tried to surrender to the law of God by playing all the notes. But the score is so demanding it breaks them, and they have to surrender to the love of God, the grace of God, the song of God—*Jesus.* We surrender to Jesus, the person of God, and He romances us. He sings over us until His life begins to grow in us and we *sing back* to Him . . . His life in us bears fruit.

If you say, "Well, I don't feel like singing," maybe God in His mercy will come alone and break up the hard soil of your heart . . . maybe even throw some dung on it, to make it open to the seed. People tend to change their songs in difficult times.

If you still don't feel like singing, read on . . .

The wheat is harvested, that is, the bread. Now something else must be harvested. I suspect it's the same two angels that do the harvesting.

REVELATION 14:17–20: *And another angel came out of the temple in heaven, and he too had a sharp sickle. Then another angel came out from the altar, the angel who has power over fire, and he called with a loud voice to him who had the sharp sickle, "Put in your sickle, and gather the clusters of the vine of the earth, for its grapes are ripe." So the angel swung his sickle on the earth and gathered the vintage of the earth, and threw it into the great wine press of the wrath of God; and the wine press was trodden outside the city, and blood flowed from the wine press, as high as a horse's bridle, for one thousand six hundred stadia.*

ONE THOUSAND SIX HUNDRED STADIA is the length of Israel. It covers Israel . . . to the depths of the horse's bridle . . . enough blood to cover all Israel and indeed to cover the entire earth.

Most commentators say this is simply a picture of judgment on the unbelieving followers of the beast, who have been told they'll "drink the wine of the fury of the wrath of God." In Isaiah and Joel, trodding the grapes is judgment on the enemies of God. In Revelation 14 it says they are the grapes of wrath.

So commentators say the grain harvest (bread) is good works that God does. Therefore, the *grape* harvest (wine) is Satan's evil works. Maybe so, but I don't think so. I don't think a harvest of evil makes sense. The farmer burns the stalks, the chaff, and the tares, but not the grain, because that's the harvest. The vinedresser prunes and burns the branches that won't bear fruit, but not the *grapes*, because they are the harvest.

Jesus tells us that He is the vine and we are the branches. When we abide in Him, we bear much fruit—that would be grapes.

The *angelos* who has the power of fire (Pentecost?) comes from the altar in the temple (which is us) and again calls to the first *angelos* with the sickle. This *angelos* comes from the temple in heaven down to earth. He harvests the grapes and throws them into the winepress of the wrath of God. Winepress and grapes make wine. Yet this wine flows out and turns into blood. Blood that is wine, wine that is blood . . . that sounds familiar.

The winepress is trodden "outside the city" where the sin offerings are made. Hebrews 13:13–16 points out that Jesus suffered *outside* the gate, *outside* the camp, *outside* the city of Jerusalem. That's where the Lamb on the throne of God was slain. And there is a river of blood that flows from that place, enough to cover all Israel and indeed the entire world.

John tells us that Jesus is "the atoning sacrifice for our sins, and not only for ours, but also for the sins of the whole world" (1 John 2:2). He *satisfies* God's wrath. I know we're skirting across incredible, theological mysteries that are far beyond us, but I believe the winepress of the fury of the wrath of God is a cross outside the walls of Jerusalem on which God in Christ bore the sins of the world, suffering His own wrath on our behalf. Now every person ever born must somehow go to that cross, visit the winepress, and see that their sins crucified the King of Glory.

If they hate God and are of the beast and the dragon they will drink the "wine of the fury of the wrath of God"—*blood*. If they *love* God they drink the "wine of the kingdom"—the forgiveness of sins.

I know from experience—I've seen this—that communion wine burns the dragon like fire. But to the children of God, it is the sweet gift of grace, the wine of the kingdom.

We were enemies of God, so our lives were infected with sin. But *confessed sin* is the fruit of abiding in Christ. Unless you abide in Christ, you don't even *see* your sins, let alone confess them or surrender your life.

In repentance and confession, broken and humbled,

> He takes our sin to His cross,
> > dies in our place,
> > > and our confessed sins are crushed
> > > > in the winepress of the fury of the wrath of God.
> > > > Crucified with Christ.

His blood is our wine. It flows from His cross, and we drink it—His life blood. Seed enters the broken, humbled soil of our hearts, life begins to grow, and we begin to sing. We join the great symphony.

My children sing love songs to me because I have loved them. My bride sings love songs to me because I have loved her. Why do you sing to Jesus? If you don't feel like singing, go to the cross and see the love of God in Christ

Jesus for you and for a world. The Lamb bears so much sin for us that war horses stop in a river of His blood.

So if you don't feel like singing, spend some time at His cross. Take His body broken and blood shed. Bride of Christ, the harvest of the earth is bread and wine, body and blood of Jesus our Lord. He is good deeds born of you, the Church. His body in Palestine two thousand years ago and His body the Church throughout the ages.

In Islam, men earn virgins in heaven. In Christianity Jesus wins you, His Bride, with sacrificial love. "By grace you have been saved through faith; . . . for good works [deeds], which God prepared beforehand, that we should walk in them" (Ephesians 2:8-10). We walk with Christ.

Islam is dependent on people and our efforts. Mohammed takes us very seriously. He's *very serious* and *very grave* and *very dead* . . . and he never sings.

Christianity is dependent on God and His furious grace. So Christians must take God *extremely seriously,* so seriously that they sing all the time.

Have you noticed? The Reaper is not grim. He is the life of the party . . . forever.

TWENTY-FIVE

THE GOSPEL OF WRATH

(Revelation 15)

I NEVER REALLY UNDERSTOOD WRATH until I had kids. It's not because they were so *bad,* but because I loved them so much.

I remember sitting on a railroad tie in a park when my daughter Elizabeth was about two, watching my priceless, precious little girl going up and down the slide, so proud of herself. Another two-year-old came along with her mother. As this toddler went up and down the slide, her mother kept saying, "Oh, that's wonderful! You're doing great!" She never even noticed Elizabeth.

Finally, Elizabeth walked to the top of the slide, sat down, and started yelling at the lady, "See me? See me? I do it! I do it! See me?" And the lady did not even turn her head. A fantasy flashed through my mind: me picking up a board and smacking that woman upside her head. It shocked me! *Wrath.* But that's part of a father's heart.

Dispensing wrath, however, is insanely difficult—how could there ever be enough of it to set things straight? If the U.S. killed Osama bin Laden to avenge the deaths at the Twin Towers and the Pentagon, that's a drop of blood for an ocean of blood. Short of blood, we make *other* people pay. The terrorists exercised indiscriminate wrath, so Americans are tempted to exercise indiscriminate wrath in return—"Make 'em all pay!" Either we underpay or we overpay. And holding onto wrath is an incredible burden. People who cling to it become angry and bitter, enslaved by their own lack of forgiveness.

Perhaps you're thinking, "That's why we must entrust wrath to God— 'Vengeance is mine,' says the Lord." But let's be honest. We have trouble entrusting our *finances* to God, let alone our *wrath.* We worry that God will underpay—the terrorist might live a comfortable life and die an easy death. Or worse, we worry that God might overpay. As a young believer, I think my

190

deepest struggle was the doctrine that God would send the reprobate to hell to be tortured with wrath forever and *ever* without end! That's a lot of wrath—even for someone that's been really naughty.

A third reason we have a hard time trusting God's wrath is because it seems so indiscriminate and random. Hurricanes, terrorist attacks, disease.

It's hard to entrust wrath to God, for we worry that He'll either dispense too little or too much or do it in the wrong place . . . indiscriminately. Even worse, deep inside we fear this the most: He might dispense wrath to absolute *perfection*.

As I sat on the timber in the park fantasizing about hitting this woman in the head with a board because she ignored my priceless little princess, I had this thought . . . I believe it came from my Father in heaven . . . "Peter, now you know just a little how I feel for all my children."

I thought, *Oh, God! How many children have I ignored?* In the Sudan . . . in Ethiopia . . . in Mexico, not sitting on slides but in garbage heaps saying, "Look at me! I'm hungry." *What if He feels over them the way I feel over my daughter? What if He thinks the lady in the park is one of His children, and He reads my thoughts?* I suppose He feels that way over Afghan children, over terrorist children, maybe even over *terrorists*. (When Elizabeth was two, sometimes she *acted* like a terrorist . . . and I still loved her.)

What if He felt about everyone on the planet the way I felt about Elizabeth sitting on that slide that day?—*so much wrath . . . so much blood . . . all* of us so guilty we merit hell.

What does a Daddy do when His own children murder each other? Rape each other? Destroy each other?

What does a Father do with His wrath?—I guess just kill them all . . . flood them all . . . drown them all. In fact, He tried that once. The problem was, Noah got away. Of course he was meant to get away, but that's a huge mystery in the Old Testament: Why are we still here? It's not a mystery in the Koran, because some people are *good*. People say, "Don't bash the Koran. There's violence in the Old Testament too." Well, there *sure is*. The mystery is why there is not *more*. At the very beginning, it's as if God Himself issues a *fatwa* against *all humanity*. He says, "If you eat the fruit of the tree, you will die." We ate, so we're either dead or dying (walking dead). Paul writes, "The wrath of God *is* [not *will be*] being revealed" (Romans 1:18 NIV).

What a nightmare. We long for justice, yet the justice we long for is our own death.

The wrath of God—what a nightmare. For years I was terrified of Revelation 15–16, where the wrath of God is poured out. So I didn't read it . . . denial of a nightmare.

ETERNITY NOW

In Revelation chapter 14, John has just watched Jesus trample the grapes of wrath outside the city where He was crucified. Blood flowed from the winepress like a river that filled the whole land to the depth of a horse's bridle. That's a lot of blood.

REVELATION 15:1–8: *Then I saw another portent in heaven, great and wonderful, seven angels with seven plagues, which are the last, for with them the wrath of God is ended.*

And I saw what appeared to be a sea of glass mingled with fire, and those who had conquered the beast and its image and the number of its name, standing beside the sea of glass with harps of God in their hands. And they sing the song of Moses, the servant of God, and the song of the Lamb, saying,

> *"Great and wonderful are thy deeds,*
>   *O Lord God the Almighty!*
> *Just and true are thy ways,*
>   *O King of the ages!*
> *Who shall not fear and glorify thy name, O Lord?*
>   *For thou alone art holy.*
> *All nations shall come and worship thee,*
>   *for thy judgments have been revealed."*

After this I looked, and the temple of the tent of witness in heaven was opened, and out of the temple came the seven angels with the seven plagues, robed in pure bright linen, and their breasts girded with golden girdles. And one of the four living creatures gave the seven angels seven golden bowls full of the wrath of God who lives for ever and ever; and the temple was filled with smoke from the glory of God and from his power, and no one could enter the temple until the seven plagues of the seven angels were ended.

NEXT JOHN WATCHES as the angels pour out the bowls of wrath upon the earth in chapter 16:

Sores.

The sea becomes blood.

The rivers become blood.

The sun scorches men and women.

The beast's kingdom is plunged into darkness.

And *nobody* repents. Demons and armies prepare for Armageddon. At the last bowl, mountains and islands flee, and all opposed to God end in the lake of fire.

These seven bowls in chapter 16 are reminiscent of the ten plagues on Egypt, which were poured out immediately before Israel passed through the Red Sea and sang the song of Moses. In chapter 15 of Revelation, the saints seem to have passed through the sea of fire and glass. They sing the song of Moses and the Lamb.

The seven bowls are also like the seven seals and seven trumpets, except with the seals, things happen in fourths, and with the trumpets, things happen in thirds. Now with the bowls, the plagues are complete (not a third, but *all* of the sea turns to blood.) Seven bowls of wrath are also like the seven days of creation, only in reverse. If you want wrath, you'll get it. And it will be perfect.

Yet this is "great and wonderful" news (15:1).

Did you notice that the seven angels come out of the temple (15:6)? We are the temple. I've wondered if these seven *angelos* are the seven *angelos* in the churches and the seven spirits before the throne who are the eyes of the Lamb, the Spirit of God sent out into the entire earth, the Holy Spirit. They are at least closely connected to the Spirit who lives in us—the temple. Each one of them is dressed as Jesus is in chapter 1—a white, linen robe with a golden sash around His chest.

In the Gospels Jesus said that on the day of judgment the king will say to those he judges, "Whatever you did to the least of these you did to me" (see Matthew 25:31–46). Perhaps that's because the king was dwelling in them. So *this* is judgment: How you treat Christ in His temple. And *you* are that temple, children of God. The angel of Yahweh is in the temple—*us*. So then these angels do not pour these bowls indiscriminately. It's perfect and absolute.

I suspect wrath was being poured out at the World Trade Center. I believe it's being poured out all the time. Paul said it in Romans 1:18, "The wrath of God is being revealed against all ungodliness and wickedness of men, who by their wickedness suppress the truth."

So I bet wrath was being poured out in New York. But not *just* wrath. I bet . . . some saw seals broken, revealing the glory of Christ. Some heard trumpets, even the last trumpet calling, "Come home! Come home!" Some heard the thunders speak wonders that cannot be uttered on earth. And yes, I imagine some drank from the cup of the fury of the wrath of God Almighty.

Seals, trumpets, thunders, bowls . . . I believe they're all happening. To the outsider they look the same and so indiscriminate. But to the receiver they're not at *all* the same. His judgments are revealed, and they are not indiscriminate but a perfect wonder.

In 15:1 John writes that the sign or portent is great and wonderful, for with these seven plagues the wrath of God is ended—*teleo*—perfected. I'm just going to believe Scripture on this one: *The wrath of God comes to an end.* That means if souls are forever tormented in hell, it's not by the wrath of God. In fact, in the second death (chap. 20), death and hell get thrown in the lake of fire. "And death shall be no more" (21:4). No living death. The wrath of God comes to an end . . . even better, a *teleos*—a perfection.

The seventh bowl is like the seventh and last trumpet. At the last trumpet, "the dead will be raised imperishable," writes Paul (1 Corinthians 15:52). The seventh bowl and the seventh trumpet anticipate the last plague on the Egyptians, which was the death of the firstborn sons. As the seventh bowl is being poured out and God's wrath is complete, mountains and hills flee away, and a voice comes out of the temple from the throne. Who is on the throne?— A slaughtered Lamb, the firstborn Son of God, only begotten of the Father. And the voice cries, "It is done!" (16:17). Lightning flashes and the earth shakes.

When Jesus hung on the cross outside Jerusalem, trampling the winepress of the wrath of God, John records that His last word was *"tetelestai,"* the conjugate of *teleo*—"It is finished *[teleo]!*" (John 19:30). And the lightning flashed and the earth shook.

On that cross, Jesus saved us not just from Satan and death, but from the wrath of God Almighty by bearing it Himself. There God fulfilled His *fatwa* against humanity, and the blood flowed a river over all the land to the depth of a horse's bridle. That is *enough blood.* On that cross Jesus didn't just die His own death, he bore the entire wrath of God for an entire "God-cursed" world. That's a lot of blood.

> Every bowl,
>> every sin,
>>> every sorrow;
> Every tear wept
>> by every child in New York City,
>>> going to bed alone;
> The anxiety of every mother
>> at the Afghan border
>>> trying to feed her children.

Every bowl . . . His blood. What does a good Father *do* with all His wrath? He bears it Himself. And on that cross the Father's wrath was *teleos*—perfected—ended.

The wrath of God *will* come to an end, either at the cross or in the lake of fire. The question is, where does it come to an end for *you?* Surrender wrath to Jesus, and it ends at the cross as grace. Harbor wrath for yourself, and it will end with you in the lake of fire.

But this is the great and wonderful news: God's wrath has a *goal* (a *teleos;* that is, a perfection). Satan's fury does not; it is a reaction. God's wrath is not simply a reaction to sin. God's wrath must be part of a glorious plan set forth at the foundation of the world—"Let us make man in our image."

In Revelation 15 it appears these saints pass through the sea of fire and glass, just like the Israelites passed through the Red Sea. The same sea that baptized, delivered, and created the Israelites consumed the Egyptians. The saints stand on the edge of the sea and sing the song of Moses and the Lamb— God's salvation. Only *they,* the children of God, can sing it.

Maybe the sea of fire not only consumes what's evil but purifies what's good . . . such as our faith, more precious than gold, which though perishable is refined by fire (1 Peter 1:7). Gold perishes. Faith, hope, and love abide forever. Maybe the fire consumes evil and purifies the good. Maybe it's how we're made in His image.

What *is* the fire? I'm not sure I really understand it. But the author of Hebrews says, "Our God is a consuming fire" (12:29). John tells us that God is love. I don't think this means that God is *part* love and *part* fire. I think it means His *love* is fire. The word *theion* in Greek can be translated both as "brimstone" and "divinity." In Revelation 14, 19, 20, and 21 we read about the lake of "fire and brimstone," or "fire and divinity," or "fire that is divinity."

In Matthew 10:34 Jesus said, "I came to cast fire upon the earth. How I am constrained until it is accomplished." Maybe He is "fire on the earth."

He taught us that His Spirit would convict the world of sin. He taught us that His cross was the judgment. Perhaps His cross is the fire. Fire did fall at Pentecost—the Spirit of the Living God.

The Church *did* go to war.

Satan *is* defeated.

The gates of hell *cannot* prevail against the Church.

Saints *do* conquer by the blood of the Lamb. He has given us His blood to drink: sweet wine to the children of God, fiery wrath to the prince of darkness, but the same fluid. The love of God in Christ is a consuming fire, and it is what we are to bleed: *forgiveness.* When we forgive, we bleed fire.

The saints don't battle any earthly kingdom. They battle the kingdom of hell with the fire of God, the blood of Christ, and the grace of God. They pour it unmixed on the head of the evil one, and it burns him like hot coals, exposing every one of his foul arguments, obstacles to the glory of God. The saints are people like John, exiled on the island of Patmos; Peter, crucified upside down; Paul, beheaded; the martyrs in the seven churches that changed the world; Saint Francis of Assisi; Mother Teresa; people like *you* every time you bleed Jesus' love for someone else. *You* are being made in His image.

The Lamb is the Lion. He *is* the consuming fire. I've seen it fall on demons in prayer, and it burns them like fire. But that very same Spirit on you is love, joy, peace, patience, kindness, goodness, gentleness . . . *life!*

So if you surrender to Him and His grace, if you surrender wrath to Him . . .

- the cup of wrath is not blood to you, but wine.
- the Word is not the sword of death, but the scalpel of healing.
- the rock does not crush you but it hides you—your refuge.
- the cross is not your judgment, but your salvation.
- the wrath of God is not your horror, but a blazing portent in the heavens of your Father's relentless love.
- the fire does not consume you, but refines you in His image. And you will stand forever with Jesus, singing to the praise of God's glorious grace in Christ for you.

That's the *teleos,* the end, the perfection of the wrath of God: In a word, it's the *Bride* of Christ, spotless and without blemish, refined and precious, like a jewel in the New Jerusalem. Like gold, refined by fire, standing with Jesus, the Great Bridegroom.

One morning my wife woke me up early and told me about a vision she had just seen and the amazing dream right before the vision. She said:

I saw thousands of people descending in a line down a spiral staircase. The people were like zombies, the walking dead. Along the line there were demons harassing them, poking them and trying to hurt them.

The people hardly even flinched because they were *used* to it. For them it was *normal* being dead.

Then I saw a woman whose eyes weren't cloudy like everyone else's. They were wide open and awake: She was *alive!* She kept protesting, "Something's wrong here. I'm not supposed to be here." The demons kept harassing her and mocking her, but she kept protesting. And the line kept moving.

At the bottom of the staircase stood one huge demon, a beast with eight arms. It would take these zombies and throw them in the lake of fire, and they'd be consumed. Then the beast threw that woman in the lake of fire. But she wasn't consumed! In fact, she kept protesting, "Something's not right; I'm not supposed to be here."

That *infuriated* the beast! He went into a rage and tried to push her into the fire, but each time she would just float back up protesting. He kept pushing her down and she kept rising up, and then gradually she began to float out of reach of the beast. It was like the whole lake shifted and she floated into this area of cool, clear water, like glass.

On the shores I began to see vegetation lush with life. Then I saw Jesus. He reached in and pulled the woman out of the water and stood her right next to Him. *She was gorgeous!* It was like she was refined, spun gold. I don't even know what spun gold *is,* but that's what she was! She was radiant.

Jesus looked at her and said, "Sweetheart, you were meant for *here."*

Susan had never read Revelation 15. She said, "Peter, what *was* that? I understand that the end was heaven, but where were those walking dead, and who was that woman?"

I said, "I think all those people are *here,* in the land of the walking dead. That woman is *us,* the Bride of Christ."

Revelation 15 is *not* a nightmare. It is one great and wonderful dream. God's dream: reality.

TWENTY-SIX

WHAT GOD WANTS

(Revelation 16)

I ONCE SAW A MOVIE ABOUT A YOUNG WOMAN who lost the love of her life at sea and sank into despair. Years later she was kidnapped by thieves and then a pirate, only to discover, in terror, that this was the man reported to have killed her lover. He held his blade up to her and said, "Life is pain," then mocked her love and described her lover's death.

Maybe you feel like that woman . . . vulnerable, plagued by terror, afraid love is a sham and death is what's real. Your world is crumbling, you feel violated, and you wonder, "What do these terrors mean?"

In the beginning, we fell, but why did God let us choose evil? Why did He give us our wish? We *died* that day! What do these plagues mean—wrath, death, hell?

REVELATION 16:1–21: *Then I heard a loud voice from the temple telling the seven angels, "Go and pour out on the earth the seven bowls of the wrath of God."*

So the first angel went and poured his bowl on the earth, and foul and evil sores came upon the men who bore the mark of the beast and worshiped its image.

The second angel poured his bowl into the sea, and it became like the blood of a dead man, and every living thing died that was in the sea.

The third angel poured his bowl into the rivers and the fountains of water, and they became blood. And I heard the angel of water say,

> *"Just art thou in these thy judgments,*
> *thou who art and wast, O Holy One.*
> *For men have shed the blood of saints and prophets,*
> *and thou hast given them blood to drink.*
> *It is their due!"*

And I heard the altar cry,
"Yea, Lord God the Almighty,
true and just are thy judgments!"

The fourth angel poured his bowl on the sun, and it was allowed to scorch men with fire; men were scorched by the fierce heat, and they cursed the name of God who had power over these plagues, and they did not repent and give him glory.

The fifth angel poured his bowl on the throne of the beast, and its kingdom was in darkness; men gnawed their tongues in anguish and cursed the God of heaven for their pain and sores, and did not repent of their deeds.

The sixth angel poured his bowl on the great river Euphrates, and its water was dried up, to prepare the way for the kings from the east. And I saw, issuing from the mouth of the dragon and from the mouth of the beast and from the mouth of the false prophet, three foul spirits like frogs; for they are demonic spirits, performing signs, who go abroad to the kings of the whole world, to assemble them for battle on the great day of God the Almighty. ("Lo, I am coming like a thief! Blessed is he who is awake, keeping his garments that he may not go naked and be seen exposed!") And they assembled them at the place which is called in Hebrew Armageddon.

The seventh angel poured his bowl into the air, and a loud voice came out of the temple, from the throne, saying, "It is done!" And there were flashes of lightning, voices, peals of thunder, and a great earthquake such as had never been since men were on the earth, so great was that earthquake. The great city was split into three parts, and the cities of the nations fell, and God remembered great Babylon, to make her drain the cup of the fury of his wrath. And every island fled away, and no mountains were to be found; and great hailstones, heavy as a hundred-weight, dropped on men from heaven, till men cursed God for the plague of the hail, so fearful was that plague.

PEOPLE HOLD MORE VIEWS THAN I CAN COUNT, of what the bowls in Revelation 16 represent. It's difficult to know what to take at face value and what is *more*. For instance, the frogs are not just frogs, they are *demons* enticing kings. There is no Armageddon that we know of; the word means "Mountains of Megiddo." Megiddo is a geographical place, but there are no mountains there. Are the sores just *sores,* or are they more?

Historists such as John Wesley and Jonathan Edwards saw the sores as atheism. They taught that chapter 16 was about the French Revolution and the downfall of the papacy in 1798—and it made remarkable sense, actually.

Preterists think chapter 16 refers to ancient Rome or Jerusalem, and their view makes remarkable sense too. Regarding the hundred-pound hailstones (v. 21), consider that Josephus described how the Romans launched hundred-pound white stones from catapults during the siege of Jerusalem in A.D. 70 Corpses turned the Sea of Galilee and city streets red with blood. And as Jesus had prophesied, Jerusalem fell.

Futurists love to speculate about a renewed Roman Empire, nuclear war, sun scorch through ozone depletion, earthquakes, and Asian hordes crossing the Euphrates from places such as Afghanistan. Now we can add new speculations involving Osama bin Laden and world trade.

What's remarkable to me is how so much of it really fits. Maybe they're all *partly* right. Maybe all these tribulations are labor pains, as Jesus called them. Labor pains come in cycles, over and over, until it's time for delivery.

Maybe history *is* repeating itself,

      all in the service of giving birth to something.

"History consists of parables," wrote Malcolm Muggeridge, "whereby God communicates in terms that the imagination rather than the mind, faith rather than knowledge, can grasp." God is using the props of history to get us to have faith in something, to give birth to something. "You know, there are many pleasures in being old and gaga," writes Muggeridge. "One of the greatest . . . is to realize that history is largely nonsensical. . . . The only reason for studying what goes on is to get at this parable that it conveys. Otherwise it is just like an interminable soap opera whose situations endlessly recur although the characters change."[1]

I've heard my eighty-four-year-old father talk this way. In fact, he was the one who first read me Muggeridge's quote. When I spoke to him soon after the 9-11 tragedy, his attitude was, *Hitler . . . Marx . . . Osama bin Laden . . . seen it all before. How are my grandkids? Tell me about love.* Maybe he is getting the parable.

People who receive the bowls in verses 9, 11, and 21 don't repent. So if you're stressed, *repent . . .* and you might get sores and get sunburned, but it's not wrath. It's a broken seal, trumpet, or thunder. Repent and Christ *takes* your wrath. "It is done," He says. *Teleo*—perfection.

These bowls are like the plagues in Egypt. When the Israelites were in bondage and Egypt was hit with plagues—sores, blood, hail, darkness, frogs, slaughter of the firstborn—God instituted the Passover: lamb's blood on the door meant that the final plague would pass over that household, and the firstborn would live. But the people were to eat the flesh of the sacrificed lamb *in haste.* They were to be packed and ready to go, for in the morning the Lord was coming to deliver them . . . rescue them.

If the plagues meant deliverance for Israel, what does all this tribulation mean for *us?* He is coming to take us home. It could be any time . . . so *stay packed.*

If the popular pretribulation view is correct, then these people in

Revelation 16 would know *exactly* when He was coming—seven years from when all those Christians were raptured. But right here between the sixth and seventh bowls, He says, "I'm coming like a thief." It could be anytime. And if He doesn't come for you at the close of the age, I believe He does come for you the day you die (John 14:3). Maybe the day a believer dies and the close of the age are always the same . . . eternity invades *your* time at that point . . . and that point for you could be tomorrow.

He is coming; stay ready. The more intense the plagues became, the closer the Israelites were to enduring freedom. The more intense the tribulation gets, the closer your Lord comes.

Is your world under siege? Maybe it's because your liberator is drawing near. Maybe you're actually imprisoned *here,* lulled to sleep by an evil prince so that you won't hear your savior's call, but now the Lord is waking you to life.

In the midst of tribulation, Jesus calls, "I'm coming soon!" Does that fill you with *fear* or *hope?* Is He your *enemy* or your *Savior?* Do you fear His wrath? Do you think He's coming to steal your life? Crush your heart? Do you think He's coming to rape you? Is *that* who you think He is?

I don't think we can begin to understand the sorrow we inflict upon our Lord Jesus when we're afraid. The opposite of fear is faith.

Your lack of faith makes you fear:

- the same fear that makes you turn to porn instead of entrusting your desires to Christ.
- the same fear that makes you eat and eat instead of stopping.
- the same fear that compels you to lie instead of depend on truth.
- the same fear that keeps you from entrusting every moment of your life to Christ in joyful obedience.
- the same fear that makes you close your heart to Him.

I bet it's the same fear that you felt on September 11. September 11 just woke you to the fear that was already there.

Many think they are courageous, but it's just that their faith hasn't been tested and their fears have never been exposed. Fear, hidden or revealed, is what robs you of life now.

Paul writes, "For God did not give us a spirit of timidity [fear] but a spirit of power and love and self-control" (2 Timothy 1:7). Fear is a false suitor. We think it offers us security, that it will guard our hearts. But for the Bride of Christ, fear is a *lie.* It can even be an evil spirit Satan sends to keep you in bondage. So when you are afraid, rebuke fear and call on Jesus. *He* is your security.

If fear of God is the "beginning of wisdom" (Proverbs 9:10), it is not the end, for "perfect love casts out fear" (1 John 4:18). *Let not your hearts be troubled,* says Jesus, *I will come for you. I will not leave you desolate* (John 14:1, 18). He was talking about His Spirit. Whenever we hope in Christ's coming for us in the end, He comes *now* in Spirit and drives out fear.

Soon after 9-11, and secretly worrying about bioterrorism, I took my kids for a walk to the minimarket. I was half-consciously praying, and the thought hit me: *We could all be dead soon.* Then I thought, *Well, Jesus, that's great! You love my children more than I do.* I looked up and the sun was shining, the mountains were glorious, and the field we were walking in was bathed in light. The kids were running through the tall grass laughing, and . . . I *lived.* I was blessed and happy. *This is glorious!* I thought. And it was—for *He* was there, transforming fear into faith.

When fear says, "You could die," Jesus says, *"You will live."*

When fear says, "You could get crucified," Jesus says, *"And I will raise you up."*

When fear says, "You could lose everything," Jesus says, *"I am giving you everything."*

When fear says, "Satan is coming to get you," Jesus says, *"I am coming to set you free."*

When fear says, "All hell has broken loose," Jesus says, *"Hell is under siege, and heaven has come to take you home."*

Fear is an insult to Christ, and it robs you of life *now!* When you're afraid, you don't dance well, you don't sing well, and you don't live well. And you certainly don't *kiss* well.

I remember the first time I kissed Susan. She was seventeen. It was like kissing . . . a post. (Don't worry, it's gotten better.) I understand why—she was afraid. She did not yet have faith in me. So her kiss was impure (infected with fear), and it lacked passion (fear guarded her heart). So that kiss ranks at just about the very bottom of my list of kisses.

Tribulation comes, but for Christians that shouldn't mean fear. What *does* it mean? In the midst of the bowls of wrath, right before the great earthquake, the voice from the temple calls out, "Behold, I come like a thief! Blessed [happy] is he who stays awake and keeps his clothes with him, so that he may not go naked and be shamefully exposed" (Revelation 16:15 NIV).

Some people think that means underground bunkers, survival gear, stashes of canned goods. But Jesus isn't talking about physical clothing (you can take a shower in *peace).* Paul tells us we are to "put on Christ (Galatians 3:27). In

Revelation 19:8 the fine linen is the "righteous deeds of the saints." Our righteous deeds are the fruit of faith, so we are to clothe ourselves with faith, not fear. With fear, Satan tempts us to cover our naked shame from the wrath of God. But with faith, Christ covers our shame with His righteousness.

Fear closes our hearts; faith opens them.

Jesus doesn't just want our bodies; He wants our hearts. If He has only our bodies, He has purchased a harlot. If He has our hearts *and* our bodies, He has won a bride. Our Lord will not ravish us until He has won our heart. For in His furious love, our pleasure is His pleasure; our sorrows His sorrows. He longs for our kisses . . . but only if they are freely given.

Do you see the suffering of Jesus? His Bride has gone to bed with the evil one, and she thinks it's *life*. He comes to set her free, and the evil one fills her with fear. He must rescue her from the evil one and also win her heart. He crushes the evil one with power but must say to His Bride, "As you wish." He must give her the freedom to surrender to Him in faith. Kisses surrendered in fear have no value to Him.

In Revelation chapter 7, the saints wash their garments white in the blood of the Lamb. Now He calls, "Keep your garments ready." In Revelation 19 the garment is white linen . . . and it is what the Bride wears. It is a *wedding dress*—He comes to elope! He wants to marry you! But only "as you wish."

With joyful hope can you say, "Come, Lord Jesus"? That's the last line of Revelation (before John's benediction). Throughout Revelation, Jesus keeps saying, "I'm coming." We keep answering with fear. But He is the Great Lover, so in the end we finally say in faith, "Come, Lord Jesus." He must answer, "As you wish," for that's *The End*. He does not want a frightened harlot; He wants a Bride full of faith, hope, and love.

In the movie I mentioned earlier, the maiden Buttercup doesn't know that her captor, Dread Pirate Roberts, is actually her true love Westley, who she thinks is dead. Westley has crossed the sea and fought horrendous battles to reach her. But now he is testing her heart by questioning her faithlessness, because in his absence she has become betrothed to the evil Prince Humperdinck. "I *died* that day," cries Buttercup, "and you can die too!" She pushes him down a steep hill. As he falls, he calls out a phrase that she immediately recognizes: "As . . . you . . . wish . . ." Buttercup flings herself down the hill to die with her beloved.

She's *The Princess Bride*, and so are we. As you may know, the two become separated again, but the entire movie is about Westley winning Buttercup's heart—her faith. For in the beginning, her heart is arrogant. She orders Westley around until she finally realizes that when he says, "As you wish," he is really saying, "I love you."

At one point Westley dies, but he's resurrected by Miracle Max for true love. He plans to storm Humperdinck's castle, where Buttercup is once again tempted to marry Humperdinck out of fear. Before the wedding she has a dream that awakens her. She dreams of marrying Humperdinck, and an old woman in the crowd keeps yelling, "Boo! Boo!" Buttercup asks the old woman, "Why do you do this?" The old woman replies, "Because you had love in your hands, and you gave it up!"

"But they would have killed Westley if I hadn't done it!" Buttercup explains.

"Your true love lives, and you marry another!" cries the old woman. "True love saved her in the fire swamp, and she treated it like garbage. And that's what she is, the Queen of Refuse. So bow down to her if you want. Bow to her. Bow to the Queen of Slime, the Queen of Filth, the Queen of Putrescence! Boo! Boo! Rubbish! Filth! Slime! Muck! Boo! Boo! Boo!"

The dream is fear (her fear), but Buttercup awakens to faith.

Bride of Christ, true love has saved you from the lake of fire. True love lives, and you have treated it as garbage. But He *will not* let you go. You will not marry another. Wake up and live now.

Early in the movie, Westley says to Buttercup, "Hear this now: I will always come for you." She asks, "How can you be sure?" He replies, "This is true love." On Buttercup's wedding day, the castle is stormed; Buttercup is saved; and the lovers are reunited at last. The moral of the movie is, true love *always conquers.*

At the end of the movie, as the dawn rises, Westley and Buttercup kiss. The narrator says, "Since the invention of the kiss, there have been five kisses that were rated the most passionate, the most pure. This one left them all behind."

If you've wondered, "Just what is it that God wants?" Jesus tells us that God seeks true "worshipers" (in the Greek, *proskuneo*) (John 4:23). Scholars agree that this basically means "a good kiss."

He is coming soon. When He arrives, may you say to Him in perfect faith without fear, "As you wish."

TWENTY-SEVEN

TO MAKE A BRIDE

(Revelation 17)

In the beginning God created the heavens and the earth" (Genesis 1:1), and as the final act of creation He said, "Let us make man in our image, after our likeness" (1:26). Many theologians argue that the image of God is to be a creator, as He is a creator. And certainly we are to love as He *is* love.

From Revelation 17 on, the end is dominated by two women separated by the Lamb and one thousand years of His reign. The two women are the great harlot (the whore of Babylon) and the Bride (the New Jerusalem). The New Jerusalem is the end. Does the end have anything to do with the beginning?

Paul writes, "[God] accomplishes all things according to the counsel of His will" (Ephesians 1:11). That means that the end *must* have something to do with the beginning. And *your* life is not plan B, because there *is* no plan B. It's all plan A.

Genesis is about you. Revelation is about you.

"For everything that was written in the past was written to teach us" (Romans 15:4 NIV). For we are the Israel of God, children of Abraham by faith, true Jews circumcised in heart, the temple of the Living God, the Bride of Christ, the New Jerusalem coming down.

So the truth is not like this American pop theology of the last hundred years that makes the Church a parenthesis in God's plan for the geopolitical state of Israel. The Church is not a parenthesis in another plan. The Church is the crowning pinnacle of God's creation. Paul said, "[God] has made [Christ] the head over all things for the church, which is his body, the fulness of him who fills all in all" (Ephesians 1:22–23). The end has everything to do with the beginning and with *you* right now.

In the beginning (Genesis 1:1-2:3) God creates *every*thing in six days. The last thing created (the pinnacle of creation, God's dream of creation) was man in His image. Then God rests on the seventh day, because all creation is finished.

We modern people tend to read that story simply as "seven days" long ago. But there's a huge problem with that: God is still creating. He's not finished. Paul even said in 1 Corinthians 15 that we're still being made into His image, the image of Christ. We're still being made into the kind of creator that Christ is. Remember, Christ called from His cross, "It is finished." Did God say, "Excuse me . . . *actually* it was finished back there on the seventh day"?

In Hebrews we read that God rested on the seventh day, but we are called to enter His rest *now* (4:4–11). So . . .

Did Christ enter God's rest at the cross?

Did Christ finish God's creating on His cross?

Are we finally perfected in His image through the cross, not just at a point in time, but when we carry His cross each day?

If so, it means we're still living in the sixth day, still being made into the image of God. And then those seven days of Genesis cover all of time, the whole canvas.

Seven churches . . . seven days . . . seven seals . . . seven bowls . . . seven trumpets . . . seven thunders . . . seven eyes of the Lamb . . . seven heads of the beast . . . that's more than just counting. It's saying, "These are the days of time, the days in which we live."

We're being painted in time, but the canvas is finished in eternity. So we have been made and are being made in His image.

Now, you may say, "Seven days is *seven days,* and I take the Bible *literally!*" (Sometimes I think that means we take the Bible *scientifically* rather than *spiritually,* by sight rather than by faith.) Well, okay, how long is seven days?

Remember what I mentioned in chapter 2? According to Einstein's theory of relativity and the calculations of physicist Gerald Schroeder, creation is 15 3/4 billion years old, but from the standpoint of creation (the big bang) the universe is not quite seven days old. That would mean we're still existing in the sixth day *being* made in God's image.

Genesis 1:1–2:3 describes the seven days and God's dream of creation: "Let us make man in our own image and after our likeness." But then in Genesis 2:4 the author goes back to day six, because he begins to describe how God made man. I believe the rest of the Bible is day six until some women go to a tomb early one Sunday morning and the stone is rolled away and Easter—eternity—day seven—begins to invade history.

Day seven—heaven—never fully invades all space and time until the end of the Revelation when the people of God say, "Come, Lord Jesus," and He says, "As you wish." Then is the kingdom of God consummated, finished, for His Bride is ready—finished—fully created. It's the wedding supper of the Lamb.

How *is* the Bride made ready? How is man made in God's image?

In Genesis 2 God makes the Garden, and God says, "But of the tree of the knowledge of good and evil you shall not eat, for in the day that you eat of it you shall die" (v. 17). Then God sees the first thing that he pronounces "not good." In the words of Milton, that thing is *loneliness*. He said, "It is not good that the man should be alone; I will make him a helper fit [suitable] for him" (v. 18).

A *helper*. Who is your helper, Christian?

Then He brought to Adam every beast and every bird. They're each male and female (I would imagine) . . . each has a partner, each has a likeness, each has a helper through whom more life will be created. Animals are created after their kind. But Adam is alone. It's as if God asks, "Who's your helper, Adam? In whose likeness are you, Adam? Who will create through you, Adam? To whom will you cleave, Adam? As you wish, Adam."

But Adam did not find a helper suitable for him. (Now, this is a deep mystery, but how could he find his helper? He did not yet know good and evil, and his helper is the Good.)

So God begins the great lesson. He puts Adam to sleep, and He takes a rib from his side and fashions it into Eve. So far, when I've said, "Adam," I was talking about you, too, women. Together, male and female, we are in the image of God. So when Adam sees Eve he says, "Hey! That's my rib! Bone of my bones and flesh of my flesh. She is me!" And she really was.

The helper Adam got was more of himself. And the helper Eve got was more of herself. In Ephesians Paul writes that this male-female thing in Genesis 2 is a picture, a lesson, about something else. You see, the helper Adam picks is more of himself. And some help *she* turns out to be! The first thing she does is help him find some fruit. She talks to a snake. But both Adam and Eve are present, and not only is Eve a lousy helper for Adam, but Adam is a lousy helper for Eve.

The snake says, "Hey, this fruit will make you like God, knowing good and evil." The thing is, it *does*. For God even says, "Behold, [they have] become like one of us, knowing good and evil" (Genesis 3:22). Isn't that God's dream? His likeness? Yet Adam and Eve sinned. They are kicked out of the Garden, sentenced to death, and they find themselves alone. They sinned.

How did they sin? Wasn't it God's dream of creation to create them in His likeness? Yes, it was God's dream, but they tried to create them*selves* without help. If God wanted them to know good and evil (like Him), perhaps He would have given them that fruit another way. (I don't know; it's a mystery.) But independent of God they took the fruit and consumed the fruit.

Not just *like* God . . . they tried to *be* God.

More than God, they wanted God's stuff . . . consumers.

More than His *self*—His *heart*—they wanted His attributes.

Instead of trusting God to create them in His image, they trusted themselves to create themselves in His image.

Instead of trusting their helper, they trusted themselves and they trusted a snake.

Instead of a bride, humanity had become a harlot . . . a consumer rather than a creator.

But that was *still day six,* and God will *still* have His dream. And God *still* "accomplishes all things according to the counsel of his will." And God was *still* making man in His image, according to plan. And God is *still* asking, "Who's your helper?"

In 1 Corinthians 15:45 Paul calls Jesus the "last Adam," that is *"eschatos* Adam," "deepest Adam," "uttermost Adam." He is also God. Bride of Christ, who's your helper?

After Genesis 2, the next time that word *helper* appears in my English Bible is a few thousand years later. A desperate man named David (hardly a model citizen, but a royal catastrophe) wrote, "Oh Lord, be my helper." And God called him a man after His own heart.

A thousand years later, another man, a son of David and the Son of God (Jesus, who referred to Himself as the *parakletos*—the "helper") said, "I am going. . . . And I will ask the Father, and He will give you another Helper. . . . You know Him because He abides with you, and will be in you" (John 14:4, 16–17 NAS).

Jesus referred to us as His Bride saying, "Apart from me you can do nothing. But abide in me and I in you and so bear much fruit" (see John 15:1–8). That is, create *much fruit*—God's dream of creation, His Bride, man in His own image and likeness, creating with love, in love, and through love.

REVELATION 17:1–18: *Then one of the seven angels who had the seven bowls came and said to me, "Come, I will show you the judgment of the great harlot who is seated upon many waters, with whom the kings of the earth have committed fornication, and with the wine of whose fornication the dwellers on earth have become drunk." And he carried me away in the Spirit into a wilderness, and I saw a woman sitting on a scarlet beast which was full of blasphemous names, and it had seven heads and ten horns. The woman was arrayed in purple and scarlet, and bedecked with gold and jewels and pearls, holding in her hand a golden cup full of abominations and the impurities of her fornication; and on her forehead was written a name of mystery: "Babylon the great, mother of harlots and of earth's abominations." And I saw the woman, drunk with the blood of the saints and the blood of the martyrs of Jesus.*

When I saw her I marveled greatly. But the angel said to me, "Why marvel? I will tell you the mystery of the woman, and of the beast with seven heads and ten horns that carries her. The beast that you saw was, and is not, and is to ascend from the bottomless pit and go to perdition; and the dwellers on earth whose names have not been written in the book of life from the foundation of the world, will marvel to behold the beast, because it was and is not and is to come. This calls for a mind with wisdom: the seven heads are seven mountains on which the woman is seated; they are also seven kings, five of whom have fallen, one is, the other has not yet come, and when he comes he must remain only a little while. As for the beast that was and is not, it is an eighth but it belongs to the seven, and it goes to perdition. And the ten horns that you saw are ten kings who have not yet received royal power, but they are to receive authority as kings for one hour, together with the beast. These are of one mind and give over their power and authority to the beast; they will make war on the Lamb, and the Lamb will conquer them, for he is Lord of lords and King of kings, and those with him are called and chosen and faithful."

And he said to me, "The waters that you saw, where the harlot is seated, are peoples and multitudes and nations and tongues. And the ten horns that you saw, they and the beast will hate the harlot; they will make her desolate and naked, and devour her flesh and burn her up with fire, for God has put it into their hearts to carry out his purpose by being of one mind and giving over their royal power to the beast, until the words of God shall be fulfilled. And the woman that you saw is the great city which has dominion over the kings of the earth."

DID YOU NOTICE that in Revelation 17, Satan's kingdom consumes itself? The beast consumes the harlot—a consumer kingdom. In verse 14, those with Christ conquer the beast! Remember—that was the huge question at the start of the book: "Who will conquer? Who will eat of the tree of life in the Paradise of God? Who will not be hurt by the second death? Who receives the morning star and will be clad in white garments? Who will be the temple, the New Jerusalem, the dwelling place of God? Who will sit with Christ on His throne? Who will conquer?" Here's the answer: *Those with Christ . . .* for He is their helper.

John is "amazed" at the harlot (17:6). The word can even mean "attracted." It's clear the harlot is evil yet attractive. She loves men for their attributes but not for themselves. She loves men as food to consume. The beast exercises power over men through intimidation. The harlot exercises power over men through seduction. In the next chapter we find God's people have been seduced.

In verse 5 the harlot is Babylon. In verse 9 she sits on seven mountains like Rome. In verse 18 she *is* (as John writes) the great city that has dominion over the kings of the earth. (She's *at least* Rome and Babylon.) In verse 6 she's drunk with the blood of the saints and martyrs. That best fits Jerusalem. Clearly this woman is the antithesis of the New Jerusalem, so maybe this is the Old Jerusalem. Remember, the Old Jerusalem killed Jesus. They had a dream of Messiah who would liberate the geopolitical entity of Israel from the dominion of Rome. And when He did not do that, they killed him. They wanted an independent Jewish state. They wanted the blessings of God, not the *person* of God. So when the *person* of God showed up, they killed Him.

Some Christians worry about blessing the geo-political state of Israel in order to be blessed. That sounds like harlotry . . . and the spirit that got Jesus crucified. I hope you bless Israel and all nations, but not for what you'll get.

In Jesus' day Jerusalem was infected with consumer religion. So Jesus went into the temple and drove out the merchants and moneychangers in an absolute fury, like a man who has found another man in his wife's bed. He said, "Destroy this temple, and in three days I will raise it up" (John 2:19). And He *did*—His Church.

Harlotry is the pinnacle of consumerism. It's buying and selling life— consuming life. When you pay with money for a person, you make them worth a finite amount, something you can pay. You make them part of your own portfolio, your own kingdom. But then everything in your kingdom is less than you . . . dead . . . and you're alone. That's the end of consumerism.

If you consume everything, purchase everything, own everything, every- thing is dead. You can pay for idols, but do you think you can *acquire God?* Acquire the blessings of God, the attributes of God, like plucking fruit from a tree? To dream of buying God is to dream your own death, God's death, and the world's death. It's to dream of hell.

Harlotry is trying to get with human energy what only God can give through grace. Harlotry is choosing a dead lover, an unsuitable helper.

As I read the Revelation, the beast doesn't really scare me; the dragon's not even that big of a deal. But the harlot really makes me nervous . . . because I find her attractive. She looks a lot like home: A world economy in bed with the kings of the earth, the great consumer culture. She looks an awful lot like America.

We Americans think we can buy and sell anything, even kings, friends, and enemies (around the world). We have come to view each other as consumer items. So we consume wives and consume husbands. It's even the way we date in America. We *shop* for love.

I watched *Happy Days* in high school, so *I* dated around. Girls were like a consumer item: You shopped around and got the best you could, for you obtained her attributes and she increased your value.

In my ninth grade year, I dumped a wonderful girlfriend because I could get *Lisa.* (I didn't even *know* Lisa, but she was a cheerleader . . . more valuable than a Pom-Pom Girl, and almost a Liberty Belle!) I was a soccer player, and I had a cheerleader, and I was *making myself.* By my tenth grade year, she dumped me and I got cut from the soccer team. Then suddenly my former girlfriend became really attractive. In fact, I found girls to be very attractive until I *had* them. Then they lost their luster.

By the eleventh grade, I was dating a girl named Susan, who was absolutely gorgeous until I thought I owned her heart. Then she lost her magic. We broke up and then once again I couldn't live without her; it became a cycle. You see, every time I thought I had her, I turned her into a harlot in my heart. Finally, during my senior year, I began thinking, "Maybe a bride isn't a consumer item. When I possess her as a consumer item, she dies. Maybe a bride is more like something I *serve,* and in serving I create."

Many Americans are getting divorced saying, "My husband or wife wasn't what I thought they would be. I'm returning the merchandise." If that's you, it reveals you didn't really marry a husband or wife. You thought you purchased a harlot. Your husband or wife is not a consumer item. They are not to be *consumed,* but *created.* We learn that in marriage.

In Ephesians 5 Paul quotes Genesis 2 about God making Adam male and female. He says, "This mystery is a profound one, and . . . it refers to Christ and the church" (v. 32). "Husbands, love your wives, as Christ loved the church and gave himself up for her, that he might sanctify her, having cleansed her by the washing of water with the word, that he might present the church to himself in splendor, without spot or wrinkle or any such thing, that she might be holy and without blemish" (vv. 25–27). *Finished.*

Christ creates His Bride—His people—by washing her with His Word—His gospel—and feeding her His very own body broken and blood shed. He washes her because she's ugly. She's become a harlot. She knows good and evil because she's chosen evil. She's sold out to evil. But with His own flesh and blood He makes her—He creates her—to choose the good—Himself—her helper—her wish.

In chapter 17 the harlot is drunk on blood. In chapter 19 the Bride has been washed in blood (the Lamb's life).

The harlot is decked with jewels, gold, and pearls; the Bride *is* jewels, gold, and pearls.

The harlot is the abode of demons; the Bride is the dwelling place of God.

The harlot is a city, an economy of consumption; the Bride is a city, an economy of creation.

The harlot consumes, and she is a consumer finally consumed in the lake of fire. The great harlot is the *spirit* of harlotry. But God loves harlots: Rahab, Mary of Magdalene, you, me, His people. Do you see that His plan for the fullness of time is to take harlots (the children of Adam) and turn them into His Bride?

We all were whores loving other gods, other lords. But Christ makes us His Bride. In Ezekiel 16 God says Jerusalem is a harlot, a whoring bride. He says, "I will deliver you to be burned by your lovers, but then I will establish with you My everlasting covenant. I will atone for your sins" (see Ezekiel 16:39, 41, 60, 62–63). That atonement is His body and blood.

God commanded Hosea to marry a harlot because Israel is a harlot. Hosea is commanded to redeem her—for fifteen shekels. Jesus has redeemed you from the evil one with His own blood. His blood is His life, not finite but infinite. He paid for your freedom, but now He is romancing your heart. He will not take you until you surrender to being taken. He does not want a harlot to consume, but a Bride to create. So with His blood He: paid for your freedom, washes you in His grace, romances your heart, establishes the covenant. And if you surrender . . . He impregnates you with His life.

You become a creator in God's image—love.

I once prayed with a Christian woman who had been sold by a family member to a very corrupt man. She didn't know of the transaction at the time, but later it was revealed. The man was now long gone, but a demon associated with the evil covenant remained. At one point, he manifested and I commanded him to go. He replied, "I paid for her." At that I held out a communion cup of wine in front of the woman and said, "What's worth more? The money or the blood of the only begotten Son of God?" The demon screeched, "The blood," and left.

If you're a believer, no price is greater than the price paid for your redemption. No covenant is more binding than the covenant established for you from the foundation of the world. I do believe that you were created from the Uttermost Adam's rib, the Bridegroom's bleeding side, the body and the blood.

Now, Eve, who's your helper? Surrender to your Helper and bear fruit as a creator in His image.

Don't believe the lie. You're not the harlot . . . you're the Bride.

Twenty-Eight

To Love the Bride

(Revelation 18:1–19:8)

Harlotry is the pinnacle of consumption—an "economy of consumption," and harlotry is a great lie—a deception. It is the belief that a person can purchase something that only comes by grace.

God created sexuality as a sacramental communion of grace in the covenant of marriage. The groom goes into his bride to commune with her in love, and in the process he implants his seed in her womb—*his life*. She bears life—creation—in the image of God. Sexuality is to be "life given" and "life created." And God designed it to be *pure ecstasy.*

Harlotry is a lie. It promises communion, life, and ecstasy, but . . .

instead of surrender, it is control;

instead of giving, it is taking;

instead of creation, it is consumption;

instead of ecstasy, it ends in depravity and tragedy;

instead of communion, it ends in isolation and death.

Harlotry uses *people* to obtain *things;* love uses *things* to serve *people.* Harlotry is consumption; Love is creation. Harlotry ends in dead hearts alone in their own private hell.

In Revelation 17 we meet the great hooker. She's not happy but drunk with blood. She rides the beast; she is dependent on the beast and his kings, and they are dependent on her. They use each other, so they *hate* each other. In the end the beast burns her and makes her fall.

She is world economy dependent on a unified political authority. She is world trade dependent on the United Nations.

She is a goddess who preaches liberty but practices licentiousness. She is a goddess who preaches freedom that is really bondage to evil.

Who is the harlot? Well, she's Babylon . . . Babel in Genesis, where they built a tower to conquer heaven. Babel is a tower that falls.

She's also Rome. Peter even refers to Rome as Babylon in 1 Peter 5. World trade flourished under Roman empirical power. The Mediterranean Sea became a free trade zone. (This then is quite a picture: John the apostle, old and exiled to Patmos by the Empire of Rome, sings a funeral dirge over Roman culture in the height of its glory.)

The harlot also appears to be Old Jerusalem. Jerusalem fell suddenly, *crushed* by the Roman beast in A.D. 70. She was called a harlot by God, because the people of God had sold out to other gods—*idolatry.*

When the voice cries in chapter 18, "Come out of her, my people" (v. 4), it sounds like Jesus. Remember that Jesus warned His disciples in Jerusalem to flee the city at the sign of its destruction. History shows that, in fact, they *did.* In Revelation 17 John describes the great harlot, how she's destroyed by the beast. In Revelation 18 he sings a funeral dirge over her destruction. Who is she?

REVELATION 18:1–3: *After this I saw another angel coming down from heaven, having great authority; and the earth was made bright with his splendor. And he called out with a mighty voice, "Fallen, fallen is Babylon the great! It has become a dwelling place of demons, a haunt of every foul spirit, a haunt of every foul and hateful bird; for all nations have drunk the wine of her impure passion, and the kings of the earth have committed fornication with her, and the merchants of the earth have grown rich with the wealth of her wantonness.*

Porneias in Greek means fornication, impure passion, harlotries. *Pornos* is "harlot" or "whore." All these words are from the same root—porn. "If you look on a woman with lust, you commit adultery in your heart," Jesus said. Sex for money or sex simply for pleasure (sex for consumption, sex outside the covenant of marriage) is *porneias.* "And the kings of the earth have committed fornication *[porneias]* with her, and the merchants of the earth have grown rich with the wealth of her wantonness" (v. 3).

Our economy runs on "wantonness." We call it "consumer confidence." This was a recent perfume ad in the window at Macy's:

You want it. You want it bad. Sometimes so much it hurts. You can taste it. You feel like you would do anything to get it. Go further than they'd suspect. Twist your soul and crush what's in your way. Then you get it. And something happens. You become the object of your desire. And it feels incredible.

Does it? Throwing licentious parties for herself alone in the dark—the great whore.

"The merchants of the earth have grown rich with the wealth of her wantonness." I bet more people around the world have tasted Coca-Cola than communion wine. But that only stands to reason, for "Coke is the real thing."

REVELATION 18:4–5: *Then I heard another voice from heaven saying, "Come out of her, my people, lest you take part in her sins, lest you share in her plagues; for her sins are heaped high as heaven."*

. . . heaped like bricks in the Tower of Babel, heaped in order to seize eternity with human energy.

REVELATION 18:5–7: *And God has remembered her iniquities. Render to her as she herself has rendered, and repay her double for her deeds; mix a double draught for her in the cup she mixed. As she glorified herself and played the wanton* [that is, "gave herself luxuries"].

I read that if we could shrink the earth' s population to a village of one hundred people, one half of the village would suffer from malnutrition, one half of the village's wealth would be in the hands of only six citizens, and all six would be American. I don't know how accurate that is, but I do know that something like a billion people subsist on the equivalent of less than a dollar a day.

"But man shall not live on bread alone but every word that proceeds from the mouth of God. His Word is life," we remind ourselves.

In the early 1990s it was reported that Americans spent 140 times as much on legalized gambling as overseas Protestant ministries. And we spent 17 times as much on diets and diet-related products. That is, while billions of unsaved people starved, we paid already wealthy people to help us not eat . . . at a rate of 17 to 1 . . . diets over the Word. We're still some of the most overweight people on earth. And a little preaching might have gone a long way in Afghanistan about ten years ago. . . .

REVELATION 18:7: *So give her a like measure of torment and mourning. Since in her heart she says, "A queen I sit, I am no widow, mourning I shall never see."*

The harlot has become *so arrogant* in her wealth she thinks she will never see suffering. "Health and wealth" theology is really strong in America: Our riches mean God's approval. This whole pretribulation rapture thing is really a recent American phenomenon. The idea is, God *surely* wouldn't let His chosen people suffer great tribulation.

So I guess that means those martyrs in the Sudan weren't chosen . . . and *of course* we're supposed to "pick up our cross and follow." In fact, you can get a nice gold-plated one on a chain at Macy's for $49.95. . . .

REVELATION 18:8–13: *So shall her plagues come in a single day, pestilence and mourning and famine, and she shall be burned with fire; for mighty is the Lord God who judges her." And the kings of the earth, who committed fornication and were wanton with her, will weep and wail over her when they see the smoke of her burning; they will stand far off, in fear of her torment, and say, "Alas! alas! thou great city, thou mighty city, Babylon! In one hour has thy judgment come. And the merchants of the earth weep and mourn for her, since no one buys their cargo any more, cargo of gold, silver, jewels and pearls, fine linen, purple, silk and scarlet, all kinds of scented wood, all articles of ivory, all articles of costly wood, bronze, iron and marble, cinnamon, spice, incense, myrrh, frankincense, wine, oil, fine flour and wheat, cattle and sheep, horses and chariots, and slaves, that is, human souls.*

In my country white people are still far richer than black people. Don't be fooled. There is a reason for that . . . slavery. And if I understand Scripture correctly, my country has systematically and hygienically aborted something like thirty-eight million human souls since 1973. Loneliness is longing for human souls.

REVELATION 18:14–21: *The fruit for which thy soul longed has gone from thee, and all thy dainties and thy splendor are lost to thee, never to be found again! The merchants of these wares, who gained wealth from her, will stand far off, in fear of her torment, weeping and mourning aloud, "Alas, alas, for the*

*great city that was clothed in fine linen, in purple and scarlet, bedecked with
gold, with jewels, and with pearls! In one hour all this wealth has been laid
waste. And all shipmasters and seafaring men, sailors and all whose trade is on
the sea, stood far off and cried out as they saw the smoke of her burning, "What
city was like the great city?" And they threw dust on their heads, as they wept and
mourned, crying out, "Alas, alas, for the great city where all who had ships at sea
grew rich by her wealth! In one hour she has been laid waste. Rejoice over her, O
heaven, O saints and apostles and prophets, for God has given judgment for you
against her!" Then a mighty angel took up a stone like a great millstone and
threw it into the sea.*

Jesus said, "Whoever causes one of these little ones who believe in Me to
stumble, it would be better for him if a millstone were hung around his neck
and he were thrown into the sea" (Mark 9:42 NKJV). In my children's school it
is illegal to talk about God. Life is explained through consumption, "survival
of the fittest." Any biologist has to admit that this principle doesn't explain
life; it explains death. Have you ever tried to teach world history without referring to Jesus? Of necessity it forces you to lie and lead children astray . . .

REVELATION 18:21–23: *Then a mighty angel took up a stone like a great
millstone and threw it into the sea, saying, "So shall Babylon the great city be
thrown down with violence, and shall be found no more; and the sound of
harpers and minstrels, of flute players and trumpeters, shall be heard in thee no
more; and a craftsman of any craft shall be found in thee no more; and the sound
of the millstone shall be heard in thee no more; and the light of a lamp shall
shine in thee no more; and the voice of bridegroom and bride shall be heard in
thee no more; for thy merchants were the great men of the earth, and all nations
were deceived by thy sorcery* [magic spell].

By graduation the average American teenager has seen 350,000 TV
commercials, amounting to one and a half years of eight-hour workdays. Not
just Americans, but all nations are sucked into our economy through commercials. It's how we rule the world . . . our magic spell. And how do they work?

Remember this one? "Is that me holding you or you holding me? I cannot
tell where you begin and I end. *Eternity.*"

What are they selling? Perfume. What can you say about perfume? It smells
good. What do they promise? Eternal communion. Now, in Eternity commer-

cials they show children running down a beach . . . eternal communion that bears life. And all it really is—*smelly water.* That's a lying promise, a magic spell, harlotry . . . and it works, for we buy the stuff.

REVELATION 18:24: *And in her was found the blood of prophets and of saints, and of all who have been slain on earth.*

Prophets and saints bled for a vision of a country, blessed like old Israel . . . "Blessed in order to be a blessing." That's the Protestant work ethic: Work with God to create for others, instead of working alone to consume in the dark.

It may look the same on the outside, but its dream is creation, not consumption. It runs on *Creator* confidence, not *consumer* confidence. It runs on *fullness* not *emptiness, giving* instead of *getting.*

Israel was *blessed* in order to be a blessing, but they turned their blessings into idols. What have you been mourning since September 11? I hope it is towers filled with priceless human souls for whom Christ died. But perhaps it is towers that represent an idol, our consumer lifestyle . . . towers of Babel. You see, my heart is awfully invested in Babylon. Planes flew into the Twin Towers (the World Trade Center) right down the street from the United Nations, in the great city. We watched them fall in one hour, behind a statue on the waters, the goddess of liberty, whose liberty has become license.

God might actually be sending me a message, even at the hands of the godless beast. And the message is, "Repent." Whenever Israel encountered disaster, their immediate temptation was arrogance: "We're God's people!" But God's message was always the same: "Repent!"

Well, the U.S. is *not Israel,* but the Church is Israel. We may be living in the most dangerous place on earth, but not because of terrorists. Jesus calls, "Come out of her, my people," and we call back, "Well, we actually kind of *like* it here."

We're like dieters who work in a doughnut shop. Is anything wrong with doughnuts? No! In fact, doughnuts can be used to save a starving man. But if you are an overweight diabetic, hanging around doughnut shops can be dangerous.

"The Lord is my shepherd, I shall not want." In America? Yeah, right. "Thou shalt have no other gods before me." In America? That's tough. And to the extent America is a harlot, she's an unhappy one. For prostitution leaves you violated, alone, and mortally depressed. Mother Teresa said several times, "The greatest poverty is in the West." She was talking about loneliness.

The suicide rate for youth in our country has tripled since the 1950s. Rightfully we mourn the deaths of Americans killed by terrorist beasts, but in the last few years, far more Americans have killed themselves. They must have died feeling like lonely harlots, not heroes.

So what is God saying? The voice cries, "Come out of her, my people." What does it mean when a man comes out of a harlot? Jesus is saying, "Stop fornicating with the harlot. She'll suck you dry and leave you desolate. Stop giving your treasure, your heart, your dreams, the deepest longings of your soul, to an economy of consumption. Your heart is only satisfied in me. And I am in the last and least of these, my brethren."

When you're depressed, do you go shopping? Jesus calls to you in that moment saying, "Come out of her. She will not give you life."

Well, a man was made to go into a woman and give life. If he is to come out of a whore, into whom is he to give life and make life?

REVELATION 19:1–8: *After this I heard what seemed to be the loud voice of a great multitude in heaven, crying, "Hallelujah! Salvation and glory and power belong to our God, for his judgments are true and just; he has judged the great harlot who corrupted the earth with her fornication, and he has avenged on her the blood of his servants." Once more they cried, "Hallelujah! The smoke from her goes up for ever and ever." And the twenty-four elders and the four living creatures fell down and worshiped God who is seated on the throne, saying, "Amen. Hallelujah!" And from the throne came a voice crying, "Praise our God, all you his servants, you who fear him, small and great." Then I heard what seemed to be the voice of a great multitude, like the sound of many waters and like the sound of mighty thunderpeals, crying, "Hallelujah! For the Lord our God the Almighty reigns. Let us rejoice and exult and give him the glory, for the marriage of the Lamb has come, and his Bride has made herself ready; it was granted her to be clothed with fine linen, bright and pure"—for the fine linen is the righteous deeds of the saints.*

In Revelation 21:24 we read, "The kings of the earth shall bring their glory" —their life, their stuff—into the New Jerusalem, the Bride of Christ. In Revelation 21:2 we read, "The new Jerusalem [*is*, present participle] coming down." I think that means the New Jerusalem has been coming down for two thousand years and is somehow among us . . . just as Jesus said that the kingdom is among us (see Luke 17:20–21). The New Jerusalem is the people of God—the Bride.

Come out of the whore and go into the Bride . . . with your seed (*sperma* in Greek) if she's your wife . . . with your treasure, heart, time, and money, if she's your Church. In other words, use *things* to love *people* and bear much fruit . . . fruit that will not be consumed in the fire, but purified for eternity.

If America is the harlot, America is also the bride. No country has ever *consumed* as much, and no country has ever *created* as much. We've built hospitals around the world; we've evangelized nations; we even rescued the world from Hitler in World War II. I hope we're doing as well now.

There is no other kingdom of this world in which I'd rather live than the United States of America. But I'm already a citizen of a better kingdom. It is not of this world, yet it invades this world when I touch lepers, defend the oppressed, and give to the poor.

America is seduced by the harlot, but she's also salted with the Bride.

God consumes the great spirit of harlotry, turning harlots into brides. His love is a consuming fire. God's people were all harlots without Him—idolaters. He creates His Bride from harlots by bleeding for them on His cross, then sending His word to conquer their hearts and impregnate them with life.

In chapter 19 the Word riding a white horse conquers the world. Then the Bride is revealed in all her glory. We are created to create in His image. It means sacrifice, it means Word—seed—spoken into broken hearts. It hurts, but done in love it's a taste of ecstasy—life. It produces life—the party—the kingdom—the New Jerusalem—even here. Come out of the whore and love the Bride.

TWENTY-NINE

THE WORD, RIDING ON
YOUR TONGUE

(Revelation 19:9–21)

WHEN JOHN SENT THE REVELATION to the saints in those seven baby churches in Asia Minor, it must have seemed like a myth. The Word of God must have seemed like a myth. Asia Minor is a long way from Palestine. Paul had planted the churches forty years earlier, but now Paul was dead and John was exiled. A few in these churches had been killed for refusing to worship the Emperor. Many were facing economic trials, such as exile from the trade guilds. They were being persecuted, yet also seduced back into their old lifestyles. These were probably the days of Emperors Vespasian or Domitian, so the coliseum in Rome would have been brand-new, soon to be filled with the blood of Christians slaughtered by Roman gladiators for entertainment.

The world had never seen an empire so glorious and powerful. But John prophesies its fall and tells the seven little churches they will *conquer* with Christ. It must have seemed like a *myth* . . . good words separated from everyday reality.

When you think about it, all good words seem separated from reality in some way. We call it *futility;* sometimes *injustice.* The word *love,* for instance, shouldn't feel like pain and suffering. Yet in this world it often does. The word *evil* shouldn't look like a handsome man in a designer suit with gold rings. Yet in this world sometimes it does.

In fairy tales the good somehow always turns out beautiful, and the evil is always exposed as a monster. Instinct tells us the word *beloved* should look like a gorgeous bride, spotless and without blemish. The words *faithful* and *true* should look like a prince on a white horse. The words *coward* and *lie* should look like a snake.

The Hebrews didn't really have a word for *word*. They used *dabar*—meaning "thing." You say or hear a "thing." The Greeks used *logos*—idea—reality—meaning, and also *rhema*—applied meaning.

The hard thing about words in this world is that they don't always line up with the reality we experience. And so we say, "Oh, it's just words." In the twentieth century, we came to believe that unless words matched what we could prove with our five senses, they weren't really true . . . just myths. People call that logical positivism, empiricism, scientism, or modernism. The only problem is that logical positivism can't be proved true with logical positivism (our flesh, our senses), for truth is not of this world.

Speaking good words in this world can be very hard. Words such as *just, faithful,* and *true* tend to get crucified. It's hard to speak the Word of God—Jesus—because . . .

- the Word seems ridiculous and weak, and our world likes demonstrations of power.

- the Word seems confused. How do you prove or define a word like *love* or *Jesus*—wrap Him up nice and tidy?

- the Word is painful. God's Word cuts against this world and into your own heart. And when it does, it lives in you with power and passion. But when you share it, it's often rejected as myth.

So many times when I'm done preaching or witnessing, I feel like a jackass . . . ridiculous, weak, confused, alone, rejected . . . by myself—my own flesh, my own five senses. I think, "How could I have *said* such things?!" *Crazy myths.* Haven't you walked out of church and said to yourself, "What was *that?*" I have.

Arguably the most influential theologian of the last century was Rudolph Bultmann. In 1941 in Germany he published an essay on "Myth in the New Testament," in which he argued that Scripture embodied a prescientific view of the world. He reasoned that to communicate the gospel to the modern mind we needed to translate Scripture into nonmythical terms. That is, we needed to demythologize the Word.

So while Hitler preached pagan myths, we (the Church) demythologized the Word.

Historically, in mainline churches, liberalism has tended to make angels and demons into psychologies and God into a great idea. They read the

Revelation like a parable. Fundamentalist churches reacted against that idea but did their own demythologizing, trying to prove the Word of God with science. They said they took the Revelation "literally," which meant scientifically or empirically. They took numbers and calendars, space and time, very seriously. But I do not think they took the meaning *(logos)* very seriously.

I think charismatic churches have done some demythologizing as well by teaching that God doesn't show up unless someone shakes, falls down, or gets up out of a wheelchair—unless there is scientific evidence—something you can see.

Mainline, fundamentalist, charismatic—I'm a bit of each. For those in the late-twentieth-century church, words just didn't cut it. In order to believe something, we needed to see it, explain it, chart it, or feel it. We needed *flesh*, not faith which came by hearing and hearing by the Word of God.

In this world, "word" is ridiculous, weak, confusing, and even painful. So speaking the Word of God is *hard*. And what *is* it?

The *logos*, the Word, is unchanging truth. It's Scripture, *at least*. The *rhema* of God is more like God's Word for a particular need or moment. How can we recognize *that* Word?

SOME PEOPLE THINK the spirit of *weird* is the Word of God (*rhema* of God). But not everything weird is holy, or we'd be worshiping Peewee Herman. Sometimes weird is just *weird*—but then, have you ever received a note or a prayer or some words from somebody and it really *was* weird . . . not because it *didn't* fit, but because it *fit so well?* Even weirder, have you ever been the one who *spoke* the word? I have, on occasion, and what's weirdest to me is that it didn't happen during those times I was trying *so hard* to hear God's Word. In fact, I wasn't even focused on me and what *I* could do, so I don't fully know how it happened.

How are we to speak God's true words in the moment?

REVELATION 19:9–10: *And the angel said to me, "Write this: Blessed are those who are invited to the marriage supper of the Lamb." And he said to me, "These are true words of God." Then I fell down at his feet to worship him, but he said to me, "You must not do that! I am a fellow servant with you and your brethren who hold the testimony of Jesus. Worship God." For the testimony of Jesus is the spirit of prophecy.*

Prophecy is speaking God's Word for the moment. "The testimony of Jesus is the spirit of prophecy" (Revelation 19:10). The spirit of prophecy is all about Jesus.

I'm a baby at all of this, but I've found that if I get all worked up about whether or not I can hear God's Word in the moment, whether or not I'm ridiculous, confused, or going to get hurt, whether or not *I* can hear . . . well, I *don't*. But if I can forget myself (my flesh) and get lost in Jesus . . .

loving Jesus—
glorifying Jesus—
thinking about Jesus—
worshiping Jesus—
testifying to Jesus—

. . . those are the times I've been shocked to find that God's Word got through, and it fit like a hand in glove.

If you go to a prayer service looking for prophecy because you want to know who to date, what stock to buy, and how to feed your flesh, you don't understand. Prophecy is the testimony of Jesus. He leads—the *Word* leads—and we follow.

When I first prayed for some people who struggled with powerful demonic spirits, I saw violent, physical reactions to words that came off my tongue. That was because other spiritual realities momentarily controlled their flesh. Now I see that many of those words were prophetic, and I spoke them when I wasn't worried about *me*. I longed to see Jesus glorified. I would speak a thought and the word was exactly like a knife sticking something in another world. The wildest part was that it felt like the word had a life of its own; it wasn't dependent on me. I was dependent on the *Word*—following the Word —which fit into a plan from before there was time. I just happened to have the incredible privilege of speaking it into history.

The spirit of prophecy is the testimony of Jesus. But the Revelation says the testimony of Jesus *is* the spirit of prophecy . . . a spirit . . . a living thing. Not just the few times I've been able to see it empirically in the flesh, but every time I truly testify to Jesus, I'm speaking a word that has a life of its own, "living and active, sharper than any two-edged sword" (Hebrews 4:12).

Sharper and stronger,
cutting into things deeper than flesh,
even beyond space and time.

Every time I focus on Jesus, watch Jesus, love Jesus (not thinking of myself) . . . every time I am lost in Jesus, following Jesus, and therefore testifying of Jesus . . . the Word actually rides out and conquers, even if I look like a *jackass* . . . and later feel like a jackass when I'm alone with myself.

REVELATION 19:11–16: *Then I saw heaven opened, and behold, a white horse! He who sat upon it is called Faithful and True, and in righteousness he judges and makes war. His eyes are like a flame of fire, and on his head are many diadems; and he has a name inscribed which no one knows but himself. He is clad in a robe dipped in blood, and the name by which he is called is The Word of God. And the armies of heaven, arrayed in fine linen, white and pure, followed him on white horses. From his mouth issues a sharp sword with which to smite the nations, and he will rule them with a rod of iron; he will tread the wine press of the fury of the wrath of God the Almighty. On his robe and on his thigh he has a name inscribed, King of kings and Lord of lords.*

LEADING UP TO CHAPTER 19, we have just witnessed the destruction of the great whore—Old Jerusalem and all those whoring moneychangers in the temple. Now, in verses 11–16 of chapter 19, the Word rides in, and soon we'll see the Bride, the New Jerusalem.

Two thousand years ago, the Word rode a jackass into old Jerusalem. He died on a cross and cleansed His harlot Bride (His temple) with His blood that is wine.

On the cross, Jesus cast out the ruler of this world. He was *judgment;* His Word *is* judgment. There, He draws all men to Himself. He does it through the Word proclaimed, and the Word *is* Himself (see John 12).

Christ died for His Bride that He might cleanse her by the washing of water with the Word, that He might present her to Himself spotless in splendor (Ephesians 5:25–27). He told His followers, "You are already made clean by the word which I have spoken to you" (John 15:3).

In this earthly realm, Jesus still rides into town on a jackass. Like then, He often looks ridiculous, weak, confused, and in pain. In this earthly realm, Jesus still rides on jackasses. But in reality, He rides the warhorse.

When you testify to Jesus (not yourself) and follow Him, you ride with the King, clothed in fine linen. You may look and feel like a jackass, but there is no greater power and glory than the one who rides out on your tongue: King of kings and Lord of lords.

If you are a mainline liberal you say, "Oh, that's a *myth.* It's not the real world!" Well, how do you know that the real world isn't a myth, and this mythical world isn't real? Maybe Jesus *is* truth, and you are the lie. Maybe there really is a world where the beloved is a "glorious Bride," where the Word, faithful and true, is a "conquering King on a white horse" where they see evil for what it is—a snake—and where good always conquers. Maybe truth *is* invading this world of lies. But He comes humbled and riding on an jackass, because God wants us to choose His world in faith . . . the freedom of love, not the constraint of fear.

One day all eyes will be opened, and the judgment is: "Did you see me when I rode into town on a jackass?"

Fundamentalists might say, "This is strictly in the *future* when all eyes will see." But Revelation 1:7 proclaims, "Behold [that means "look!"], he is coming, and all eyes will see him." He already *is* coming; it's just that not all eyes can yet see Him.

Paul prayed for Ephesus and Asia Minor (the seven churches) that God would give them a spirit of wisdom and revelation in the knowledge of Him, that the eyes of their hearts would be opened and they would know, among other things, the immeasurable greatness of His power at work in us who believe (Ephesians 1:17–19). I think that prayer was answered forty years later when John sent them a letter called the Revelation. Heaven is opened and behold, He is coming.

Some will accuse me of spiritualizing the text. Maybe we need to stop *flesh*atizing the text, as if the spirit is nothing and the flesh availeth much. "It is the spirit that gives life, the flesh is of no avail; the words that I have spoken to you are spirit and life" (John 6:63).

Charismatics may say, "We didn't see anybody shake, and no one got healed." You realize that when Jesus, the Word, rode into Jerusalem and crushed the head of the dragon, ransoming you from hell (that is, cleansing His harlot Bride for all time, washing her with the blood of His eternal covenant), nobody shook with joy, nobody spoke in tongues, and nobody's back was healed. It looked irrelevant, weak, wretched, confused, and painful. He rode a jackass. And everyone abandoned Him, thinking He had failed.

He is the Word. He does not return void.

The twentieth century is over, and modernity turned out to be absurd. Maybe we need to "remythologize" the Word (as if we ever could have demythologized it). We need to remythologize ourselves. We need to believe the Word and not our flesh.

REVELATION 19:17–21: *Then I saw an angel standing in the sun, and with a loud voice he called to all the birds that fly in midheaven, "Come, gather for the great supper of God, to eat the flesh of kings, the flesh of captains, the flesh of mighty men, the flesh of horses and their riders, and the flesh of all men, both free and slave, both small and great." And I saw the beast and the kings of the earth with their armies gathered to make war against him who sits upon the horse and against his army. And the beast was captured, and with it the false prophet who in its presence had worked the signs by which he deceived those who had received the mark of the beast and those who worshiped its image. These two were thrown alive into the lake of fire that burns with sulphur. And the rest were slain by the sword of him who sits upon the horse, the sword that issues from his mouth; and all the birds were gorged with their flesh.*

"Flesh and blood cannot inherit the kingdom of God nor does the perishable inherit the imperishable" (1 Corinthians 15:50). The beast and the false prophet are thrown into the lake of fire. But the rest—the remnant—the kings of the earth—are slain by the Word *(logos)* with the Word *(rhema),* and the birds devour their flesh. Check this out: In Revelation 21:24, the kings of the earth bring their glory into the New Jerusalem. *They must have been slain in order that they might live.*

"The Word became [sinless] flesh and dwelt among us, full of grace," wrote John (John 1:14). Christ went to the cross to absorb *our* sinful flesh and die in our place. And there, God "condemned sin in the flesh" (Romans 8:3).

If we are crucified with Christ, we will be raised with Christ. Old flesh is stripped away, and we will receive a new body. But the Word slays us—crucifies us. The testimony of Jesus is His death and resurrection, the gospel. The Word came to save sinners, so He reveals my sin, my flesh, my arrogance, my pride . . . and crucifies it so I can live.

Speaking the Word can feel ridiculous, weak, confusing, and lonely, and it *hurts* because it cuts your own pride—your flesh, and it cuts those to whom you speak. So you may feel like a jackass, but in reality nothing is more glorious, and nothing is more powerful.

Sometimes you can even see it in this world of lies, for the kingdom of this world has become the kingdom of our God and of His Christ. He has taken His great power and begun to reign.

At the end of the first century in Asia Minor, the Revelation must have seemed like a ridiculous myth. Yet in A.D. 312, the emperor Constantine confessed Christ as "King of kings and Lord of lords." By the end of the fourth century, most of the Roman Empire was at least nominally Christian.

Around that time in the region of the seven churches, a weak little monk named Telemachus felt called to Rome. When he arrived he went to the coliseum and saw the gladiators salute the emperor and prepare to die for the glory of Rome. Compelled by love, the monk jumped the wall and ran to the middle of the field. He looked like a jackass, but he yelled, "In the name of Christ, stop!" They all mocked him, the gladiators abused him, and the crowd chanted, "Run him through!" Then a gladiator did.

Legend says that with his dying breath, Telemachus invoked the Word: "In the name of Christ, stop!"[1] In silence, Rome stared at the body broken and blood shed. One by one the spectators got up and left.

According to historians, that was the last gladiator contest in the Roman Coliseum.[2] It was won by the Last Gladiator. He set an ambush and rode out on the tongue of a ridiculous little monk.

According to the U.S. Center for World Missions . . .

- in A.D. 1420 there was one Bible-believing Christian for every ninety-nine people on the planet;
- by 1790 there was one for every forty-nine people on the planet;
- by 1940 it was one in thirty-two;
- by 1970 it was one in nineteen;
- by 1980 it was one in ten;
- by 1999 it was one in eight.

He is coming. There is no greater power and no greater glory. Speak the Word. Sticks and stones may break your bones, but the kingdom of God comes with a Word—*the Word.* Some day sticks and stones will disintegrate in fire, but the Word of God abides forever.

THIRTY

DON'T MISS THE MILLENNIUM

(Revelation 20:1–10)

W HAT KIND OF WORLD ARE WE LIVING IN? *Wars, rumors of war,*
terrorism. Plagues, immorality, abortion. Drugs, promiscuity, divorce. . . . And on
top of all this, the Church has lost its place in society, the courts, and the
schools. Belittled in the media, stripped of power and authority, Christians
have become victims in a hostile world. *Victims!*

How ironic: God's plan was that we would rule the world from a paradise
garden. For in the beginning God created man in His own image and said to
them, "Be fruitful and multiply . . . and have dominion [rule] . . . over every
living thing that moves upon the earth" (Genesis 1:28). That would *certainly*
include *snakes.* But you know what happened—*deception.* The punishment
was death, futility, and snake bites—dragon bites, bruised heels—and we were
banished from the Garden.

This world is hardly a garden now.

REVELATION 20:1–10 (NKJV): *Then I saw an angel coming down from*
heaven, having the key to the bottomless pit, and a great chain in his hand. He
laid hold of the dragon, that serpent of old, who is the Devil and Satan, and
bound him for a thousand years; and he cast him into the bottomless pit, and
shut him up, and set a seal on him, so that he should deceive the nations no more
till the thousand years were finished. But after these things he must be released
for a little while.

And I saw thrones, and they sat on them, and judgment was committed to
them. Then I saw the souls of those who had been beheaded for their witness to
Jesus and for the word of God, who had not worshiped the beast or his image,
and had not received his mark on their foreheads or on their hands. And they
lived [some translations say, "they came to life," but the Greek is simple—

aorist active indicative: "they lived"] *and reigned with Christ for a thousand years. But the rest of the dead did not live again until the thousand years were finished. This is the first resurrection. Over such the second death has no power, but they shall be priests of God and of Christ, and shall reign with Him a thousand years.*

Now when the thousand years have expired, Satan will be released from his prison and will go out to deceive the nations which are in the four corners of the earth, Gog and Magog, to gather them together to battle, whose number is as the sand of the sea. They went up on the breadth of the earth and surrounded the camp of the saints and the beloved city. And fire came down from God out of heaven and devoured them. The devil, who deceived them, was cast into the lake of fire and brimstone where the beast and the false prophet are. And they will be tormented day and night forever and ever.

REVELATION 20 is probably the most controversial chapter in all of Scripture. Remember that millennium means a thousand years, and Christians certainly don't agree on what those thousand years mean. There have been four dominant millennial views.

The historic *premillennial* view, held by many of the early church fathers, attests that Christ will return in bodily form *at the start of* the millennium, reign for a thousand years from an earthly throne, and then the final judgment will come.

Amillennialism, a position held by other early church fathers, teaches that this present age is the millennium, and Christ reigns on earth *now through* His Church. As Christ taught in the parable of the wheat and the tares, the kingdom of heaven and the kingdom of Satan both grow in history until the end when Jesus returns, and the earth is reaped on the last day. Augustine argued for this view in *The City of God.* At a church council in A.D. 431, the premillennial view was denounced as superstitious and unbiblical. The amillennial view was the dominant and official church position for fourteen hundred years. It was the view of Augustine, Martin Luther, John Calvin, and as always, the Roman Catholic Church.

In the nineteenth century, *postmillennialism* became the dominant view in America. It is the view that the thousand-year reign of Christ happens in the future, but that it occurs through the "ordinary means of grace." Therefore, Christ's bodily return is after the millennium at the final judgment. Postmillennialists believe a day will come when Christ, through the Church, will convert the nations and usher in a thousand-year period of spiritual blessings and physical prosperity previously unknown on earth. This view gave rise to abolition, temperance, and the great missionary thrust of the nineteenth century. It was behind the Great Awakening and the second Great Awakening: the great American revivals. Both Charles Finney and the Puritan Jonathan Edwards were avid postmillennialists. Over time, however, much of this view devolved into optimistic liberalism—the belief in utopia through human energy.

None of these views is popular in America today. In the mid-nineteenth century in England, John Darby developed dispensational theology and added an "extraordinary innovation" to his premillennial scheme: the heretofore unheard-of pretribulation rapture. This form of dispensationalism teaches that Christians are mysteriously "raptured" prior to a seven-year tribulation. (Some forms have Christians raptured "midtrib" or "post-trib.") They usually argue that the tribulation has to do with the conversion of ethnic Jews, and that this is what most of the Revelation is about. After the tribulation, Christ returns with His raptured Church. They set up an earthly government in Jerusalem and reign a thousand years on earth, fulfilling Old Testament and messianic prophecies. *After that,* the other dead from throughout history are raised and are judged. Then the end comes: New Heaven and New Earth.

Traditionally, there has also been a fifth view: the igno-apothomillennial position, which means roughly, "I don't know and I don't care." For most of my life that has been my staunch position. Well, now I have to care and I've come to care, because I care about good news. Unfortunately I may be unpopular, because I have real problems with the popular view.

I want to tell you what the problems are because our view of the end changes how we live *now.* I want to tell you, but I don't want you to be offended or feel attacked. We're all learning, and I could be *wrong.* Very simply, here are some of my problems with the popular view:

First, the popular view is part of dispensationalism, a scheme that usually argues that certain gifts of the Spirit, like prophecy, are no longer for today. Peter teaches in Acts 2 that these *are* the last days, and your sons and daughters shall prophesy.

Second, the popular view also teaches that Israel and the Church are separate groups, and that the Old Testament and most of Revelation is about the State of Israel, not about *me.* But I *am* Israel, a child of Abraham by faith, one of the chosen people. Old branches were broken off, and I was grafted in. Scripture is extremely clear on that, especially in Romans. The Church is why the Lamb bleeds on the throne. She is His Bride, His temple, His body, His suffering presence in this world.

Third, the popular view doesn't take Scripture literally, even though its proponents *say* they do. I think they take it empirically, scientifically—in a worldly manner. Taking it literally should mean taking it according to its literal form, how the author intended it. It's clear to me that the Revelation is not meant to be understood as a calendar. And the one thing the popular view takes as obvious is the one thing Scripture says is *not* obvious. Peter tells us, "But do not ignore this one fact, beloved, that with the Lord one day is as a thousand years, and a thousand years as one day" (2 Peter 3:8). Who's counting—God, us? Are we traveling at the speed of light?

John writes of those who live: "kings and priests" who reign with Christ one thousand years. Then he stops his description and says, "Hey, this is the first resurrection" (v. 5)—as if those folks in Ephesus and Colossae and Asia Minor knew very well what that is. . . .

- To the Ephesians, Paul said that we have been raised with Christ and seated in the heavenly places (2:6).

- To the Colossians, he wrote that if we have been raised with Christ, we should seek the things above (3:1).

- If you have ever read John's Gospel and epistles, you know that he is Mr. Born Again—he is always talking about how we have passed from death to eternal life (1 John 3:14).

- Jesus tells Nicodemus that we must be born of the Spirit—born again. Nicodemus says, You mean I have to go back inside my mother's womb? Jesus responds, "Come on, Nicodemus. Take a shot at abstract reasoning." Actually, He says, "If I have told you earthly things and you do not believe, how can you believe if I tell you heavenly things?" (John 3:12).

In Revelation 20, John is now speaking of heavenly things, for heaven has been opened. But we don't believe it. We don't take it seriously. I think the modern Church is infected with Nicodemitis—spiritual blindness. So we pull out our calendars and start counting a thousand years in space and time. John stops and says, "This is the first resurrection" (v. 5).

Have you not been raised with Christ? Do you not have eternal life now? You're His Body; the living Christ is in you, and He's not dead.

Fourth, the popular view takes this world way *too* seriously. It takes space and time and of empirical evidence way too seriously and spiritual realities not seriously enough. I'm afraid it walks by sight, not by faith. So we think the kingdom comes with "signs to be observed," and we're always asking, "When does the kingdom come?"—just as the Pharisees did in Luke 17. And Jesus says,

"The kingdom of God is not coming with signs to be observed; . . . the kingdom of God is in the midst of you" (Luke 17:21). Jesus says, "In this world you will have tribulation, but be of good cheer [don't take it so seriously], I have overcome [conquered—same word] the world" (John 16:33 NKJV).

The popular view usually says, "Jesus won't let us suffer tribulation." It's not that He conquers and rules the world through us *in* tribulation, but that He takes us out of the world—rapture time! I believe the idea of a pretribulation rapture is unbiblical. It sends an awful message to the world . . . not that Christ suffers *for* the world, but that He hightails it *out* of the world. We "fill up the measure of his sufferings," writes Paul. That must be in the world. He overcomes the world *in* us, *in* tribulation.

I have Romanian friends who bear the scars of torture on their bodies. What do I tell the husband who held his dying wife in his arms, because of her refusal to renounce her faith? What do we say to them? "Be of good cheer, because God will rapture His faithful Church *before* the tribulation"?

Americans taught this doctrine to the Church in China in the 1940s. When the Communists took over and started torturing the Church, many Chinese Christians thought they had missed the rapture. According to Brother Andrew, many missionaries were barred from returning by Chinese Christians who said, "You told us that before tribulation we'd be raptured. You're liars." The cross is tribulation, and we are crucified with Christ.

Fifth, the popular view makes the cross *small* by discounting what God has already done and is doing. *"Now* is the judgment of this world," said Jesus. *"'Now* shall the ruler of this world be cast out; and I, when I am lifted up from the earth, will draw all men to myself.' He said this to show by what death he was to die" (John 12:31, emphasis added).

On the cross Jesus bore our judgment, conquered the enemy, and conquered the world. And we are "more than conquerors through him who loved us" (Romans 8:37). On the cross He "disarmed the principalities and powers" (Colossians 2:15). He told us, "Whatever you bind on earth shall be bound in heaven" (Matthew 16:19). In Luke 10:18–19, He said, "I saw Satan fall like lightning from heaven. Behold, I have given you authority to tread upon serpents and scorpions, and over all the power of the enemy; and nothing shall hurt you." "If God is for us, who is against us?" (Romans 8:31). "For all things are yours . . . and you are Christ's; and Christ is God's" (1 Corinthians 3:21–23). By loving us and washing us in His blood, He has "made us kings and priests unto God and his Father" (Revelation 1:5–6 KJV).

Wow—if you really took the cross seriously and took Scripture *literally* and didn't take this world so *seriously,* you might figure that the millennium is *now.*

Technically, I suppose this puts me in the amillennial camp. But "amillennial" means "no millennium" to most, and I believe in the millennium. I believe the millennial reign of Christ happens whenever we walk by faith: Whenever we walk by faith, the kingdom of God is upon us, and eternity *(kairos)* invades temporality *(chronos)*.

I do believe all chronology will end some day. Jesus will return with fire . . . *as* fire consuming the earth and His adversaries. And there will be judgment at the last day, and He will raise us up on the last day (John 6, 12). And it will be the *last* day, not 365,000 days (and seven years) *before* the last day. Until then, believers are to reign and rule. Child kings reign with a regent. We reign with Christ. But we do reign:

- *over sin in our own flesh* (Romans 6:12). The world is enslaved to sin, but as a child of God you are forgiven, no longer condemned, so you rule it through grace.

- *over the accuser, Satan.* Satan is *bound* by the gospel Word that rides on your tongue. He is bound in hell; yet I suspect hell is among us, just as heaven is among us. Satan's only hope is to get you to believe lies. He is unbound at the end to mislead the nations. (I imagine that's outright satanism . . . when he no longer needs the beast and false prophet.) But he is still bound by the Word that rides on your tongue.

- *over creation.* All things work for the good with those who love God and are called according to His purpose. Sure—those things can *hurt* a lot. But for you, tribulation has been transformed from wrath into grace. In trials God shapes you into the image of Christ the King. In trials you exhibit the gospel. In trials Christ communes with you in suffering. Every moment you receive in gratitude by faith becomes an eternal moment, and you walk with God, as in the Garden. Your prayers rise before the throne as he speaks creation into existence. You rule the world through faith. Don't let it rule you.

- *over the hearts of men and women.* We are priests; that is, we bring them to God. We are the body of Christ in this world, and when *His* body is broken and *His* blood is shed—when His Body (us) is crucified and we suffer in love—He draws all men to Himself even through us.

"Thanks be to God, who in Christ always leads us in triumph, and through us spreads the fragrance of the knowledge of him everywhere" (2 Corinthians 2:14).

I may be wrong about the millennium, but I am right about this: Believers are "a chosen race, a royal [kingly] priesthood, a holy nation, God's own people." *Why?* "That you may declare the wonderful deeds of him who called you out of darkness into his marvelous light" (1 Peter 2:9). The resurrected Jesus *did* appear to His victimized, seemingly powerless disciples and say, "All authority [rule, reign] in heaven and on earth has been given to me. Go therefore and make disciples of all nations [They're no longer bound by Satan] . . . and lo, I am with you always, to the close of the age" (Matthew 28:18–20).

You, believer, have been made one of the kings and priests who live and reign and declare the Word—the Rider on the white horse. Satan's only hope is to convince you it's not true . . . so you'll get depressed, fearful, and anxious; so you'll close your heart and mouth, keeping the Rider inside; so you'll stockpile food and hoard resources and wring your hands as you wait for the rapture and dream of the millennium.

Satan's only hope is to convince you that you're a *victim,* when in reality you are a *victor.* His only hope is to convince you that *the world rules you,* when in reality *you* rule the world.

In 1949 when Mao Tse Tung took over China, many American Christians wrung their hands and thought, *That's it. The Church is powerless in China.* It's a good thing Chinese Christians didn't believe that. There were an estimated 750,000 Chinese Christians in 1949. China is now the second largest evangelical Christian community in the world with a conservative estimate of 35 million believers. I've read numbers as high as 100 million believers, which would make it the largest Christian community in the world. In the U.S., the Church is stagnant; in China, Africa, and South America, it grows at an unprecedented rate.

While Lindsey wrote *The Late Great Planet Earth* and we worried about the "yellow peril," Pastor George Chen was shoveling human sewage in a Chinese prison camp. They thought putting him deep in the cesspool was the best punishment for a pastor. But George Chen loved it there because he was left alone with Jesus, the King of kings. When he was released from prison after eighteen years, he found his churches had grown from three hundred to five thousand people. He had reigned in the cesspool.

That's *crazy!* Just about as crazy as the King born in a stable and placed in a manger . . . or the King stripped naked and nailed to a cross. Even there, *especially there,* He conquers. Look who sits on the throne.

Years ago a friend got to hear a pastor named Y. Chan share his testimony. I don't know if "Y. Chan" is the same man as "G. Chen," but Chan was sentenced to labor deep in the prison camps cesspool as well. Y. Chan said:

I enjoyed it there in the cesspool because I could pray as loud as I wanted, I could recite Scripture, and no one would come near me, I could sing hymns with all my energy. One of my favorite hymns was "In the Garden"—"I come to the garden alone, while the dew is still on the roses, and the voice I hear falling on my ear the Son of God discloses. And He walks with me and He talks with me, and He tells me I am His own. And the joy we share as we tarry there, no other has ever known!" When I sang this hymn in the cesspool, I understood the meaning of the garden. I met my Lord in the garden of the cesspool.

Instead of being defeated by death, futility, and snakebites, he lived, reigned, and stomped on the old dragon. Just think of it! On earth (in the cesspool) he exercised dominion as he walked with God in the garden.

THIRTY-ONE

LIVING BY THE BOOK
AND DYING BY THE BOOK

(Revelation 20:11–15)

ONE WEEKEND I carried a huge bag of books in with me to worship. At the start of the sermon, I explained that although they were very heavy and hard to carry around, I needed them in order to know what's good . . . I want to be good.

I explained that these books were the Books of Judgment. They are extremely complicated, so I simplified and reproduced one page onto an overhead transparency so that all could see.

I showed them a particular page for a particular moment of one day in the fall of 1975. Each page looked a bit like an accounting spreadsheet. Across the top were listed the people in my world, my neighbors. For simplicity I edited this list to include only three people: Bobby, Dave, and myself. In the left-hand column was the Table of Good Deeds (or as it was called in 1975, the Categories of "Cool"). Under each name, the Record of Good Deeds is tabulated in UGUs (Universal Goodness Units).

Scores were constantly tabulated, updated, and factored into historical records kept in the supercomputer (the library of books) that was my tenth-grade brain. For the sake of understanding, on the overhead, we plotted scores for one particular moment, assuming that Bobby, Dave, and I all started at zero.

It went like this:

> *Ski Tags* (on your jacket): Bobby always had ski tags on his jacket = 2 points; I usually had ski tags on my jacket = 1 point; Dave . . . no ski tags = 0 points.

Sports: Bobby was a great jock = 3 points; I was on the soccer team, but not that good = 2 points; Dave didn't do sports = no points.

Girls: All the girls loved Bobby = 3 points; a cheerleader once talked to me = 2 points; Dave = 1 point.

Pimples: Bobby didn't have any pimples = 3 points; I had some = 2 points; once Dave came to school with dried Clearasil on his face = minus 1 point.

Dumb Instruments: Bobby didn't play any dumb instruments = 3 points; I didn't play an instrument (well) = 3 points; Dave was a state champion cello player = minus 3 points.

Body Function Noises: Bobby and I each got about a 2, but Dave could belch the entire alphabet = 10 points.

Well, you get the picture. Each moment you calculate the relative scores of each person. Then, just a point or two under your own score, you draw the Universal Geek Line. Those above the line are "Cool" (the good), and those below it are "Dweebs" (the bad).

I was ruled by this Book of Judgment in tenth grade. It determined whom I sat with in the cafeteria or said "Hey dude" to in the hallway. It was why I went out for sports I hated and quit the piano. I was driven in fear by this book—*enslaved.* It even determined my moods. If Bobby got a big zit, I rejoiced (I was *that much closer* to my idol). If I was feeling down, I could think about Dave carrying his cello across the football field while I practiced soccer—I could judge him "last and least," which made me feel better about myself.

Later that year I got cut from the soccer team. I don't know if I have ever been so depressed—not because I missed soccer, but because it knocked me down into the Dweeb Zone. I went behind our house beside the railroad tracks and wept for hours thinking, "How am I going to explain to my children and my grandchildren that I was a *dweeb?*"

That really hurt, but after a few weeks of mourning I just changed a few categories in the Table of Good Deeds, and that lowered the Universal Geek Line. That's the beauty of it . . . but also why it's so much *work:* all the computations! It keeps you in constant anxiety, wondering, "What if *my* computations are inaccurate?" Or, "I bet *Dave's* Book of Judgment is different from *mine."* Or, "What if I am *Bobby's* dweeb—the 'last and the least' who makes him feel good about how cool he is?"

I also brought a page out of the Book of Judgment for the Standard American Adult Male. I laid one transparency on top of the other—exactly the same layout, same operating system, but the categories of "the Good" had changed. Instead of *Ski Tags, Sports,* etc., it was: *Business Success; Wife; Kids; Landscaping; Snowblower Horsepower.* The Universal Geek Line was now called the Invite-Them-Over-for-Dinner Line. Above the line was the Responsible Citizen zone; below the line were the Less Fortunate. You could check your social standing by plotting for friends and family . . . and be sure to calculate someone like Osama bin Laden (he doesn't have a snowblower; his landscaping stinks). Relative to him, you can feel good about yourself.

On the overhead I then showed the congregation a page out of a book for the standard Taliban warrior and one for the standard Jewish Pharisee. They could see that they were all the same and operated the same. Each just had different categories of cool and a different list of neighbors.

Then we looked at a page from the Standard American Christian's Book of Judgment. It has the same operating system (competition, envy, judgment, fear), and the same layout. But the categories of "the Good" have changed. Instead of *Business Success,* etc., we find: *No Gross Sins; No Cussing; Neat-o Christian Words* (such as "bless you" and "propitiation"); *Quality Bible Cover; Short-term Mission Experience; Doesn't Read* Harry Potter. The Geek Line is now the Saved Line. Born-again Christians are above the line. Below the line —well, we're not supposed to judge, so we call it the I-Wonder-If-They-Know-the-Lord zone.

You may be thinking, *Oh, that is so true of Christians. I'm so glad I'm not a legalistic Christian.* I also showed them a page from the Standard American Non-Legalistic Christian Book of Judgment. The Table of Good Deeds includes: *Understands Freedom in Christ; Nonjudgmental; Graciousness; Number of Philip Yancey Books Read; Niceness to the "Last and Least."* But the operating system is just the same—competition, envy, judgment, fear—so we are enslaved to trying to be "free in Christ." We judge people on how judgmental *they* are. We're driven to be *most* gracious. We use niceness to the "last and the least" in order to earn points.

I then showed them a page from *my* Book of Judgment today. The Table of Good Deeds is now . . . *Preaching Well; Church Size; Model Christian Family; Evangelism.* The Geek Line is the God-Is-Pleased Line; above is the Good Pastor zone; below is the Bad Pastor zone. The neighbors I judge myself by are friends, brothers, and fellow pastors, such as Dave, Andrew, and Tom.

Actually, Dave turned out to be my best friend and one of the greatest guys I've ever known. We worked in youth ministry together. But when kids liked him more than me, or one of his talks went better than mine, I didn't rejoice. I competed.

Andrew, an evangelist, is like my adopted brother. When he leads more people to the Lord than I do, I struggle not to resent it. How sick is that? I might as well just wish them all to hell.

My pastor friend Tom is another that I measured myself by. One day, depressed, he killed himself, leaving behind a young family and a church. Something horrid in me wanted to rejoice because now I scored higher than he. How sick can I be? "Oh, wretched man that I am. Who will deliver me from this body of death?"

I think Scripture calls all these books "the law." And the energy by which I play this game is called "the flesh." When I live by the Book of Judgments I walk in death. I can't live grace fully. Lugging all these heavy books around means I can't dance well, sing well, laugh well, live well. Ironically, in trying to be good I *can't* be good. I'm always preoccupied with how I measure up: calculating, scheming, posturing, posing. It's a terrible burden—I'm enslaved to *myself.*

Jesus said, "Unless you lose your life you'll never find it." I'm unable to get beyond myself, so I certainly can't love others, I can't love God, and I hate myself. "He who does not love abides in death" (1 John 3:14). *Death.* The walking dead.

In Genesis 2:16 God said to Adam [man], "You may freely eat of every tree of the garden; but of the tree of the knowledge of good and evil you shall not eat, for in the day that you eat of it you shall surely die." I believe "the knowledge of good and evil" is also called "the law." At the dragon's tempting, Adam doubted God's goodness, trusting the law instead of God. He ate and he got the law library and lost God. He ate and got "the knowledge of good and evil" . . . the knowledge that he was naked, bad, and dead. The walking dead.

In Revelation 20, John has just seen the living, who "reigned with Christ a thousand years" (v. 4).

REVELATION 20:11–12 (NASB): *And I saw a great white throne and Him who sat upon it, from whose presence earth and heaven fled away, and no place was found for them. And I saw the dead, the great and the small, standing before the throne, and books were opened; and another book was opened, which is the book of life; and the dead were judged from the things which were written in the books, according to their deeds.*

The dead are judged by the things in the books according to their deeds. Jesus said, "Judge not that you be not judged. For with the judgment you pronounce you will be judged" (Matthew 7:1–2). That is, "If you want to play by the book, you'll get the book."

Have you ever wondered why we all have an innate sense of good and evil? We argue about the details, but we live with these books in our hearts and minds, constantly keeping score, trying to be good. It's because we all know deep inside that we have a Creator: He *is* good, and He has books. We live in fear, constantly preparing our defense, for we know that one day the books will be opened and there will be an accounting.

Jesus revealed on what that accounting is based. He said, "Love the Lord your God with all your heart, and with all your soul, and with all your mind. This is the great and first commandment. And a second is like it, You shall love your neighbor as yourself. On these two commandments depend all the law and prophets" (Matthew 22:37–40).

By loving your neighbor you love God. Ouch!

In Matthew 25 Jesus said:

> "When the Son of man comes in his glory, and all the angels with him, then he will sit on his glorious throne. Before him will be gathered all the nations, and he will separate them one from another as a shepherd separates the sheep from the goats, and he will place the sheep at his right hand, but the goats at the left. . . . He will say to those at his left hand, 'Depart from me, you cursed, into the eternal fire prepared for the devil and his angels; for I was hungry and you gave me no food, I was thirsty and you gave me no drink, I was a stranger and you did not welcome me, naked and you did not clothe me, sick and in prison and you did not visit me.' Then they also will answer, 'Lord, when did we see you hungry or thirsty or a stranger or naked or sick or in prison, and did not minister to you?' Then he will answer them, 'Truly, I say to you, as you did it not to one of the least of these, you did it not to me.'" (vv. 31-33, 41–45)

If you want to live by the book, God *is* keeping score. He's in Lazarus by the gate; He's in the "last and the least." They sit on thrones judging nations. He's in them in judgment. You may even do many mighty works in His name . . . feed the "last and the least," but He may still say, "Depart, I never knew you" (Matthew 7).

The goats say, "When did we see you?" Well, they *didn't* see Him . . . *ever!* They just saw the "last and the least" and a way to score points. (Just by

241

judging someone "the last and the least" I judge Jesus Christ "last and least." Remember that when He walked this earth, almost everyone judged Him "last and least" . . . a baby in a food trough . . . a peasant on a cross—cursed.)

So living by the book, God is everywhere in my world as *judgment.* Just by playing the game and trusting the books, I hate my neighbor, I hate God, and I hate myself. And I broadcast to the heavenlies, "Yes, I stole the fruit of the tree of the knowledge of good and evil." *Guilty.*

Well, if we dare guess at God's Book of Judgment, I imagine it would be something like this: The categories of "the Good" would be summed up as *"Love . . .* the Lord with all you are, and your neighbor as yourself. The neighbors would be everyone I meet, even Samaritans. When I compute "the Good" and "the Bad," what does God require? Perfection. How are we doing? Well, Osama bin Laden is dead. Mother Teresa, apart from God, is also dead. You, me . . . dead, in our trespasses and sins. All dead. Absolutely dead. Unable to conquer.

So what good are the books or the knowledge of the books? They tell us we need a Savior. They tell Adam [humankind] that a walk with God is better than a law library, "And now Adam, you will meet the pinnacle of good— Jesus." *Jesus* means "God saves." "Adam, now you can meet the Savior."

In Revelation 20, on the last day, books are opened (Tables of the Good and Records of Good Deeds) and "another book" is opened: one book—the Book of Life. We know from chapters 13 and 17 of the Revelation that this book contains names written from the foundation of the world, before Adam fell—*names,* not *deeds.*

To the Hebrews, names were persons. These are persons who have entrusted themselves to the Lamb on the throne. It's the *Lamb's* Book of Life. Jesus said, "Truly, truly, . . . he who hears my word [Remember that the Word rode out at the beginning of this chapter] and believes him who sent me, has eternal life [already alive!]; he does not come into judgment [condemnation], but has passed from death to life" (John 5:24). Whoever hears the Word and believes is already alive.

How can that be? Paul tells us: "For our sake [God] made [Jesus] to be sin who knew no sin, so that in him we might become the righteousness of God" (2 Corinthians 5:21). Jesus is called the Last Adam *(eschatos* Adam: eschatological ultimate Adam—1 Corinthians 15:45). His righteousness is imputed to us through faith as a *gift* from God. The operating system is *grace,* and He *is* "the Good"—not a *what,* but a *who.*

"Christ redeemed us from the curse of the law, having become a curse for us," wrote Paul, "for it is written, 'Cursed be every one who hangs on a tree'" (Galatians 3:13). I suspect that tree, the cross on which Jesus was crucified was the tree of the knowledge of good and evil. Jesus was crucified, cursed by the law and nailed to the law on our behalf. "And you, who were dead in trespasses and the uncircumcision of your flesh, God made alive together with him, having forgiven us all our trespasses, having canceled the bond which stood against us with its legal demands; this he set aside, nailing it to the cross" (Colossians 2:13–14).

At the cross, God opens His books. For the children of God, judgment is the cross of Christ. Jesus said of His death, *"Now* is this world judged." At the cross, God opens your books, (with all their legal demands), and with His own blood through all your entire history—past, present, and future—He stamps CANCELED on every debt. *Greed*—CANCELED. *Lust*—CANCELED. *Fornication*—CANCELED. *Abortion*—CANCELED. *Judging Dave at the soccer field*—CANCELED.

Canceled . . . Canceled . . . "By My blood" . . . "Drink of it, all of you."

Paul continues, "This he set aside, nailing it to the cross. He disarmed the principalities and powers and made a public example of them, triumphing over them in him [Jesus]" (Colossians 2:14-15).

Do you see what Paul is saying? This is not just "Be Happy" psychology. This is the very heart of your battle with the ancient dragon. You conquer Him by "the blood of the Lamb and the word of your testimony," claiming the blood of the Lamb over every moment of your life. You must believe that you are *entirely* forgiven and *thoroughly* loved. Then every point of sin is transformed into a point of grace.

Instead of God everywhere, waiting in judgment, He's everywhere, waiting to show you His grace. Every sin is transformed from shame into a demonstration of love, for every sin was on that cross and now reminds you of Easter, and tells you how much God loves you and how good He truly is. Every moment you step on the head of the old serpent, for the dragon has no ground on which to accuse.

Satan has been disarmed, yet he is still the accuser and father of lies. So even though your certificate of debt has been canceled, Satan tries to make copies. His only hope against you is to make you believe falsified documents, make you doubt the grace of God and the blood of Christ—that you're totally forgiven and thoroughly loved. For then you will live by the old books. You'll begin condemning yourself and will walk in death, doing the work of the accuser *for* him. That's how he takes us out of the battle and keeps us from doing the "works of God."

They asked Jesus, "What must we do, to be doing the works of God?" And Jesus said, "This is the work of God, that you believe in him whom he has sent" (John 6:28–29).

ETERNITY NOW

REVELATION 20:13–15 (NASB): *And the sea gave up the dead which were in it, and death and Hades gave up the dead which were in them; and they were judged, every one of them according to their deeds. And death and Hades were thrown into the lake of fire. This is the second death, the lake of fire. And if anyone's name was not found written in the book of life, he was thrown into the lake of fire.*

Theologians argue about whether the saints (the sheep) are even *in* this scene. If we *are,* we're not being condemned for sinful deeds. However, in Revelation 22:12 Jesus says, "Behold, I am coming soon, bringing my recompense [reward] to repay every one for what he has done [deeds]." If my evil deeds were judged and paid for at the cross, what deeds are *these?* If my record of condemnation is canceled, what record is *this?* If I'm not paid for evil deeds, what deeds *am* I paid for?

"The King will say to those at his right hand, 'Come, O blessed of my Father, inherit the kingdom prepared for you from the foundation of the world; for I was hungry and you gave me food, I was thirsty and you gave me drink, I was a stranger and you welcomed me, I was naked and you clothed me, I was sick and you visited me, I was in prison and you came to me.'

"Then the righteous will answer him, 'Lord, when did we see you hungry and feed you, or thirsty and give you drink? And when did we see you a stranger and welcome you, or naked and clothe you? And when did we see you sick or in prison and visit you?' And the King will answer them, 'Truly, I say to you, as you did it to one of the least of these, my brethren, you did it to me.'" (Matthew 25:34–40)

I bet they don't even remember . . . because they *weren't keeping score.*
They weren't conscious of the Books;
They weren't conscious of themselves;
They weren't conscious of the "last or least";
They were conscious of Christ.
So they loved because they had been loved by Christ. In short, they weren't trying to be good, they just *were* good. It wasn't even them being good. It was the good (Jesus) in them, being good. Perhaps they weren't even conscious of Christ, but they did have Christ's consciousness.

I work so hard at trying to be good to impress God and impress you. On

244

Judgment Day trumpets will sound and Jesus will say something like this:

> "Peter Hiett, on August 7, 1987, at 5:15 P.M., you gave Me a cup of cold water. Enter the kingdom."
>
> And I'll say, "But what about the sermons? I don't even *remember* giving You cold water."
>
> "Exactly. You weren't trying to be good. You *just were*. And now you know good and evil, not because you are evil and dead, but because you're forgiven and alive and I've made you good. You actually love."

So what am I saying? Try harder to love!? No. Confess that you don't . . . and receive His love. It's called *grace*. Jesus taught, "The one forgiven much loves much."

THIRTY-TWO

YOU CAN GO HOME
(Revelation 21:1–8)

As a child, I could barely wait until Christmas, because I knew I would get *new stuff*—and if I got what I wanted, my life would be complete and my world filled with wonder, wonder-full. I remember that my race car set was such paradise and ecstasy on Christmas morning, but by about 7:00 P.M., after watching cars go round and round, it had gotten old.

Material possessions get *old*. So we should be less materialistic and appreciate the wonder and beauty of God's creation—sky and land, heaven and earth, the wonder of life . . . fewer toys and more of getting the kids into nature.

One evening, my wife and I returned from a date to find all the lights on and the hamster cage broken and lying open on the floor. No hamsters, but hamster bedding and refuse was spilled on the new carpet. It looked like a bomb had gone off.

We heard Poppy (Grandpa, my dad) upstairs reading stories to the children. He would explain to us later that the neighbor girl brought *her* turtle over to see *our* turtle and then decided to bring *her* hamster to visit *our* hamsters. In fact, the children had already done this a few months earlier—and learned about the wonder of reproduction. So our neighbor's hamster had new babies, which technically are my kids' grandbabies, and Poppy told them they shouldn't hold the babies, but they did.

About that time my son's gecko escaped from its cage and couldn't be found. My son was distraught . . . I imagine the dog was barking . . . and then the mother hamster got so nervous she began to do uncivilized cannibalistic hamster things to her babies.

The kids were so horrified to see this that our daughter's friend went into a hysterical rage and threw her hamster off the top deck. Somehow, *our* hamsters got out. Everyone was screaming and yelling, and Poppy was on his oxygen and couldn't move too fast. He told them to calm down, and my son yelled, "You don't understand our pain!" One child fell on the floor screaming in uncontrollable agony; there was open wailing and general pandemonium. My father said it was such chaos that he decided to sit down and read a book. Finally, when the chaos had died down, my two youngest came to Poppy and said, "We need some Bible stories. Would you say our prayers?"

If you idolize nature, go spend some time on a farm, or get yourself some hamsters—and even nature can get old really quickly.

In every new experience, we hope for fulfillment and ecstasy. We may even *taste* it for a moment, but then it gets old.

Church gets old. New people will sometimes say, "Oh, I'm so glad we found this church. The worship, the preaching, the programs!" And I wonder, *Will they leave when it gets old?*

Religion gets old. At the time of the Revelation, Judaism was thousands of years old and had become cynical and dead, *so* dead that Jerusalem had murdered the Messiah.

People get old. How many times have you met someone and thought, "This person has it all together." Then what was new about them gets old.

What is it that makes a thing old?

- On a physical level, it's when a thing decays and breaks down—entropy.

- On a personal level, things get old when they get old to us, when we think we have them figured out, when there's no mystery left . . . no wonder, no newness. People's physical bodies get old, and when we think we have them figured out, they get old to us. For some, God is old news and not wonderful, because they think they have God figured out. The higher the percentage of things you have figured out in your world, the older you are, the older your world is, and the closer it is to dead. A toddler has nothing figured out, and everything is wonder-full.

- Decay and a loss of wonder makes things old. In short, anything in time (chronos) gets old.

We all want the new and wonderful, but the older we get, the more we know that *new* gets *old.* So we get cynical. We all want the new, but we're all fearful of the new, because to get the new is to lose the old (that was new).

So we say:

"Give me that old-time religion! It's good enough for me."

"Careful of that *new* stuff."

"Play it safe."

"Stay at home."

So then, somewhere in life we switch strategies: We give up on the new and hang onto the old. Instead of a new house, we want a home. Instead of longing for new experiences, we guard the old. But just as the new becomes old, we can't stop the old from being replaced by the new. We cannot stop time.

Sometimes I drive by the house where I grew up in Littleton and think, *You can never go home. Dad will never work in that yard again while I play in my fort, while Lydia and Rachel play with the rabbit, and while Mom makes fried mushroom sandwiches in our kitchen with the mustard yellow countertops and the avocado refrigerator. I'll never go home.* Then I want to grab my dad and hang on, because he's eighty-four with heart trouble and a lung disease. But like they say: "You can't go home."

The folks in the seven churches in Asia Minor were probably mostly the Diaspora (dispersed Jews). Jerusalem was their *real* home: Abraham, the Exodus, David, Solomon, the exile . . . the twelve tribes and also the twelve apostles . . . the temple, where they met God, and where John had memories of meeting Jesus. Jerusalem was history, energy, and religion for two thousand years, and in A.D. 70 the Romans laid siege to it. They plowed the temple into the ground. All that energy gone, laid waste . . . all that labor in vain. They must have thought, "You can never go home."

I remember when my bride came down the aisle. I was afraid—that the new would get old, that the old was being replaced by the new; that is, I wasn't going home. In fear, hanging on to the past and worried about the future, I almost *missed* the bride coming down the aisle. I remember thinking to myself, "Stop it! Stop worrying! Live this moment. Don't miss this moment. Live *now!*"

The "now" is what is actually new. And if I don't live in the now (which is new) it will never be the old. I won't have the new *or* the old, and I will have never lived. And I will have missed the bride coming down, because I was preoccupied with fear. And at the end of our marriage she will say, "Depart! I never knew you. You never made our house a home."

Now is when I can know another.

Now is when I live.

Now is when I make choices.

Now is when I create.

Now is when the new is created into the form of the old.

Now is when I enjoy a gift or make a home or see a bride.

Now is the moment eternity touches time.

Scientists say that if we traveled at the speed of light, all time would be eternally present; all past and all future would be eternally new; all old would then be forever new . . . at the speed of light.

God said: "Let there be light. . . . Moses, my name is *I AM* . . . . *Now* is the acceptable time; *now* is the day of salvation."

Jesus means "God saves," and Jesus said, "I came that they might have life and have it abundantly" (John 10:10): eternal life; new life; a life of newness.

At His cross Jesus redeems every page of our book, every moment of our lives. He makes all things new. When we're with Him in each moment, we live new.

Recently I had a burrito with my dad. He's getting pretty old and I worry that one day he may die. But though he's getting old, I remember one moment, looking into his eyes. He was so *excited* and *animated* and *grateful* about something, and, well, he just seemed so . . . *new.* Maybe he's not totally living in time.

My bride just turned forty-two. But to me she's more new and wonderful than ever. She's still coming down that aisle.

REVELATION 21:1: *Then I saw a new heaven and a new earth; for the first heaven and the first earth had passed away, and the sea was no more. And I saw the holy city, new Jerusalem, coming down out of heaven from God, prepared as a bride adorned for her husband.*

John sees "a new heaven and a new earth." This new world violates our laws of physics, not because it is *less* real, but because it is more real than this world. Jesus' resurrected body wasn't *less* real; it was *more* real than brick walls.

"A new heaven and a new earth" . . . I have a theory that it is disproportionately populated with goldfish and hamsters set free from their bondage to decay, having obtained the glorious liberty of the children of God through little pet-loving children saying their prayers before bed.

It's back to the Garden, but not just the Garden: John sees a city. Cities are made with human hands, but this city comes from God. Maybe it's built like a good work, which God prepared beforehand for us to walk in. It is adorned with the "righteous deeds of the saints" (19:8). At the end of the chapter, "the kings of the earth . . . bring their glory into it" (21:24)—stuff like computers and microwave ovens and electric trains, I suppose. So I fully expect to see my electric racecar set in heaven, and it will never get old, and it will never get old to me.

I asked my dad, "Are you scared to die?"

"Oh no," he said. "In fact, I had a dream—I think it was a dream of heaven. At the old farmhouse . . . Mom and Dad and my brothers and sisters . . . we were all having such fun. I dreamed of home." Maybe you can go home.

John sees a city, but not just *any* city: he sees Jerusalem—the *New* Jerusalem. Maybe you *can* go home, but it's never old . . . it's always new.

REVELATION 21:2–3: *And I saw the . . . new Jerusalem, coming down out of heaven from God, prepared as a bride adorned for her husband; and I heard a loud voice from the throne saying, "Behold, the dwelling of God is with men."*

"God with us." In Hebrew, that is pronounced "Emmanuel." That's what they called the baby in the manger.

REVELATION 21:3–8: *He will dwell with them, and they shall be his people, and God himself will be with them; he will wipe away every tear from their eyes, and death shall be no more, neither shall there be mourning nor crying nor pain any more, for the former things have passed away.*

And he who sat upon the throne said, "Behold, I make all things new." Also he said, "Write this, for these words are trustworthy and true." And he said to me, "It is done! I am the Alpha and the Omega, the beginning and the end. To the thirsty I will give from the fountain of the water of life without payment. He who conquers shall have this heritage, and I will be his God and he shall be my son. But as for the cowardly [fearful], *the faithless, the polluted, as for murderers, fornicators* [fornication is sex outside of marriage], *sorcerers, idolaters, and all liars, their lot shall be in the lake that burns with fire and sulphur, which is the second death."*

But He said He makes all things new. That must mean "all *kinds of* things new," or "all new, He makes new" or that some things are made new after the second death . . . or that those people and the dragon and the beast aren't really "things" but vessels of wrath and shadows of things. I don't know, but He makes all things new . . . old but forever new.

REVELATION 21:9–14: *Then came one of the seven angels who had the seven bowls full of the seven last plagues, and spoke to me, saying, "Come, I will show you the Bride, the wife of the Lamb." And in the Spirit he carried me away to a*

*great, high mountain, and showed me the holy city Jerusalem coming down out
of heaven from God, having the glory of God, its radiance like a most rare jewel,
like a jasper, clear as crystal. It had a great, high wall, with twelve gates, and at
the gates twelve angels, and on the gates the names of the twelve tribes of the sons
of Israel were inscribed; on the east three gates, on the north three gates, on the
south three gates, and on the west three gates. And the wall of the city had twelve
foundations, and on them the twelve names of the twelve apostles of the Lamb.*

In Revelation 3:11 Jesus says, "He who conquers, I will make a pillar in the
temple of my God." This Jerusalem appears to be that temple. It is built with
people. Names are inscribed on the gates and on the foundations . . .

- names such as Judah, who sold his brother Joseph into slavery and fornicated with his daughter-in-law Tamar.
- names such as Peter, who lied about Jesus and ran like a coward.
- names such as John, who wanted to murder an entire Samaritan village,
  who is also seeing this vision.

The city is built with fornicators, liars, and murderers who have been
redeemed. It's built with John, who must have wondered at times as he was
exiled on Patmos, "Is all my work and struggle and ministry just in vain? Was
Jerusalem all in vain?"

All the people, all the faith, all the hope, all the love that went into building
that old Jerusalem was not in vain. In time they built a Jerusalem of stone,
which the Romans destroyed. But with their faith, hope, and love God built
the heavenly Jerusalem in eternity.

We think of faith, hope, and love as tools they used to build the city.
Maybe building the city was the tool God used for building their faith, hope,
and love—the eternal city.

He makes all things new, so *nothing you give Him is wasted.* You may be
discouraged, tired, confused, or feeling wretched because of sin. *Surrender it.*
Give each moment to Jesus in the obedience of faith, and that moment
becomes gold brick in the eternal city. It fits perfectly, for it was prepared
before time by God.

History is like a backward explosion. Have you ever watched an explosion
on film in reverse? All the burnt, confused, old pieces miraculously fly together,
from the end to the beginning, and make something new that was old.

Jesus is end and beginning (21:6). He can play the big bang forward and backward. I think the biggest bang is not the *beginning* but the *end* of time, when it all comes together in wonder through His cross. He is playing the biggest bang backwards.

The night the hamster bomb went off at my house and all hell broke loose and then my children repented, read Bible stories, and prayed—that will be part of all the pieces coming together in the new creation . . . hamsters everywhere and a city built with the faith, hope, and love of children.

Well, the New Jerusalem is already here in God's people. My dad's body is old, but his spirit is new. Church will get old or new . . . unless you realize Church is God's people, and then the old is forever new. "From now on, therefore, we regard no one from a human point of view," writes Paul. "Even though we once regarded Christ from a human point of view, we regard him thus no longer. Therefore, if any one is in Christ, he is a new creation" (2 Corinthians 5:16–17).

The new creation has already invaded the old creation. It was born into an old dirty stable and placed in a manger. In that manger, in human flesh, lay the bottomless depths of the Lord God, mysteries unimaginable and wonders that will never cease.

The New Jerusalem is coming down (Revelation 21:3). Do you have eyes to see it? Most people walked past the stable that Christmas. But some shepherds entered in through that stable door, and they wondered, and they lived.

"You have come to Mount Zion and to the city of the living God, the heavenly Jerusalem, . . . and to Jesus, the mediator of a new covenant, . . . See that you do not refuse him who is speaking" (Hebrews 12:22, 24–25). When we hear the Word in faith, New Jerusalem comes down. In faith, hope, and love, the New Jerusalem builds us.

Paul wrote, "The Jerusalem above . . . is our mother" (Galatians 4:26). Eternity gives birth to our new temporality. *Kairos* is the meaning of all our *chronos.* "If any one is in Christ, he is a new creation; the old has passed away, behold, the new has come" (2 Corinthians 5:17). For those people, even now . . . their world must be wonder-full.

My dad came over to my house recently. All he does any more is talk about how *won*derful everything is. "Peter, gosh, that church is *wonderful,* and those people are wonderful. Oh, Peter, I love this house, and your kids are so *wonderful.* Susan is *wonderful.* I love driving up and down C-470," he said. "I *love* those foothills. They are just *wonderful.*"

Sometimes I think my dad is kooky. But he's not. I think he's starting to see the New Jerusalem. Maybe *he's* getting so new that everything is new to him.

Whenever we receive a moment in faith instead of fear, we live in that moment. That moment is *now* and eternal and new, and that's where "I AM" is—Emmanuel, "God with us"—and He makes all things new.

Maybe whenever we believe the new covenant and sing the new song with a new heart and new spirit, walking in newness of life . . . maybe we begin walking into the New Jerusalem, or at least we glimpse it by faith through a stable door.

Whatever the case, one day a trumpet will sound, and there will be no doubt. You'll see the city of God with a new body and new eyes. And you'll say, "This is *it!* I'm *home!*" For everything old is new, and you recognize it, for you have visited this country in faith, hope, and love. You can go home.

THIRTY-THREE

YOU CAN COME OUT NOW

(Revelation 21:9–22:5)

IN GENESIS 2 God makes man, and then He makes his bride from the man's bleeding, wounded side. "Therefore a man leaves his father and his mother and cleaves to his wife, and they become one flesh" (v. 24).

In Ephesians 5:32 Paul writes, "This mystery is a profound one, and I am saying it refers to Christ and the church."

"And the man and his wife were both naked, and were not ashamed. Now the serpent was more subtle than any other wild creature that the LORD God had made" (Genesis 2:25–3:1).

The serpent tempts Eve. Eve takes the fruit and gives some to Adam. "Then the eyes of both were opened, and they knew that they were naked; and they sewed fig leaves together and made themselves aprons. And they heard the sound of the LORD God walking in the garden in the cool of the day" (Genesis 3:7–8). In the presence of the Lord there is fullness of joy; at His right hand are pleasures forevermore (Psalm 16:11).

They heard the sound of the Lord walking in the garden . . . "and the man and his wife hid themselves from the presence of the LORD God among the trees of the garden. But the LORD God called to the man and said to him, 'Where are you?' And he said, 'I heard the sound of thee in the garden, and I was afraid, because I was naked; and I hid myself'" (Genesis 3:8–10).

In the Revelation Jesus declares, "Behold, I stand at the door and knock" (3:20).

Why *don't* we open the door and invite Him in—not just with our heads, but our hearts? Why *don't* we surrender in absolute and joyful obedience? Why *don't* we invite Him into every dark corner of our souls so every breath we take is the ecstasy of unadulterated, passionate surrender?

Because of shame. And we've had reason for shame.

We take after our mother, Eve, who trusted the snake and became a harlot. So we hide from God, but we're desperate for communion and fulfillment. And so we join ourselves to idols—cars, houses, jobs, pornography, adultery—but that makes us only *more* ashamed. Then the presence of the Lord makes us aware of our shame and drives us deeper into hiding. His glory becomes our criticism. That is the story of Israel.

Through the law God reveals: "Israel, you're being a harlot." Through the prophets God cries: "Israel, you've become a harlot!" But it only drives Israel deeper into the dark, and she *will not* open the door and let Him in. She has too much pride to surrender her shame.

According to Stephen in Acts 7:51, the problem with the Jews was an "uncircumcised heart"—the unsympathetic genital of the soul—a heart unfeeling, sealed off to God, hiding in the trees. The law was criticism, driving them deeper into shame.

Husbands, you know that if you want to make love to your wife, the last thing you should say when she puts on the lingerie is, "Hey, you put on a few pounds this week." That may be true, and it may be best if she hadn't, and you may love her thoroughly and absolutely, but *that* comment will slam the door. She may comply out of obedience, but it will not be joyful surrender. Her heart will be far from you.

Jesus said, "This people [Israel] honors me with their lips, but their heart is far from me" (Matthew 15:8). He was quoting Isaiah, who goes on to say, "Therefore, behold, I will again do marvelous things with this people" (29:14).

Ezekiel prophesied to God's harlot Bride: "I will establish with you an everlasting covenant. . . . that you may . . . be confounded . . . when I forgive all you have done" (Ezekiel 16:60).

God said through the prophet: "Therefore, behold, I will allure her [entice her, romance her] and bring her into the wilderness and speak tenderly to her. And there I will give her her vineyards; there I will . . . make the Valley of Achor [Valley of Trouble] a door of hope" (Hosea 2:14). That is, "I'll take my harlot Bride through trouble, and there in that wilderness I'll provide a door. I will show my grace and romance her heart out of the darkness."

Israel of God, we were *born* into the wilderness. And Christ is the door. He has entered the shadows and I believe He whispers, "Eve, Eve . . . You handed Me the evil fruit, for I am always with you, Emmanuel. I was not deceived . . . But I took the curse for the love of you . . . I was nailed to the tree, crucified to fulfill the law. I died in your place . . . I am the last Adam, ultimate Adam, *eschatos* Adam. So see My face . . . your scars on My brow; your bruises on My back. Now see the glory of God shining in My face. Yes, My Eve, you've sinned immeasurably. But I have already loved you immeasurably more."¹

Even so, "Husbands, love your wives, as Christ loved the church and gave himself up for her, that he might sanctify her, having cleansed her by the washing of water with the word, that he might present the church to himself in splendor without spot or wrinkle or any such thing, that she might be holy and without blemish" (Ephesians 5:25–27).

Jesus whispers, "Eve, Eve . . . come out of the darkness. I bear your curse, and now look in *My* mirror . . . not the old law but My perfect law—the law of liberty—My grace . . . and see yourself clothed in My righteousness. No more shame. And now, Eve, it's our wedding day. Say 'I do' with all your heart, so you would laugh with joy as I enter you and give you life for evermore. Look in *My* mirror and believe."

Revelation 21:9 is the last vision in the Revelation, the last vision in Scripture. This tells us what God is making . . . *why* the wilderness, *why* the Valley of Achor, *why* the curse, *why* the pain, the seals, the trumpets, the bowls of wrath. You'll never understand the gospel until you get a glimpse of what God wants.

"Eve, look in the mirror and see who you are."

REVELATION 21:9–22:5: *Then came one of the seven angels who had the seven bowls full of the seven last plagues, and spoke to me, saying, "Come, I will show you the Bride, the wife of the Lamb." And in the Spirit he carried me away to a great, high mountain, and showed me the holy city Jerusalem coming down out of heaven from God, having the glory of God, its radiance like a most rare jewel, like a jasper, clear as crystal. It had a great, high wall, with twelve gates, and at the gates twelve angels, and on the gates the names of the twelve tribes of the sons of Israel were inscribed; on the east three gates, on the north three gates, on the south three gates, and on the west three gates. And the wall of the city had twelve foundations, and on them the twelve names of the twelve apostles of the Lamb.* [That means John looked and saw his name! This was a mirror.] *And he who talked to me had a measuring rod of gold to measure the city and its gates and walls. The city lies foursquare, its length the same as its breadth; and he measured the city with his rod, twelve thousand stadia; its length and breadth and height are equal. He also measured its wall, a hundred and forty-four cubits by a man's measure, that is, an angel's. The wall was built of jasper, while the city was pure gold, clear as glass. The foundations of the wall of the city were adorned with every jewel; the first was jasper, the second sapphire, the third agate, the fourth emerald, the fifth onyx, the sixth carnelian, the seventh chryso-*

lite, the eighth beryl, the ninth topaz, the tenth chrysoprase, the eleventh jacinth, the twelfth amethyst. And the twelve gates were twelve pearls, each of the gates made of a single pearl, and the street of the city was pure gold, transparent as glass.

And I saw no temple in the city, for its temple is the Lord God the Almighty and the Lamb. And the city has no need of sun or moon to shine upon it, for the glory of God is its light, and its lamp is the Lamb. By its light shall the nations walk; and the kings of the earth shall bring their glory into it, and its gates shall never be shut by day—and there shall be no night there; they shall bring into it the glory and the honor of the nations. But nothing unclean shall enter it, nor any one who practices abomination or falsehood, but only those who are written in the Lamb's book of life.

Then he showed me the river of the water of life, bright as crystal, flowing from the throne of God and of the Lamb through the middle of the street of the city; also, on either side of the river, the tree of life with its twelve kinds of fruit, yielding its fruit each month; and the leaves of the tree were for the healing of the nations. There shall no more be anything accursed, but the throne of God and of the Lamb shall be in it, and his servants shall worship him; they shall see his face, and his name shall be on their foreheads. And night shall be no more; they need no light of lamp or sun, for the Lord God will be their light, and they shall reign for ever and ever.

It's *all here* . . . "the hopes and fears of all the years." Little children, there is no night here, and there is no curse here. We're back to the Garden.

But Eve is not just in the Garden; the Garden is in Eve. The Garden and the city are the Bride of Christ. And she is radiant (every precious stone; supernatural gold; pearls for gates). She fulfills the prophecies of Ezekiel, Hosea, and Isaiah; the words of Jesus—Living Water, Light of the World. She is twelve tribes and twelve apostles (Israel and the Church). She is a cube, just like the sanctuary in the temple, but 1,500 miles wide, 1,500 miles deep, and 1,500 miles high. A *big gal* . . . she contains the throne of God; she is His temple and He is hers. She sees His face, and she has His glory.

"Eve, look in the mirror and believe who you are."

This final scene is the future, for the first earth has passed away. Yet John writes, "By its light shall the nations walk" (Revelation 21:24). *What* nations?

In 22:14 he writes, "Blessed are those who wash their robes, that they may have the right to the tree of life and that they may enter the city by the gates [those pearls]. Outside are the dogs and sorcerers and fornicators and murderers and idolaters, and every one who loves and practices falsehood." That sounds like *now*.

We already *are* the temple of God, according to Paul. We *are* the Bride of Christ. Jesus said that whoever believes in Him, out of their heart will flow rivers of living water. If we believe, we have eternal life *now.* Jesus said we *are* the light of the world. He is a pearl merchant who has paid everything for the greatest pearl.

- A pearl is God's miracle,
  wrapped around a wound
    in an oyster buried in the mud.
- The Church is God's people,
  wrapped around the *wound* of Jesus,
    on the cross in this fallen world.
- A Christian is God's grace: Jesus
  wrapped around our sin
    turning our wounds into treasure.
- Your testimony of Christ's grace
  is a door to the kingdom,
    a gate to the city for others.

The twelve gates are twelve pearls: the Church *now.* "You have come to Mount Zion, to the city of the living God, the heavenly Jerusalem" (Hebrews 12:22). Eternity is *now* by faith.

Jesus is not the Ghost of Christmas Future. He is the Alpha and Omega. This is not what *could* be; this is what *is . . . now . . .* in eternity. *You* are Christ's glorious inheritance . . . *now.* I used to feel sorry for Jesus that *we* were His inheritance, His gift—how depressing! But maybe we don't know what glory or beauty really is.

In the fairy-tale movie *Shrek,* the princess Fiona is under a curse that turns her into an ogre at night. But she falls in love with the ogre Shrek, who saved her from the dragon. She begins to think Shrek is beautiful, although the world thinks he's ugly. When Shrek kisses her, the curse is broken and she is forever gorgeous: That is, she is an ogre during the day as well as during the night. What we thought was ugly is the greatest beauty to Shrek.

If beauty is in the eye of the beholder, *there is only one beholder:* the Lord God. The world thought Jesus on His cross was an ogre, but He is the romance of God. Nothing is more glorious, and we reflect His glory. But unlike the movie, with Christ the curse on *all creation* is broken. All will see that we've been blinded by the God of this age . . . and nothing is more beautiful than Christ and His Bride. The Bride is redeemed people, and redeemed people reflect the glory of God through grace.

The great city is a harlot redeemed, a bride in love. In the fairy tale, the happy ending almost didn't happen, because the princess thought the *beautiful* was *ugly*. She thought *she* was ugly, so she hid herself every night in shame.

Maybe we don't know what real beauty is . . . so we listen to the world . . . displaying our pride, vanity, and dead works, yet hiding our faith, hope, and love for Jesus, who saves us. We hide our testimony of His grace.

Jesus says, "Eve, please look into *My* face. Look in *My* mirror—*My* Word —and see what I have made you: My Bride. Believe, and come out of the shadows and into the light."

People of God, do you have any idea how gorgeous you are to Him? How beautiful you are in eternity? How valuable you are right now? He cannot love you more than He already has and does. He desires you like the most passionate groom longs for his bride on his wedding night.

But He will not storm the closet and rape you.

He will not rip you from the bushes and tear off your garments. He wants you to *want* Him. He wants you to give yourself to Him as a gift. He wants you to stop hiding in shame.

What is it that He wants? *A loving Bride.*

A groom's worst nightmare on his wedding night is that the bride will come out all wrapped in flannel, hiding herself in shame. He wants the bride to dance into the room saying, "I'm yours—take me now. I'm God's gift to you." What is a bride's worst nightmare? That she will dance into the room with desire and the groom will say, "Yuck." Jesus will not say that to His naked Bride.

To confess your sins is to be naked before Jesus. If you've confessed yourself to Him, He has washed you with His blood. Believe the Gospel: You are the gift of God *for God*.

> You are the gift of the Father
> given to the Son: the Bride.
> You are the gift of the Son
> given to the Father: His children.

Believing your value is not arrogant. Calling yourself a "piece of garbage" is arrogant. How dare you curse yourself, condemn yourself, hate yourself, abuse yourself, demean yourself, when God calls you "Bride"! He did not suffer hell for a piece of *garbage*.

Believing your value is not arrogant, for the value doesn't come from you. The New Jerusalem is the creation of *God*. Your righteousness is the righteousness of Christ. Believing your value is believing the cross of Christ and the sanctifying work of His Spirit. "He who began a good work in you will bring it to completion" (Philippians 1:6). It's already complete in eternity; complete in the *now* of faith.

Did you notice it was one of the seven bowl angels who showed John the harlot and the Bride? The seven angels reminded us of the sevenfold Spirit: the Holy Spirit—the Spirit in each church, working sanctification. The Spirit of Christ transforms us.

He makes us His body. When we curse ourselves, we curse Christ and His body. Look at His side. Where did He get His scars? They're *your* curses. Your scars are His scars—scars on His body. Why would He do it? To romance you out of hiding, so you would look and believe He has made you gorgeous, spotless, and without blemish. He finds you thoroughly sexy in the best possible sense of the word. So He whispers, "Come out." "Show me your face, let me hear your voice; for your voice is sweet, and your face is lovely" (Song of Songs 2:14 NIV).

It's the end of the story . . . and what did God want: obedient robots? knowledgeable scholars? soldiers to accomplish His mission? No. *A Bride.*

My bride has no mission statement. She has no purpose. I mean, I did not marry her for some *other goal.* She herself is the treasure, the pearl—my mission, purpose, and goal.

You are God's treasure *now,* as you are. Believe who you are already, eternally, and then you will give yourself joyfully in the freedom of love.

When you do that, every mission will be accomplished, and every purpose will be fulfilled in time. For the Lord enters His temple, and a river of life will flow, and the Bride will begin to produce fruit.

When you do that, the King takes up residence, and you shine. The "light of the world"; "a city set on a hill." The world sees the pearl of great price and longs to enter. Satan's only hope is to make you hide the glory under a bushel. "Hide it under a bushel? No! I'm gonna let it shine."

When you surrender your heart, you conquer. "This is the victory that overcomes the world," says John, "our faith" (1 John 5:4). Believe the gospel and stop hating yourself. Everyday, look in the mirror and say, "God is *nuts* about you. Jesus died for the love of you. He gives everything for you. You are created for His glory. You are priceless." When you pray, confess everything to Him (naked) and then bask in His love.

Believing His love is the greatest gift—yet I have such a hard time doing it, and now I know why. It is the heart of my warfare against the ancient dragon. A snake is trying desperately to scare me back into hiding: *Stop preaching. Stop smiling. Get self-conscious.* He has no weapons except lies and my own shame, but he is subtle, and I have believed his lies.

My wife and I have spent a lot of time praying for our friend whose father was a satanist and raised her in a coven. She is a profoundly beautiful believer, but she has had a hard time seeing it. I don't, and you wouldn't either. Her story is so painful I wouldn't have believed it except that in praying for her I've encountered the demonic in ways that have blown my mind. But more than that, I've seen the glory and power of Christ in her like nowhere else in my experience.

I suspect that at times my friend has battled Satan himself. He tempts her to hide in shame, to curl up in a ball and curse herself by saying, "I hate myself. I despise myself." As a child she was terribly abused and left in a closet; as a young woman she suffered it again. Satan tells her that she belongs in the closet, hiding in the dark with Eve. But it's the *dragon* who inhabits the closet.

Jesus has shown her that He has gone to the closet, too, to suffer with her. She is terrified by shame to let Him, but He has shown her in visions that her scars are His scars. Her blood is on His body; He's romanced her out of the closet and covered her in righteousness.

Into the vision I've prayed, "Jesus, would you show her how *You* see her?" He holds up a mirror, and she sees herself in a pure white wedding dress. She gasps in awe and wonder. *It's a dress she owns.* She bought it as an act of faith and devotion.

A few years ago, she was in the intense heat of battle. I told her to hang the wedding dress on her bedroom door and remember that Jesus told her how priceless she is. And remember to invite Him into her room to hold her and love her, to be her forever Bridegroom.

When the dress was on the door and she believed the gospel, the dragon was bound.

I've watched it unfold. She is not the product of her past. She is the presence of the future. She is redeemed. It's the most beautiful and stunning faith I've ever seen. She has walked through the door in the wilderness, and nothing is more beautiful in all creation than the Bride of Christ.

Bride of Christ, *believe* the gospel;

step on the snake's head;

and never, ever hide in shame again.

We're at the end of the Revelation now, the evening of the sixth day, and man has been created in the image of God with God's glory. What *is* man? A Bride that reflects the glory of her Groom. She is created at the bleeding side of Jesus, and *nothing* is more glorious in all creation.

So the last Adam whispers, "Eve, Eve . . . look what I've done! Come out of the shadows. Two shall become one flesh, and we will dance in glory forever." Our wedding day is at hand. Say "I do" with all your heart.

THIRTY-FOUR

"COME, LORD JESUS"
(BUT THERE'S A LION IN THE WAY)
(Revelation 22)

IN THE BEGINNING there was a great veiling: "God drove out the man; and at the east of the garden of Eden he placed the cherubim, and a flaming sword which turned every way, to guard the way to the tree of life" (Genesis 3:24).

REVELATION 22:1–5 (RSV): *Then he showed me the river of the water of life, bright as crystal, flowing from the throne of God and of the Lamb through the middle of the street of the city; also, on either side of the river, the tree of life with its twelve kinds of fruit, yielding its fruit each month; and the leaves of the tree were for the healing of the nations. There shall no more be anything accursed, but the throne of God and of the Lamb shall be in it, and his servants shall worship him; they shall see his face, and his name shall be on their foreheads. And night shall be no more; they need no light of lamp or sun, for the Lord God will be their light, and they shall reign for ever and ever.*

WE SURE WOULD LIKE TO GET TO THAT TREE OF LIFE and that river of the water of life, because sometimes it feels as if we're just going to *die* of thirst.

In C. S. Lewis's *The Silver Chair,* the girl Jill finds herself alone and guilty in a strange world, having just done a very prideful and stupid thing. After she cries, she is terribly thirsty. The sight of a beautiful stream across a meadow intensifies her thirst tenfold. But as she moves toward it, she is stopped in her tracks by an immense lion standing in front of the stream, like the flaming sword before the tree of life.

The lion looks at her as if it knows her. She is frozen, caught between fear

262

of the lion and longing for the water. Then it speaks in a powerful voice—twice, telling her she may come to the stream and drink. It does not make her any less frightened than she had been before, but it makes her frightened in rather a different way.

> "Are you not thirsty?" said the Lion.
> "I'm *dying* of thirst," said Jill.
> "Then drink," said the Lion.
> "May I—could I—would you mind going away while I do?" said Jill.
> The Lion answered this only by a look and a very low growl. And as Jill gazed at its motionless bulk, she realised that she might as well have asked the whole mountain to move aside for her convenience.
> The delicious rippling noise of the stream was driving her nearly frantic.
> "Will you promise not to—do anything to me, if I do come?" said Jill.
> "I make no promise," said the Lion.
> Jill was so thirsty now that, without noticing it, she had come a step nearer.
> "*Do* you eat girls?" she said.
> "I have swallowed up girls and boys, women and men, kings and emperors, cities and realms," said the Lion. It didn't say this as if it were boasting, nor as if it were sorry, nor as if it were angry. It just said it.
> "I daren't come and drink," said Jill.
> "Then you will die of thirst," said the Lion.
> "Oh dear!" said Jill, coming another step nearer. "I suppose I must go and look for another stream then."
> "There is no other stream," said the Lion.[1]

Jesus is the lion, and He's not a *tame* lion. Like Mr. Beaver told the children in Narnia, "Safe? . . . who said anything about safe? 'Course he isn't safe."[2]

Jesus is the lion. We're dreadfully thirsty, and we've just glimpsed the river and the tree of life. We're beginning to see the New Jerusalem coming down. Jesus says, "Let him who is thirsty come" (22:17), and we say, "Thank you! But —there's a *lion* in the way. Could it just go somewhere else, please?"

Or else we try to tame the Lion. Human religion is the human quest to make the holy God tame, to make the awesome God trivial. "We have very efficiently pared the claws of the Lion of Judah," wrote Dorothy Sayers, "certified Him 'Meek and mild,' and recommended Him as a fitting household pet for pale curates and pious old ladies."[3]

I've always longed for the water of life and the tree of life: the power of God. But I remember the first time I saw a demon cast out of a man. It wasn't subtle, or some manipulative hype; it was obviously real and incredibly powerful. I was *terrified* . . . not of the demon but of the One who cast it out, the One whose name my friend Scott invoked: Jesus, the Lion of Judah. It was obvious that at any moment He could *eat* me, if He so desired. I tried to remember how He looked on the flannel graph in Sunday school. I had an insatiable longing for trivia (meaningless things). I prayed, "God, could I just watch *I Love Lucy* for a while?"

Maybe we're *starting* to believe the Meaning, so we hide from the Meaning in trivia. Maybe the Lion begins to scare us because He's *not* trivial, so we hide in trivia.

Maybe He's not just words. Maybe He's not just metaphors. "These words are faithful and true" (22:6).

The Revelation is not a metaphor. In 19:11 Jesus, the Word, is named "faithful and true." He's alive. Jesus is not a metaphor; He's the Meaning. And from His mouth comes a sword. The sword pierces to the division of soul and spirit, joint and marrow. He cuts us; we don't cut Him. He is the Word that cuts us before the tree of life, like the flaming sword at the east of Eden. He is the Lion in the way. He is "the Way."

REVELATION 22:6–7 (NKJV): *Then he said to me, "These words are faithful and true." And the Lord God of the holy prophets sent His angel to show His servants the things which must shortly take place.*

"Behold, I am coming quickly. Blessed is he who keeps the words of the prophecy of this book."

The Lion scares us, so we try to keep Him trivial. And we try to keep Him distant. But these things must "shortly" take place (22:7)—the Greek word *tachu* doesn't mean "soon" as much as "without delay, at once." It's the word used by the angel at the tomb on Easter morning when he says to the women, "Go tell the disciples *at once.*" The Revelation of Jesus has been happening ever since that morning. The *kairos* is at hand (Revelation 22:10). *Chronos* shall be no more (Revelation 10:6).

The prophet Daniel was instructed to seal up the scroll because it pertained to the distant future and the time of the end (Daniel 12:4). In the Revelation, John is told *not* to seal up the scroll, because the time is at hand. Eternity now. Jesus and His kingdom are not distant—in space or time.

Jesus is *the Bridegroom* standing with longing at the bedroom door.

He is *the Wind* that blows through your soul, crying "Abba, Daddy."

He is *the Word* that upholds every fiber of your being.

He is *the Meaning* in every sentence.

He is *the Light* that enlightens all men and women.

"He is closer to everything than anything is to itself," said Martin Luther.

And when we first see it, it fills us with *terror.* We say, "Could the Lion please stand . . . some place else?"—*Distant.*

REVELATION 22:8–10 (NKJV): *Now I, John, saw and heard these things. And when I heard and saw, I fell down to worship before the feet of the angel who showed me these things.*

Then he said to me, "See that you do not do that! For I am your fellow servant, and of your brethren the prophets, and of those who keep the words of this book. Worship God."

And he said to me, "Do not seal the words of the prophecy of this book, for the time is at hand."

John falls at the feet of the revealing angel, who says, "Stop that! Worship God!"

We tend to worship the Revelation rather than the One revealed, because the One revealed is a dangerous, wild Lion. We try to tame the Lion by turning Him into trivia. So we buy books, attend prophecy seminars, stuff our heads with endless trivia speculating that Jesus will come to Jerusalem in 2059 or whatever . . . and ignore Jesus, who has already come to us in our wife and kids and the "last and the least," who is already lifted up, who is already the judgment, who is already romancing us into communion and the sacrificial, passionate surrender of His love.

Even worse, some folks seal up the book, saying such things as "This is for Israel, not you." "This was for Asia Minor, not you."

- Some worship the letter in order to hide from is meaning. They search the Scripture . . . but refuse to come to Jesus (John 5:39–40).
- Some worship the revealing angel. An adulterous generation seeks a sign, not the bridegroom (Matthew 12:39).
- Don't worship the mailman; don't worship the mail.

This is "The Revelation of Jesus" . . . worship God.

REVELATION 22:11 (NKJV): *He who is unjust, let him be unjust still; he who is filthy, let him be filthy still; he who is righteous, let him be righteous still; he who is holy. Let him be holy still."*

After all the warfare, after all the talk of conquering, "Let him be unjust still"? "Let him be righteous still"? You worship God.

We try to tame the Lion by turning Him and his kingdom into "our project." For if it's something we can do, at least we're in control. Then the project is trivial, but safe . . . and we can feel good about ourselves. We are so tempted to be the savior rather than worship the Savior. If you want a project, read Marx or Mohammed. But if you want to conquer, you must be conquered by the Lion.

Jesus saves the unjust; He cleanses the filthy; He builds His Church. If you want to be part of His project, you must be in Him—in the Lion. Worship God and fruit happens.

REVELATION 22:12 (NKJV): *And behold, I am coming quickly, and My reward is with Me, to give to every one according to his work."*

These must be the righteous deeds of he saints granted to the bride, the fruit that grows when I abide in Him. For apart from Him I can do nothing. I can't comprehend the meaning, but the meaning comprehends me. He reveals mystery.

REVELATION 22:13–15 (NKJV): *"I am the Alpha and the Omega, the Beginning and the End, the First and the Last." Blessed are those who do His commandments, that they may have the right to the tree of life, and may enter through the gates into the city. But outside are dogs and sorcerers and sexually immoral and murderers and idolaters, and whoever loves and practices a lie.*

In the last chapter we read that their lot was the lake of fire. Three verses earlier, Jesus said, "Behold, I make all things new." In 5:13 John hears "every creature in heaven and on earth and under the earth praising God." I don't understand that.

There are many mysteries in the Revelation that I don't understand.

Sometimes John speaks as though *every* creature gets saved; other times he doesn't. I wonder about the mystery of God's sovereign will expressed in our own free will. I can't explain where I end and Jesus begins. I still wonder about the seven angel messengers in the seven churches, and is that the sevenfold Spirit of God? I wonder about evil and judgment: Is the fire in Christ's eyes the lake of fire into which evil is thrown? Is that also the fire that purifies the children of God? Is that the fire that falls at Pentecost and rides on the words of our tongues? Is it the fire on the flaming sword that guards the way to the tree of life and pierces to the division of soul and spirit? "Our God is a consuming fire"—mystery. And the seven thunders are commanded mysteries.

I can't comprehend all this. If I respected Scripture *less,* I could. I would simply say, "John didn't really mean it here, but he did there." I know that I've written many things you didn't comprehend, because I've written many things I didn't comprehend. But I wrote them because they're true, because we could see meaning in the mystery. I just couldn't tame the meaning for you. It's been said that mystery is not the absence of meaning, but the presence of more meaning than we can comprehend.

We are very uncomfortable with mystery. We want to capture the meaning by killing the mystery, so we hire pastors and teachers to hunt it down and kill it. It's how we tame the Lion and make Him safe. A tame lion is a predictable lion, a dead lion . . . not *the* lion (maybe).

REVELATION 22:16 (NKJV): *"I, Jesus, have sent My angel to testify to you these things in the churches. I am the Root and the Offspring of David, the Bright and Morning Star."*

He is the Root of David, the source of David. Revelation 5:5 tells us that the Root of David is the Lion of Judah. To get to the water we try to make Him tame . . . try to make Him a metaphor . . . try to keep Him at a distance . . . try to turn Him into a lesson or a feeling or a project we do . . . try to turn Him into something trivial—something small—that fits in our own self-centered, little world. In short, we try to *kill* Him. And here's the most astounding thing of all:

He has already made Himself small.
He already allowed us to kill Him.

"Behold, the Lion of Judah has conquered!" says John, who looks and sees "a lamb standing, as though it had been slain." The Word became flesh and dwelt among us, and He still wasn't small enough—trivial enough—tame enough—understood enough. So the religious people carved Him up, strung Him up, and killed Him.

It was probably there, when He was small, as a baby in a manger, as a flannel graph Jesus, or as a slaughtered Lamb on a cross, that you picked Him up and said, "Be my Lord."

He didn't deceive you; He told you He was "King of kings and Lord of lords." He told you He was the "Lion of the tribe of Judah." It's just that you were blind and in a stupor. You were dreaming your own dreams.

You have been asleep in the insane dream of your own sovereignty. But now He has entered your dream—only one that great can become that small.

A friend of mine tells about a night his brother-in-law and his drunken buddies hit a deer with their car. As they stared at the deer lying still in the road, one of then said, "Let's take him home and eat him." They put the body in the front seat and all but the driver climbed in back. A few miles down the road, the deer began to move . . . a lot. It wasn't dead. Before they could stop the car, the deer cracked the windshield, smashed the dashboard, broke the side window, and produced much tribulation for the dreamy drunken boys in the backseat.

My friend, you've run into something far more terrible than a deer. You've hit the Lion. Driving drunk and dreamy you careened into the Living God and killed Him. You thought He was dead, just body broken and blood shed. So you picked Him up. But it is not as if it wasn't planned.

He planned it before time . . . an ambush. The baby in the manger grows. The battered man on the cross rises from the dead. The slaughtered Lamb is *still* the Lion. He's waking up . . . or I should say He's waking *you* up.

You try to tame Him, but it's too late! You've already picked Him up . . . and He will not leave you. This is the Revelation—the Apocalypse—the unveiling of Jesus. His love is a consuming fire, and He *will have* all of you.

Perhaps you picked up this book on Revelation because you wanted some information . . .

You came looking for meaning, and He is the Meaning.

You wanted some words, and He is the Word.

You wanted revelation, and He is the Revelation.

You wanted to know when, and He is when: I AM.

You wanted directions, and He is the Way.

You wanted answers, and He is the Truth.

You wanted the water of life, and the Lion in the way is the Way, the Truth, and the Life.

You wanted to conquer, and He conquers you.

You wanted a drink, and it turns out you're not the only one thirsty.

REVELATION 22:17 (NKJV): *And the Spirit and the Bride say, "Come!" And let him who hears say, "Come!" And let him who thirsts come. Whoever desires, let him take the water of life freely.*

Who is thirsty . . . really?

In John 4 *Jesus* is thirsty. He asks the Samaritan woman for water, and then He tells her He has living water. Yet to get that water, she must surrender her heart and confess her five husbands and her own thirst. Jesus tells her that God is thirsty for worshipers. We never know if Jesus gets His drink until the end of John. On the cross Jesus says, "I thirst" . . . and then He cries, "It is finished."

"The Spirit and the Bride [perhaps the Spirit in the Bride] say, "Come!" the Bride calls to the Groom. He's waited for her call, for her thirst to grow. The Groom will not rape her, but He has romanced her thirst.

Then we read, "Let him who thirsts come." Who's thirsty? The thirsty could be you, for the next line is, "Whoever desires, let him take the water of life freely." So the thirsty may be the Bride, the thirsty may be you, but the one most thirsty is the Lion—Jesus—God. You drink living water and Jesus drinks you. You're thirsty, but He is so thirsty He died for you. He is thirsty for worshipers. Worship is to surrender your heart in love.

If you read the Revelation and diagram every chapter, explain every paradox, are visited by revealing angels, and die with the martyrs on the street of the Great City, but don't love Jesus more at the end of the book . . .then it's worthless—a noisy gong, a clanging symbol. You've read and haven't heard.

REVELATION 22:18–19 (NKJV): *For I testify to everyone who hears the words of the prophecy of this book: If anyone adds to these things, God will add to him the plagues that are written in this book; and if anyone takes away from the words of the book of this prophecy, God shall take away his part from the Book of Life, from the holy city, and from the things which are written in this book.*

I am glad the warning is there . . . or this book would have been tamed and trivialized long ago. Eugene Peterson says the Revelation is "medicine for trivial people like us."[4] Don't trivialize Jesus. Don't try to tame Jesus. *Read. Hear. Worship.*

REVELATION 22:20–21: *He who testifies to these things says, "Surely I am coming quickly."*

Amen. Even so, come, Lord Jesus!

The grace of our Lord Jesus Christ be with you all. Amen.

He is coming "quickly."

He is "at hand." Yes, it's scary, but like Mr. Beaver said, "'Course he isn't safe. But he's good."

He is *the Good.* Not the dead good (law), but the living good (life).[5] He is the way to the tree of life (a cross). And He is the Life.

In the midst of the eternal city is the "tree of life." It can also be translated "the cross of Life." At His cross we know the good, He is the Good. At His cross we receive life, He is the Life. In Eden there were two trees in the midst of the garden. In the eternal city, there is one tree and no curse. At His cross we are made in God's image, and there is no curse. We are made in God's image and His image is Jesus.

In Revelation 22:2, tree is the Greek *xulon* rather than *dedron. Xulon* also means "cross." I believe "the tree of the knowledge of good and evil" (law) and the "tree of life" become or always were somehow one *xulon:* the cross. At the cross Jesus bears our curse for idolizing ourselves through the law. Now we go back to the cross and receive life. But we not only receive life, we receive the knowledge of the good; I should say we *know* the good, for the good is not a thing but a person: Jesus.

At the cross we receive the knowledge of evil (that we were evil—we crucified Jesus) and the knowledge of good (that He let us). But more than that, we know the Good. Commune with the Good. He is the Good. We know the Good not because we took "it" (flesh) but because the Man on the tree gave "it" to us as a gift of grace: His body broken and His blood shed—the fruit of the tree for all people (twelve kinds), the life (leaves) which heal the nations . . . Himself. At the tree the nations worship and the lion gets His drink. To drink and be drunk by the lion—true worship—no greater ecstasy.

The Revelation is a call to worship, to say, "Come, Lord Jesus!" in faith, hope, and love. In the early Church it was the practice to say, *"Maranatha—* Come, Lord Jesus"—at the Lord's table. One scholarly theory is that the

Revelation was read as a call to worship at the Lord's table, for the Revelation ends with *Maranatha,* and it explains the Lord's table. It reveals Jesus.

Here the world is judged.

Here the ruler of this world is cast out.

Here He romances all men to Himself.

Here the saints sing on Mount Zion.

Here the grapes of wrath are trampled and the river flows.

Here the Bridegroom enters His Bride with His life.

Here eternity invades time.

Here the Lion and Lamb conquer at the cross.

Here we come to the cross.

At the cross God reconciles to Himself all things, making peace through His blood. The life is in the blood, and the river of life flows from the throne, for on the throne sits a bleeding Lamb. He is the Lion, who bleeds for you.

"Eat, oh friends, and drink deeply, oh lovers" (Song of Solomon 5:1 RSV). "Eat, friends, drink and be drunk with love" (Song of Solomon 5:1 NRSV). That is: *Drink and be drunk by God.*

SO SEVEN LITTLE CHURCHES IN ASIA MINOR who wondered, "Where is God? Does He know? Do we even matter?" read the Revelation and then ate His broken body and drank His blood, and they were caught up not only in history (after all, God did use them to change the world), but in His Story. They were caught up in Him. Drunk by Him.

Go to worship this weekend. Believe the gospel. Take the bread. Drink the wine. Be caught up in the Meaning. Be caught up in Him.

"Eat the body and drink the blood, and you will be His body and bleed His blood."

If you have never prayed this before, pray it now: "Jesus, I need You. I want You. I give You my sins. I give You my life. Thank You for saving me at Your cross. Thank You for the water of life without price. *Maranatha.* Come, Lord Jesus."

And *now:* May the eyes of your heart be enlightened, "that you may know what is the hope to which he has called you, what are the riches of his glorious inheritance in the saints, and what is the immeasurable greatness of his power in us who believe, according to the working of his great might which he accomplished in Christ when he raised him from the dead and made him sit at his right hand in the heavenly places, far above all rule and authority and power and dominion, and above every name that is named, not only in this age but also in that which is to come" (Ephesians 1:18–21).

NOTES

PREFACE

1. G. K. Chesterton, *Orthodoxy* (New York: Doubleday, 1908), 17.

CHAPTER 1

1. Hal Lindsey, *The Late, Great Planet Earth* (Grand Rapids: Zondervan, 1970).

2. Hal Lindsey, *The 1980s: Countdown to Armageddon* (New York: Bantam, 1983).

3. Edgar Whisenant, quoted in Craig Keener, *Revelation: The NIV Application Commentary* (Grand Rapids: Zondervan, 2000), 63.

4. Ibid.

5. Tim LaHaye and Jerry Jenkins, *Left Behind* (Carol Stream, Ill.: Tyndale, 1996), first in a multibook series.

6. Guy Chevreau, *Catch the Fire* (Toronto: HarperCollins, 1994), 49.

7. Quote attributed to Albert Einstein came in a private e-mail correspondence. I was unable to find the original source.

8. Private correspondence, reprinted by permission.

CHAPTER 2

1. Bill Scanlon, "Coloradans Believe Truth Is Out There, Poll Shows," *Rocky Mountain News,* 21 August 2000.

2. This is a remarkable implication of modern day astronomy and Einstein's laws of relativity. For a wonderful detailed treatment of this topic, read *The Science of God or Genesis and the Big Bang* by Gerald Schroeder.

3. Scanlon, "Coloradans Believe."

4. Edwin Abbott, *Flatland: A Romance in Many Dimensions* (New York: Penguin, 1998; first published, 1880).

CHAPTER 5

1. Philip Yancey, *Where Is God When It Hurts* (Grand Rapids: Zondervan, 1997), 56.

2. "Salutation," *The Encyclical Epistle of the Church at Smyrnom, Concerning the Martyrdom of the Holy Polycarp,* http://ccel.org/fathers2/ANF-01/anf01-13.htm (February 2001).

Notes

CHAPTER 8

1. I think this is an utterly fascinating idea, but I couldn't find it in any commentaries. It's not only substitutionary atonement, but substitutionary sanctification. The identity of the angel in Revelation 19:10 who commands John not to worship him is an important issue here. Is that a bowl angel? Are bowl angels the sevenfold spirit and the sevenfold messengers in the churches? And even if that is the case, would the Holy Spirit (who is God) ever tell us to worship the Father and Jesus (yes) but not Him, for He is a fellow servant, holding the testimony, for "the testimony of Jesus is the spirit of prophecy"?

CHAPTER 9

1. Sister Mary Rose McGeady, *Does God Still Love Me?* (New York: Covenant House, 1995), 15–19.

CHAPTER 10

1. Jeffrey Kluger, "Fighting Phobias," *Time,* 2 April 2001, 52–62.
2. Ibid., 52.
3. C. S. Lewis, *The Silver Chair* (New York: MacMillan, 1953), 153.
4. Ibid.
5. Ibid., 157.
6. Ibid., 158.

CHAPTER 12

1. Bertrand Russell, quoted in Donald Carson, "Praise to the Lamb," sermon, Preaching Today series, no. 194 (*Christianity Today,* 1999). © 1999 Donald A. Carson.

CHAPTER 13

1. Eugene Boring, *Revelation: Interpretation: A Bible Commentary for Teaching and Preaching* (Louisville, Ky.: John Knox, 1989), 111.

CHAPTER 15

1. C. S. Lewis, *The Horse and His Boy* (New York: HarperCollins, 1954), 174.
2. Madeleine L'Engle, *Walking on Water: Reflections on Faith and Art* (Wheaton, Ill.: Harold Shaw, 1980), 147.

CHAPTER 19

1. Richard Wurmbrand, *In God's Underground* (Glendale, Calif.: Diane Books, 1968), 123–24.

CHAPTER 20

1. Sydney Carter, quoted in Philip Yancey, *The Jesus I Never Knew* (Grand Rapids: Zondervan, 1995), 264.

CHAPTER 21

1. J. R. R. Tolkien, *The Hobbit* (Boston: Houghton Mifflin, 1966), 123.
2. J. R. R. Tolkien, *The Fellowship of the Ring* (New York: Ballantine, 1965), 352–53.

NOTES

3. C. S. Lewis, *Parelandra* (New York: Collier, 1944; paperback edition, 1965), 155–56.

CHAPTER 22

1. Hendrik Berkhof, *Christ and the Powers,* trans. John H. Yoder (Scottsdale, Pa.: Herald, 1962, 1977; first published Nijkerk: Callenboch, 1952).

2. Richard Wurmbrand, *Marx and Satan* (Bartlesville, Ohio: Voice of the Martyrs, 1986).

3. Trevor Ravenscroft, *The Spear of Destiny* (York Beach, Maine: Samuel Weiser, Inc., 1973), 8–9.

CHAPTER 26

1. Malcolm Muggeridge, *The End of Christendom* (Grand Rapids: Eerdmans, 1980), 9–10.

CHAPTER 29

1. Charles Colson, *Loving God* (Grand Rapids: Zondervan Publishing Company, 1983), 241–44.

2. Kenneth Scott Latourette, *A History of Christianity,* vol. 1 (New York: HarperCollins, 1953), 144.

CHAPTER 33

1. Because Paul writes that the story of Adam and Eve somehow refers to the Church and because Paul calls Christ the *eschatos* Adam, that is the eschatological, last or uttermost Adam, I suspect that the story can be read on at least two levels. First, it can be read in regard to the first Adam (typical Adam: Romans 5:14). Second, it can be read in light of the "*eschatos* Adam" (eschatological, uttermost, last Adam: 1 Corinthians 15:45), the one the type refers to. In that case, the fall of Adam is a type or picture of the incarnation and atonement of Christ. Christ took the fruit (the curse) from Eve and died (crucified) in our place, because He convenanted Himself to us (His Bride) from the foundation of the world in the eternal covenant ratified in space and time on the cross. He will not leave or forsake His Bride. He was and is "with her."

This gives new meaning to passages such as 1 Timothy 2:13–15: "Adam was not deceived"—Christ was not deceived; He knew He was taking the curse. "Woman [Eve] will be saved through bearing children"—God's people give birth to the last Adam as a particular event in Bethlehem, and as Christ is formed and birthed in us and throughout history (Revelation 12).

CHAPTER 34

1. Lewis, *The Silver Chair,* 17.

2. C. S. Lewis, *The Lion, the Witch, and the Wardrobe* (New York: MacMillan, 1950), 75–76.

3. Dorothy L. Sayers, *Creed or Chaos* (New York: Harcourt, Brace & Co., 1949), 5.

4. Eugene Peterson, "Learning to Worship from St. John's Revelation," *Christianity Today* (28 October 1991), 56. Peterson makes a wonderful case for the idea that the Revelation is a call to worship as a prescription against the trivialization of the Gnostics.

FURTHER READING

THIS BOOK IS TAKEN from a series of lessons and sermons that I gave over a thirteen-month period. In order to fit the material into one book, much of the original manuscript had to be edited out. This included additional stories, exegesis, insights, and quotes. If you would like a copy of the unabridged version of this manuscript, you may obtain one by contacting Lookout Mountain Community Church, 534 Commons Drive, Golden, CO 80401; (303)526-9287.

A slew of books have been written on the Revelation. Below I've listed a few that I found most helpful.

Aune, David E. *Revelation: Word Biblical Commentary,* 3 vols. Dallas: Word, 1997. This is a very thorough and high quality critical commentary.

Bauckham, Richard. *The Theology of Revelation.* Cambridge: Cambridge University Press, 1993. A marvelous theological treatment of some of the major theological themes of the Revelation

Boring, M. Eugene. *Revelation: Interpretation, A Bible Commentary for Teaching and Preaching.* Louisville, Ky.: John Knox, 1989. Not "boring," but very thought provoking.

Downie, Rex, Jr. *Jesus Jumpstarts Revelation: A Lawyer Sees Structure and Meaning.* Self published. Beaver Falls, Penn.: Rex Downie Jr., 1994. This is a unique and utterly fascinating treatment of the Revelation. Downie is focused on the centrality of Jesus, alert to the corruptions of a modernist mind-set, and brilliant at uncovering patterns of meaning in the text.

Eller, Vernard. *The Most Revealing Book of the Bible.* Grand Rapids: Eerdmans, 1974. A popular commentary. I don't agree with Eller's overall scheme, but he has some wonderful insights that first lit my fire regarding the Revelation.

Gregg, Steve. *Revelation: Four Views, a Parallel Commentary.* Nashville: Thomas Nelson, 1997. This is one of the first commentaries you should read on this topic. Gregg provides commentary from all four of the classical views of the Revelation in parallel form.

FURTHER READING

Grenz, Stanley J. *The Millennial Maze: Sorting out Evangelical Options.* Downers
Grove, Ill.: InterVarsity, 1992. A great help for understanding the history and
theological issues surrounding the various millennial doctrines.

Keener, Craig S. Revelation: *The NIV Application Commentary.* Grand Rapids:
Zondervan, 2000. A quality all-purpose commentary.

Peterson, Eugene. *Reversed Thunder: The Revelation of John and the Praying
Imagination.* San Francisco: HarperCollins, 1988. A wonderful commentary for
reflection, meditation, and worship.

Sock, Mr. and Nathan D. Wilson, *Right Behind: A Parody of Last Days Goofiness.*
Moscow, Idaho: Canon Press, 2001. For a good laugh . . . at yourself.

ACKNOWLEDGMENTS

THIS SCARES ME, for in no way can I thank enough people or the right people or do it in just the right way. Furthermore, the truly good thoughts in this book are the Lord's. That's a theological necessity, and a rather surprising reality that in places I've been amazed to witness. I'm sure there is also confusion and error, yet God's Truth is born in a manger, and at times that manger is me. But it's certainly not just me. This book was birthed by the Church, and especially Lookout Mountain Community Church.

Therefore I want to thank my particular church: LMCC. This book is the product of God's Spirit at work in community. I want to thank all those who prayed for me, encouraged me, and lived out the revelation of Jesus in their daily life. Thank you, Elaine, Marcia, Kate, Andrew, Phillip, my small group, and the session and staff of LMCC.

I also want to thank all those who helped with the more technical parts of this book: Stephanie Trahant, my assistant at church who helps me with all my messages; Kathryn Helmers, who encouraged me greatly as my agent and later condensed and edited this material; Janis Whipple, a most agreeable and helpful copy editor; and the wonderful people at Integrity Publishers and Alive Communications.

Thank you, Mom and Dad. You were the first revelation of Jesus for me and continue to be His artwork.

Thank you, Jonathan, Elizabeth, Rebekah, and Coleman (my kids), for tolerating me when I was tired and grumpy from working on this book, and thank you for the places you let me use you as illustrations. Most of all, thank you, Susan, my bride. You edit all my sermons (that's usually a very good thing). You believe in Jesus in me, even though you see me as I am. You are God's messenger of grace to me and a beautiful picture of why Jesus loves His Church so deeply.